CHALLENGES

LEADERSHIP IN TWO WARS, WASHINGTON DC, AND INDUSTRY

MAJ. GEN. HARRY W. JENKINS, USMC (RET.)

FORTIS

AN ADDUCENT NONFICTION IMPRINT
TITLES DISTRIBUTED IN
NORTH AMERICA
UNITED KINGDOM
WESTERN EUROPE
SOUTH AMERICA
AUSTRALIA
CHINA
INDIA

CHALLENGES

LEADERSHIP IN TWO WARS, WASHINGTON DC, AND INDUSTRY

MAJ. GEN. HARRY W. JENKINS, USMC (RET.)

HARDBACK ISBN: 9781937592912

PAPERBACK ISBN: 9781937592929

PUBLISHED BY FORTIS (AN ADDUCENT NONFICTION IMPRINT)

WWW.ADDUCENTCREATIVE.COM

DEDICATION

To Sue, Anne and Brady, TJ and Crystal, and especially to our grandchildren Maya and Max who have brightened my life throughout this journey

This hung at the entrance to the Headquarters, Marine Corps Mountain Warfare Training Center, Bridgeport, California, in 1965.

Bring Me Men to Match My Mountains:

Bring Me Men to Match My Plains:

Men with Empires in Their Purpose

And New Eras in Their Brains.

In Whiffs from Wild Meadows, 1895
Sam Walter Foss, an American Librarian, and Poet

ACKNOWLEDGMENTS

This has been a work in progress that has gone on for the better part of two years. It grew out of a desire to record what has gone on in my life from the very beginning to the present. Several friends in the service and elsewhere have said I needed to write about my experiences. Still, for many years I was not convinced such a project was worth it. Who would want to read it other than members of my family? But in a society where much of what we experience today gets tossed out in the relentless charge to move forward, who is left to record events that could provide some insight for the future? There are several experiences in this book that provide both historical and human examples of what can be accomplished for those who are coming behind and facing the challenges of the future.

There is no question that one cannot complete such a project without a large dose of assistance. That has certainly been the case with me, and I owe a large amount of gratitude to my daughter-in-law, Crystal Penney, who has advanced degrees in creative writing. She kept me going in the right direction in terms of advice at the beginning of the text as well as the prose. She has been extremely helpful in research of our family tree, some of which appear in this book. I owe a special degree of thanks to Melinda Bargreen, who is an accomplished author in her own right, and who holds a Ph.D. in English literature. Her comments and suggestions regarding the text were extremely valuable. She provided insight into how to illustrate and bring to life several of the characters that exist in this story. Brady Hypes, a devoted friend of the family, has been especially helpful with technical and photo-related issues that occasionally occurred as I progressed through the text. Finally, I owe a special debt of gratitude to Dennis Lowery, president of Adducent. He has provided me with continuous guidance and support as this book was being constructed.

Being new at this game, he has kept me on the straight and narrow to complete this project.

None of this effort would have been possible without the experiences of several members of my family from the early years to the present. I owe a special thanks to those who made me what I am. This book is a historical record for them. To the thousands of men and women with whom I served in the United States Marine Corps and the United States Navy, a special salute to you for your dedication, perseverance, and patriotism. Much of my professional success over the years is attributed directly to you.

TABLE OF CONTENTS

Author's Note

Our lives are comprised of experiences that often include challenges. I've endured many of these challenges during combat leadership in Vietnam and the Persian Gulf, winter operations in the Arctic during the Cold War, and observations in war-torn Afghanistan, all at different ages and levels of experience and responsibility. Some were harrowing in how they occurred overseas. Others were humorous as they played out. Still more were highly educational in my attempts to achieve success in a myriad of assignments from combat in faraway lands, to the bureaucratic in-fighting on the political battlefields of Washington, DC My transition to industry was another kind of experience. After 34 years in the U.S. Marine Corps, I entered an unknown world with unfamiliar languages, processes, and radically different cultural experiences.

I share what I've learned in this narrative and within it are insights for all to absorb.

I enjoyed most of my experiences, especially when working with Americans from dissimilar backgrounds and aspirations both in the Marine Corps and throughout industry. This country is rich in traditions unlike anywhere else in the world, which makes it a special place to grow up and live. Even though we have our internal problems, being able to travel the world made me—as have many others—realize that the country is special in its own way.

What I hope the reader takes away from these pages is that history can teach us much if we will just consider the past and learn and grow from it. When we ignore the lessons of history, as we have done in recent years, we repeat mistakes with costly outcomes.

Harry W. Jenkins

REFERENCE MAPS / PHOTOS

MAPS

PHOTO SECTIONS

Prologue

It was during the second week of June 1968. Mike Company, 3rd battalion 26th Marines, pressed through the dense jungle, winding upwards along a steep ridge. As we climbed, the heat and humidity clung to the 109 Marines, who were each loaded down with about seventy-five pounds of ammunition, water, and rations. Veterans of the siege at Khe Sanh, we were now three weeks into a brand-new mission to seek out and destroy North Vietnamese Army (NVA) base camps hidden in the mountains southwest of Da Nang. As company commander, it was my job to make sure we accomplished the mission.

Our experience from Khe Sanh provided little applicability to our current environment. Six weeks earlier, we were dug in and defending open, burned off hilltops against artillery, rockets, and mortars. Now we were penetrating through triple canopy mountainous jungle, searching out hidden enemy base camps, causing us to adapt as necessary as we went along.

Following a scout dog, we moved slowly and deliberately, gaining about a half-mile a day. The point of the company sets the pace, stopping, listening, and moving forward again. Moving too fast risked running unexpectedly into NVA. A sense of isolation set in as we moved further away from the battalion command post, which was currently one thousand meters to the rear.

Walking point for the company took its toll, so I rotated platoons daily. Third platoon had been on the point the day prior, so 1st platoon moved up to take the lead guiding us up the mountain.

I had relied heavily on the leadership in the 1st platoon. It was led by one of my best noncommissioned officers, Staff Sergeant Ron Echols. He was an exceptional combat leader with unparalleled instincts for smelling out potential trouble, instincts honed by

1

extensive combat experience against the NVA from Con Thien to Khe Sanh. He was a hard-nosed Kentuckian, built like a bulldog who took care of his Marines but did not suffer fools.

1st platoon neared the top of the ridge when they came across a slight trail cutting through the jungle. I told Staff Sergeant Echols to move left since the 3rd platoon was already located to the right at our rear. I directed them to proceed carefully along the trail and be alert for any sounds that might indicate another base camp.

The 3rd platoon, holding up the rear, was led by Second Lieutenant Dennis Andrews, a quiet stocky guy who carried out his assignments without any fanfare. He was a good platoon commander and one of my few remaining officers. With Lieutenant Andrews was my executive officer, First Lieutenant Bill Hutsler, a former Gunnery Sergeant who was elevated to lieutenant because of the shortage of junior officers. Hutsler was another one of those superb staff NCOs who developed into a terrific company level officer with the instincts of a cat in the field.

The stillness as we proceeded along the ridgeline was unnerving. The Marines were trying to move along without making any noise. There was an unusual amount of rock and boulders along the trail, which made it difficult.

The scout dog on the point suddenly froze in place, and the Marines quickly motioned the column to stop. They quietly pointed to something off in the canyon below us. There was no wind, and in the silence of the jungle, they heard noises. As we listened, we could hear talking in Vietnamese and the sounds of someone cutting wood or bamboo.

I passed the word for the company to go to ground and directed my radio operator to call back to the battalion and request an airstrike on where we thought the noises were coming from.

The company was now positioned along the trail as we waited for the planes to arrive on station. The noises continued. It was obvious the NVA did not know we were there yet.

The forward air controller (FAC) with the battalion called my radio operator and stated that two planes were inbound and had acknowledged the brief on the target.

I was standing behind a huge boulder, taller than me, with the 2nd platoon in front of me and the 3rd platoon behind me on the other side of the boulder.

Looking down on the target from above the triple canopy, as would be the pilots' view, gave the impression that the ground was much more moderate and not too steep. It did not show the terrain features like the razor-thin ridgeline that we were strung out on. Nothing in training or my imagination prepared me for what happened next.

The screech of the first Marine jet surprised me as he rolled in on the target, dropping two 250-pound Snake-Eye bombs, which went off in the canyon. A few minutes later, the second jet rolled in and dropped two bombs as he roared right over our position.

Then a huge explosion occurred. The extreme overpressure stunned me.

I was disoriented, and my ears were ringing badly. I felt like I had been caught in a giant cymbal.

What the hell just happened?

Our battalion was used to being under attack by artillery, rockets, and mortars, but this was something different.

I focused first on the boulder shielding me from the explosion and then grappled to regain control over the situation.

The radios were silent. Everyone was trying to figure out what was going on. My platoon commanders struggled to cut through the chaos. The blast sent Staff Sergeant Echols airborne. Some members of the 2nd platoon did not fare much better.

Instead of clearing the canopy, the two bombs went off in the treetops and right over the 3rd platoon's position on the ridgeline. Climbing around the shattered rock, the scene was one of utter destruction.

The smell of cordite hung in the air. Bodies, body parts, smashed weapons, and equipment were everywhere. There was a headless torso of a Marine lying under a shattered tree, and the moans of the wounded were terrifying. The 3rd platoon had eight dead and five critically wounded, with the other eighteen Marines in the platoon slightly injured or in shock.

I had been Mike Company's commander for the past four months. I had solid faith in those Marines, and they had trusted me to get them through safely. I had never thought that something like this could happen to me. My responsibility now was to render as much aid as possible immediately and then try to figure out how we were going to get both the wounded and the dead back to the rear. That was the challenge because there was no landing zone within a thousand meters of our position, and the trees along the ridgeline were 75 to 100 feet high in triple canopy jungle. I had run medevacs before up north at Khe Sanh, but all never involved more than two casualties, and the landing zones were easy to access by helicopter. I was on my own, but we had to work fast to get the wounded out to prevent any further fatalities.

The first thing I did was call off the jets that had been orbiting over our position on the ridge. Next, we brought every available Navy corpsman in the company to assist the injured and try to identify the dead. Both Lieutenants Andrews and Hutsler, despite being dizzy from the blast overpressure, worked to get control of the situation and establish some order.

Whatever we could do to get the casualties out had to be done from that position. There was no other way that we could move them to another location in that jungle with the NVA being active in that area.

I requested assistance for a mass casualty evacuation, and the air wing responded initially with two CH-46 helicopters.

The improvised plan was to have the first helicopter come in and hover in the treetops while the other would orbit around the position. The first bird would lower a "jungle penetrator" or a "Neal Robinson Sling" to the ground. Either would be used on one casualty depending on the severity of the injuries to the casualty. He would then be placed on or in one of the devices and hoisted 90 feet up through the treetops to the hovering helicopter. It was a slow process, but it was the only way we could get them out. I was concerned that we would take fire from the NVA, but fortunately, that never happened. After an hour, the severely wounded were in the CH-46 and flown to medical facilities in Da Nang. The skill of the pilots hovering in the treetops for that period of time was amazing.

Evacuating the dead was another matter. We could not carry the remains along with the equipment and weapons that belonged to them.

I requested another CH-46 helicopter with a cargo net slung under the bird. The improvised plan approved by the battalion was to have the helicopter come in and hover again in the treetops over our position. The net was lowered by cable to the ground and spread out.

The remains of the dead were placed carefully along with the body parts in the net. Next, the smashed weapons and equipment were also secured in the net. When that was accomplished, the net was carefully drawn up and retracted back up through the trees and secured to the bottom of the CH-46.

The helicopter then flew off toward the rear with the cargo net slowly rotating under the bird. That was one sight I never wanted to see again.

Things were very quiet that night all around the company position on the ridge. We were all lost in our thoughts and exhausted from the day's events. I did not sleep much and kept mulling over whether there had been a better way of handling the catastrophe.

What caused me to persevere in that grim situation? Training and teamwork were part of it. The superb loyalty to one another among those Marines in the worst of situations was another factor. Perhaps the ability to be resourceful and persevere that had been the hallmark of my ancestors who migrated from Europe, and then across the plains to California in the 1800s was another.

Whatever the cause, it had been a life-altering experience.

PART 1: IN THE BEGINNING

Chapter 1

The Early Years

My journey began in California in the last year of the Great Depression. Born into a newspaper family in 1938, they were decedents of migrants who came from England and Ireland in the middle 1800s. Following the discovery of gold in California in 1849, most of them continued west across the plains to the Sierra Nevada Mountains in California. Settling in Nevada City, they worked in the goldfields of the Mother Lode for a period before migrating out of the mountains and down to the San Francisco Bay Area.

My mother and dad were born in Oakland, California, and lived there for over thirty-five years before moving to San José. Life during the war (1942 - 1945) in Oakland was difficult due to the perceived threat of Japanese attack, and the shortages in everything generated by the impact of the Depression along with the requirement to supply the fighting forces in the Pacific. We lived on East 38th Street in Oakland, and I can remember watching convoys of troops moving through town on the way to the Oakland Army Terminal for shipment overseas. We used to wave at them as they rolled by, and they would always wave back or shout something that was usually funny. This was really the beginning of my fascination with some things military. In those days in Oakland, the majority of the men were in one uniform or another.

My dad joined the Marine Corps in late 1944 and went through Boot Camp in San Diego at the age of thirty. To ease the burden on my mother and sister while dad was gone, I went to live with my grandparents in the mountain town of Paradise in northern California. This was my initial exposure to mountain living. Learning to live and sustain myself there set the stage for experiences that I would face in several parts of the world in the years to come. I quickly grew to enjoy that environment immensely.

My grandfather, James Walton Finchley, was a fiercely independent individual, who had spent most of his career in logging, surveying for the railroad in the Sierras, and as a lineman and supervisor for the P.G. & E around Sacramento. He was also an excellent fisherman who tried mightily to make me into one at the same level. What I remember best about him was that he was demanding but fair when it came to managing his grandson. He did not take any lip from me but was always on hand to guide me through one experience or another. His two acres of Ponderosa Pines was a great location for learning how to cut down a large pine tree, buck the limbs off, saw the trunk into sections, and then split the logs up into firewood with sledgehammers. He did not give me any slack in this process, but I started to develop my self-confidence for working in the woods as well as fishing on the West Branch of the Feather River. I ended up living with them until my dad returned from the war in 1945, and then for every summer over the next six years.

The Finchley property was always a great place to run and play in the woods. When we were not splitting logs for firewood, we were maintaining a large garden they had developed over time. It consisted of apple, peach, and apricot trees along with an extensive array of vegetables and berries. This was necessary due to the shortages that existed. If you could not buy some of the things you wanted for food, the only solution was to grow your own. I had access to all of it, providing whatever I took was ripe. Meat was very hard to get, so grandfather raised ducks, chickens, and turkeys. You could not buy bacon, so he cured his own. Butter was very scarce, so he made his own as well. Eggs came from the chicken house daily. My grandparents' approach to sustaining themselves really grew out of experiences they both had while growing up in and around the mining camps in the Sierras. If you wanted to survive, you had to provide for yourself when times get hard.

James Finchley was also an ardent fly fisherman who knew every stream in our area, as well as the surrounding mountains. He would only fish for trout on certain days to "give the fish a rest from all the damned fools that spoiled the streams over the weekends." I became a decent fisherman, but he would not be happy if I came in without any trout. On numerous fishing trips into the mountains above Paradise, my grandmother, Oleta, who had been raised in the gold towns of Grass Valley and Nevada City, would go along and do the cooking over an open campfire while we were out on a stream. She could cook anything over a fire and often did.

Coming home in 1945, my dad joined the Marine Corps League with several other veterans. They would frequently meet in the Marine Memorial Club in San Francisco for various social activities. He was proud of his service in the Corps and used to tell tales about his Drill Instructors in boot camp because they were all veterans of battles in the Pacific. He returned to his old job in the Circulation Department at the *Post Enquirer*. Over the next three years, the family moved four times around Oakland and eventually to San José in 1948. This was in response to a lucrative job offer with the *San Jose Shopping News* in that city. He was totally dedicated to his job at the *Post Enquirer* in Oakland, and later at the *San Jose Shopping News*. He was very good at what he did in that business, but at times he did nothing else. His attention to my activities waned as I grew older and entered high school. I thought some of the single-mindedness toward work tracked back to the impact the Depression had on the population. At the same time, this provided more pressure on my mother, who tried to pay more attention to Susan and me. Dad spent the next thirty-four years in the newspaper business in San José and Southern California before retiring in 1982.

I started my formal education in a little country school in Paradise in 1944 and can say I was an average student for several years after that. Going for the highest of educational honors was never my goal, and I pretty much lived up to those standards all the way to high school. As we moved around, I attended four different grammar and mid-level schools, as well as two different High Schools in San José. This was necessary, but it meant starting all over again with new friends.

The final three years in Willow Glen High School were in the same place, so that worked out well. I competed in varsity track and football and managed to letter in both sports three years in a row. I was better in track and field, and I went undefeated in the hurdles in my senior year, reaching the state semi-final championships. I also ran the 800 meters and various relays. On occasion, my parents would attend the football games in San José, along with some of the track meets in my senior year at Willow Glen. My grades began to creep up during this period as I was placing a little more emphasis on academics. My mother was really the driver regarding my grades at home, which increased my chances of getting into San José State College. I was accepted by the school and started in the fall of 1956. Graduating from high school, I entered San José State as the first member of the family ever to attend college. My rationale for going to State was that tuition was almost free, and I could easily live at home. Actually, the only real expense was for books. Life at that level of education was a very different environment than high school, and it was easy to get distracted by all kinds of activities. I quickly discovered there was nobody around to keep you on the right track as far as grades went because you were on your own. I went out for the San José State track team initially but had to drop it to make money to support myself in college.

I was not getting financial assistance from my family, which was not unusual in those days. It did give me a growing sense of independence as I had to work with several jobs to support myself through college. At this point, being old enough and motivated, I was drawn toward working in the mountains of California. My father thought it was a good idea and told me so. My mother, on the other hand, withheld judgment until she could see what I was able to turn up. This began a two-summer effort with the National Park Service in Yosemite National Park. Although I was underage the summer before my freshman year, my cousin, Lee Shackelton, who was a ranger in Sequoia National Park, made some connections that got me a job on a Blister Rust Crew (BRC) based at Crane Flat in Yosemite. The crew had around twenty-five men, and we were working in the backcountry against a tree disease that was killing the "Five Finger Pine" (White Pine) in the park. We were paid by the hour, and the food prepared by a veteran "Bull Cook" at the camp was terrific. If we were ever called out on a fire, the pay would be time and a half per hour. In 1955, that was really good money.

The foreman on the BRC crew at Crane Flat gave us the instructions for fighting brush or timber fires. This involved the use of several specifically designed tools for cutting fire breaks in all kinds of terrain. We were called out on one fast-moving fire in steep canyons above the Merced River just outside of the park. That was my first experience in firefighting, and it was hot, hard, dirty work as we had to create firebreaks on the flanks of the brush-covered slopes. On this fire, breaks had to be cleared by hand because the terrain was too steep to support bulldozers usually used for clearing fire lines. This had been a very demanding experience that I enjoyed.

After my sophomore year at San José State, I went back for the full summer on another BRC crew, this time in a camp located at Chinquapin in Yosemite. This was another great summer where we were in the woods combating tree diseases in different locations in the park. We had the same firefighting mission, except experiences that summer involved moving deep into the backcountry in 2- or 3-man strike crews to put out small fires started by lightning. In one instance, thunderstorms coming up the backbone of the Sierras produced 18 lighting strikes within the park that started small fires. They all had to be contained by several crews working independently. This was different from what I had experienced during my first year. Here we were out on our own, deep into the high country of Yosemite, going in to check out the lightning strikes and putting the fire out if, in fact, one had started. The sense of responsibility and growing confidence were awesome, not to mention independence in dealing with such a potential series of threats out in the wilderness. I really had no qualms about what I was doing and still had visions of a career in the Park Service following college.

During my second year in Yosemite in I was the proud owner of a customized 1948 Lincoln Coupe. I had driven it to the camp at Chinquapin. While back in San José, the V-12 engine had been replaced with a 1952 Mercury V-8. The car had a custom paint job in Mandarin Red, along with straight pipes and moon hubcaps on white wall tires. It was a beautiful car, a little slow from a standing start, but once it gained speed, that Lincoln could stay up with anybody. After work, I would often take it to the Yosemite Valley in the evenings. On the downhill grade through the Wawona Tunnel, I would gear down just to hear the roar of the pipes in the tunnel. This got the attention of the rangers, but I was never caught. Later that summer, four of us decided to take the car over the Tioga Pass and down to the ghost town of Body. From there, we continued east toward the town of Walker, Nevada. About halfway to our destination, I began to hear noises followed by smoke coming out from the underbelly of the car. We pulled the Lincoln off to the side of the road and caught a ride 20 miles into Walker. I sent one wrecker out to get the car and had to send a second wrecker as well because the steering system was broken. This was after we had just crossed over the Tioga Pass, the road of which moved along the narrow canyon wall 1,000 feet above the river. It took both wreckers, with the Lincoln swinging in the breeze between them, to get the car back to town. Spare parts were not available anywhere near Walker, and we had to get back to our jobs in the park. That led to a decision I did not want to make but had no choice. The car was sold off for a "clunker" that would get us back to Chinquapin. So ended the story of the '48 Lincoln. I did see it sometime later, sitting in a gas station in Tracy, California, as I was passing through town. As that summer came to a close in Yosemite, the BRC Camps in the park were shut down for the season. Those of us who were going back to college headed for home. In my case, it was in the "clunker."

CHAPTER TWO
JOINING THE MARINES

One day in the early spring of 1957, I was walking across the inner quadrangle between classes at San José State. The campus was located in a part of town that would be called a middle-class area today. It was a beautiful campus with an ivy-covered bell tower overlooking the inner quadrangle. The area around the Quad had been decorated with Spanish tile on benches, which were bordered with grass and palm trees. This did provide some shade for those who wanted to sit and study there. It was a quiet, pleasing area one would hope to find on a college campus in California.

As I was passing through the Quad, I spotted a team of Marines in Dress Blues that were manning a table with all the normal recruiting material at the time. They were an Officer Selection Team from San Francisco looking for potential candidates who could qualify through the Platoon Leaders Class (PLC) for commissions in the U.S. Marine Corps. Bill McCluskey, a close friend through high school and at San José State, had told me about this program that he had joined a few months earlier. This was intriguing to me, and after talking to them for some time, I went off to think about it. Our family was not a traditional military family, but several of my relatives have served over the years. My grandfather, William P Jenkins, had been in the Navy and had been on the battleship USS Pennsylvania from 1910 to 1912 during the First Nicaraguan Campaign. One of my uncles, Harry R Jenkins, had served in the 346th field artillery in the AEF in France in 1917. Another uncle, Fred Wagner, had gone into France with the Army following the Normandy Landings in 1944 and had worked with German POWs. My dad had served in the Marines during World War II in 1944-1945. This had been the thing to do, but it was not a tradition where a family has a succession of general officers serving down through the generations. My interest in the

14

Marines up to this point consisted of movies like the Sands of Iwo Jima or games involving the infantry. I had read extensively about the major battles the Marines had fought from Guadalcanal to Okinawa in the Pacific, as well as the Inchon Landings and Chosin Reservoir Campaign in Korea in 1950. My interest in the Navy had developed after reading about the sea battles in the South Pacific during the war. Life on Navy destroyers seemed appealing as well, but that was about the extent of any career aspirations involving the military. Going back to the OSO Team later, I decided to take the necessary tests to see if I could qualify.

At this point in my life, having fun in school, making average grades as a freshman, and possibly working in the mountains with either the US Forest Service or possibly the National Park Service during the summers was clearly an option. The draw of the mountains in some occupations following college was always on my mind. That was about as far as I had gone regarding any occupation in the future. There was no deep thought on joining the Marines, other than it looked like a challenge, and clearly, the uniforms were really sharp. While my father had served in the Marine Corps, he had no impact on my decision to start off in this direction. At this point, it seemed like the thing to try. The OSO Team gave me the written test right there in the Quad, and I passed it. Then they gave me a date when I could go to San Francisco to be sworn into the PLC Program by the Director of the 12th Marine Corps District. Shortly after that, orders arrived directing me to report for the first six weeks of summer training at a place called the Marine Corps Schools at Quantico, Virginia. The location of this place remained a mystery, but training would start in June 1957 after school let out. My dad took this in stride and was pleased. My mother, who was working for the San José Mercury News at the time, was supportive, but a little uneasy at the prospect of my joining the Marines.

* * *

Late in the afternoon on June 16, 1957, my parents took me to the airport in San Francisco for the flight to Washington, DC Along with several other PLC candidates, I boarded a United Airlines DC-7 for the long overnight flight. We landed at the National Airport early the next morning and were told we would be met at the Capital Airlines desk in the main terminal. In those days, the main terminal at National resembled more of a country airport terminal than what it grew to be.

As we approached the designated location in the middle of the terminal, we noticed a very sharp Marine captain in uniform with a "swagger stick" as part of his uniform. He asked, "Are you people going to Quantico?" I made the mistake of answering, "Yeah," after which he yelled, "Yeah shit, and get out the door and on to the bus." Needless to say, that got everyone's attention, including all the civilians in the area who were not going to Quantico.

The bus ride to the base was the next rude awakening. I-95 did not exist, nor did air conditioning. We were all in suits with the windows of the bus rolled down to at least get fresh air. All of those candidates from California were used to moderate temperatures with little humidity. Virginia in June can be miserable with excessive heat and high humidity. Both were present on that miserable bus ride. I recall I was soaked by the time we reach our destination at a facility called Camp Barrett. This was to be home for the next six weeks. The camp was located out on the fringes of the base and isolated among pine forests that existed everywhere. It felt like the humidity was hanging off of the trees. On the first three trips to the unconditioned mess hall, I did nothing but drink cold liquids by the quart. All I accomplished by so much was to just sweat it right back out.

We were separated into training platoons and assigned to World War II Quonset huts, which served as the squad bays for the training. A Quonset hut was an aluminum-covered half-moon shaped building with a door at each end of the structure. They had been famous in the South Pacific and in Korea as billets for the troops. Each one had one large fan, which kept the air circulating to a degree, and each officer candidate had an iron rack, a footlocker, and a wall locker. Anything else one brought along was put in storage until you left for home. Many of the Sergeant Instructors (Drill Instructors today) were veterans of the Pacific and Korean campaigns. My platoon sergeant had been on Iwo Jima in 1945, and the sergeant instructor had served in Korea. They brought much experience, color, and psychological pressure to the officer candidates in training. They knew what they were doing, and when to apply real pressure when it was required. On occasion, someone in the platoon would screw up, and the entire platoon of 40 candidates would pay for it. This could be increased physical exercise, more close order drill on the Grinder, or calisthenics. Even standing at attention for prolonged periods was used on occasion to make a point. This was routinely done doing periods of high heat and humidity.

The rationale was to try to determine who would break under pressure but was far less stressful than anything a lieutenant would face in combat. The instructors were careful to not push anyone too far and cause a casualty. They had another little trick that called for placing as many candidates as possible in a "Dempsey Dumpster," which was a large steel garbage receptacle for all kinds of trash. It could hold up to about nine candidates. The instructors would then close the door then beat on it with sticks or shovels. The purpose was to make the candidates think this was fun, which it was to a degree; however, what they were really after was to see who could not take the psychological pressure of being locked up. These were qualities that were not desired in a Marine officer.

There had been a period within the culture of the Corps, when Marines serving before World War II, or during that war and the Korean conflict, were considered the "Old Corps" or the "Old Breed." Many of the senior staff NCOs at Barrett were definitely "Old Corps" in their thinking and training approach to the candidates. The days were long, but we gradually got used to both the harassment and environmental conditions during training. By the end of the six weeks, the platoons had gradually pulled together as teams, and most of the candidates who did not wash out began to carry themselves like Marines. One does not rate the title of Marine until he or she successfully completes either boot camp or Officer Candidate School (OCS).

The Officer Candidate School training is not the same as the traditional boot camp for the enlisted. It can be just as hard, but the instructors are trying to identify the potential leaders who will become good officers and get rid of those who don't show the potential. The Boot Camps at either Parris Island or San Diego are more rote in the training approach, and most recruits make it through the process. Recruits stay locked up in boot camp for the duration of their training. In contrast, officer candidates are allowed time off, usually for a couple of weekends (providing they have completed their required assignments). On those occasions, we often went into Quantico town for laundry or a beer at Diamond Lou's or some other beer joint. Diamond Lou's was famous throughout the Corps for years and even made it into Leon Uris's book, *Battle Cry*. It was a gathering place for Marines whenever they were passing through Quantico. To emphasize its popularity, Diamond Lou sent up a keg of beer for our wedding reception at Whaler Hall years later. As always, it was "on the house."

A few of us ventured into Washington for one weekend, which was also an education of sorts. While it was the nation's capital, there were still things like the Blue Laws, which seemed restrictive for anyone who had come from California. The Blue Laws were a puritanical set of laws originally put in place following religious restrictions on alcohol and other items in public. In 1957 one could not compare Virginia with California. The former had most of the history but was completely backward in some of the practical ways of living and service to the public. It has since come a very long way. I only went into Washington on one occasion during this period of training at OCS. The thing that capped off the first six weeks of PLC training was the 20-mile tactical hike we went on at the end of the course. It was difficult, but it was obvious to me I had acclimated well to the environmental conditions at Quantico. Carrying a full pack with heavy weapons did not bother me. Also, I was not consuming anywhere near the amount of liquid I had done upon arrival at Camp Barrett six weeks earlier. My confidence was up as I headed back to California for my sophomore year at San José State.

Now in school, my focus increased thanks to the training at Quantico. I was paying more attention to grades, although I still did not have much of an idea of what my future might turn out to be. PLC training had provided a challenge that appealed to me. Knowing now what to expect at Quantico could point me toward preparations for the second six weeks of training following my junior year in school. I began to understand what was being said when the recruiting posters all stated to interested youth, "we never promised you a rose garden." This phrase had a certain appeal or challenge that many young men and women responded to. If someone was looking for a very demanding kind of lifestyle, the Marine Corps was it. They did not offer you anything except discipline, hard and dirty training, a great sense of purpose and camaraderie few organizations possess. If one made it through recruit training or OCS, he or she was a Marine for life, whether for a normal tour of duty or a career. This whole attitude and philosophy were appealing to me, although I still did not really understand the leadership responsibilities that came with it. I started to see a potential sense of service when we left Quantico after the first six weeks of training. My desire was to continue to develop the process of preparation for the second six-week period at OCS.

I returned to Quantico during the summer of 1959, well prepared for the second round of summer training. This time we were billeted in old wooden barracks alongside the Richmond, Fredericksburg, and Potomac (RF&P) Railroad tracks that ran right through the main part of the base and along the banks of the Potomac River. We all swore the Marine Corps had a contract with the RF&P requiring the engineers on the trains to lay on their horns as they approached our barracks. This was especially true at night. The horns would sound, and as you become awake, the lights from the engines would flash through the windows giving you the impression the train was coming right through your squad bay. The buildings would shake and did unnerve more than a few candidates until you got used to the game. One of the first things I noticed was that all the candidates in formation the first night all looked really good in appearance, in coats and ties. After looking around, I thought to myself this was going to be really competitive. As time wore on, it became rather obvious one can't tell from the outside of what a person is made of. Some of the biggest candidates in the formation could not take the psychological pressure and dropped out of the program.

On the other hand, some of the smaller, frailer candidates had huge hearts and refused to quit. They had the potential to become good officers. The key to all of this was to never give up and keep going no matter how tired and miserable one might be.

Physical activity during this session was heavy on forced marches over such forest-covered tracks as the Hill Trail or the Power Line Trail. Both ran out across the training areas but concentrated on steep hills and an occasional stream crossing usually caused by heavy rain. They all went through thick forests with lots of concentrated heat and humidity, thanks to the dense thickness of the vegetation. This part of the training was designed to see who could get through the terrain and climate without falling out. There was also a heavy emphasis on obstacle courses to increase upper body and strength coordination skills when negotiating obstacles. Much emphasis was placed on leadership billets for tactical problems. The same applied to hikes to determine how individuals reacted under both physical and psychological stress.

We all were assigned platoon, squad and fire team billets during training, and then graded on how well we performed in those assignments. Candidates who were determined to make it and who were in good physical conditioning were generally successful. Those who were not in good shape very often did not make the cut. I really came into my own during this six-week period. My confidence was up, and my physical condition was excellent. The billets assigned to me were interesting, and I began to see what leadership responsibilities required. I had been assigned as a candidate squad leader as well as a candidate platoon leader on two different occasions. As a squad leader on a hike over the Hill Trail, my responsibility was to make sure the other candidates in my squad stayed closed up and together as we went along. I was required to get other candidates to react to my leadership and problem-solving techniques. The more times I functioned in either capacity, my confidence continued to increase. I even had a good time in some of it, especially on field problems. Our final inspection was conducted in the barracks by the Commanding Officer of the Training and Test Regiment (T&T), Colonel Louis H Wilson. He was a tall, domineering officer from Mississippi who had won the Medal of Honor on Guam during World War II. When he stopped in front of you, one did not dare to glance up when answering his questions. I would meet him again in later years. By the time we processed out of this summer session, the comradery among candidates had grown because we knew we had made it.

Upon successful completion of the second session of PLC training, we moved out to National Airport for the flights home. I flew back to San Francisco to be greeted by the family, including both grandmothers. My grandfather had passed away two years earlier. In his later years, he had been plagued with heart problems that finally caught up with him while still living in Paradise. I was sure he would have approved.

With half of the summer left, there was still time to find a job. I quickly put in for apposition with the Californian Division of Forestry as a member of a firefighting crew. This was successful primarily because of my experience with the National Park Service in Yosemite. I got lucky and was assigned to the CDF fire station out in the small town of Almaden, which was only 15 miles for our home. The last six weeks of the summer of 1959 were spent at the station in Almaden.

We were called out on a couple of occasions on small grass fires that did not amount to much. However, this experience gave me some insight as to how a State level firefighting agency operates, which is somewhat different from the Park Service. Specialized equipment and off-the-road firefighting trucks to combat some of the biggest fires in the country every season belonged to the State Division of Forestry. I still had potential aspirations for following a career with the forest service or the Park Service.

I was really prepared and focused on my senior year at San José State. The course load was not too bad, which left me time to work on the side. I applied for and was accepted as a deliveryman for the San José Paint and Wallpaper Company. This job kept me busy all through my senior year. The grades began to come up as well, as I was now really pointing toward graduation. On June 10, 1960, I graduated from college with a degree in Education and was commissioned as a second lieutenant in the U.S. Marine Corps Reserve. The graduation ceremony was held outside Spartan Stadium in bright warm sunshine. There were eight or nine of us, including 2nd Lt William C. McCluskey, whom more will be learned later. We all graduated in our dress whites that day, and after the awarding of diplomas, we had a separate commissioning ceremony, where we were sworn into the service by the Director of the 12th Marine Corps District. My dad pinned on the gold bars, and there was a small reception following the ceremony. Most of my family was present, and we all went back to the house for more celebrating.

It had been a very good day, but now it was time to focus on the next chapter of life. Three of us, 2nd Lt's Bill Scarborough, Tom Betz, and I all commissioned together, had decided to drive across the country to Quantico in one car. This was the beginning of a relationship which has lasted down through the years. We had roughly thirty days from the graduation date to check-in at the Basic School for six months of instruction on how to be an officer. As I now recall, we each took about a week to get things together and then started for the east coast with roughly three weeks to spare.

CHAPTER 3
PREPARING FOR THE FAR EAST

The summer of 1960 was the beginning of an adventure. Three brand-new lieutenants drove together across the country on the way to the Basic School (TBS) at Quantico. We traveled the southern route across the United States with stops in El Paso, New Orleans, and Fort Jackson, South Carolina. From there, it was north to Quantico. One memorable incident occurred in Monroe, Louisiana. We had stopped there after a long drive across Texas and were thirsty. I went into a local store to buy a six-pack of beer and was refused service because I was wearing Bermuda shorts. The lady behind the counter would not budge from her position, so I left empty-handed. This was my first experience in the Deep South with the local peculiarities.

Our Basic Class 3-60 (the 3rd class started in 1960) commenced study in July of that year. This was where the Marine Corps trained all new officers to be leaders. It became quickly obvious that life as an officer, albeit a lieutenant, was radically different from what we had experienced as candidates at OCS. The officers living in the Bachelor Officers Quarters (BOQ) were assigned individual rooms with an adjoining bathroom between two bedrooms. The curriculum emphasized leadership problems, customs and courtesies, military law, and marksmanship with several types of weapons, as well as a variety of field exercises. We were assigned various billets to increase our level of experience in leading others in a variety of situations, both in garrison and in the field. It also began to emphasize the importance of Marine Corps Aviation along with all other supporting arms that were available to the infantry. Young officers were required to know how to employ all of them separately as well as together on the battlefield. I really enjoyed the weapons instruction, including the live firing that went along with it. The only trepidation I had was firing the portable flamethrower. An awesome weapon but a fearful one, it has since been dropped from the inventory. Our officer instructors were all high-quality individuals who were veterans of the Korean War and specifically selected for assignment to the Basic School.

Social life, while at the Basic School, was really active. In addition to the normal military ceremonial responsibilities, the lieutenants had most of the weekends off. On several occasions, we would pile into our cars and head for Mary Washington College in Fredericksburg. At the time, the school was an all-girls institution and an obvious source for dates for several social activities. We could do what we pleased on the weekends, although it usually required a great amount of study due to the academic requirements for the Basic School. I had developed a friendship with 2ndLt Vincent R Lee, a Princeton graduate with a degree in architecture, who arrived at TBS in a customized 1939 Chevrolet 2-door sedan. This car, "the Hot Nine," was painted forest green and had a '55 Corvette engine in it. The Chevy could really fly as we rolled down U.S. Route One toward Fredericksburg and Mary Washington. Riding in that car brought back many memories of experiences with my '48 Lincoln. He and I went overseas together in 1961 and served the next year on Okinawa. Our time at TBS passed quickly as everyone was trying to withstand the demanding training schedule while preparing for assignments following graduation. There was not a lot of competition between lieutenants in the beginning, but this gradually increased as class standing at the end of the school became important.

The final field exercise was a three-day event staged in the dead of winter in January 1961. It was bitter cold with some snow and ice on the ponds in the training areas. Quantico can be just as miserable during winter, due to the damp environment in the state. When the event was over, we prepared for graduation from the Basic School and the assignments to our first duty stations. Two days after graduation, my mother, who had flown from California to attend the ceremony, accompanied me to the inauguration of President John F. Kennedy on a very cold and snowy day in Washington, DC It was quite an experience. We had a family relative, a congressman from California, who had given us tickets to sit near the podium and right behind the Marine Band. We were only about thirty-five yards from President Eisenhower, Kennedy, and Lyndon Johnson during the ceremony. Kennedy gave a very inspirational speech during the inauguration, which has resonated for years since then.

Following the ceremony, my mother and I then proceeded down Pennsylvania Avenue to find seats for the traditional parade in what continued to be freezing temperatures. Shortly after the parade, she prepared to fly back to San Francisco. I went back to Quantico to get ready for another road trip across the country with two other Basic School graduates. One was 2nd Lt Reginald George Ponsford III, a former bronc rider from Colorado State University, who served with distinction later in Vietnam. We all had orders to the 1st Marine Division and ended up going overseas together on this first deployment.

My friend, 2nd Lt Bill McCluskey, had reported to the Basic School at the same time, but he was in a different company. He graduated from TBS with orders to the 1st Marine Division, 5th Marine Regiment, in preparation for going overseas. He deployed for a one-year tour with his battalion to Okinawa, and later as the Special Landing Force (SLF) in the Far East operating in various locations to include deep patrolling in Thailand along the Laotian border. Upon return to Camp Pendleton, he requested orders to flight school. Upon graduation from flight school, Bill flew H-34 helicopters in the early stages of the Vietnam War, operating out of Chu Lai in 1965.

My orders were to report to the 1st Battalion, 5th Marine Regiment, 1st Marine Division at Camp Pendleton, California. Three of us drove back across the country in three days at a time when there were no interstate highways or clusters of gas stations and fast-food establishments in existence. Each of us took a four-hour shift behind the wheel. We made it to Denver in two days and stopped for the night there. The next day it was on to the San Francisco Bay Area to see relatives. After a short period with the family, we moved further south to the sprawling Marine base just outside of Oceanside, California.

Upon the arrival at my unit, Alpha Company, 1st Battalion, 5th Marines, I was assigned as a weapons platoon commander in charge of some forty-eight Marines and one Navy corpsman. In those days, a Marine rifle company (normally about 200 Marines) consisted of three rifle platoons and one weapons platoon. The weapons platoon consisted of three machine-gun sections and three rocket launcher sections, each assigned out to one of the rifle platoons for exercises or combat. The company was commanded by Captain Earl Pierson, a pleasant individual but one who was not very outgoing or overly close to his officers. He could be very prickly if something minor was bothering him.

Each platoon was commanded by a second lieutenant. This is where the rubber meets the road, and heavy responsibility starts. The troops belonged to me, and I was responsible for just about everything they did, good or bad. The Marine Corps gives newly commissioned lieutenants assignments like that routinely and expects them to perform up to the highest standards as leaders. At this level, the key to one's success often depends on your platoon sergeant, who is normally an experienced Gunnery Sergeant. I was fortunate in that I had GySgt Paul Bauer, a no-nonsense professional who knew all the ropes for success. Some other new officers were not so lucky, which caused them problems within their platoons.

On one occasion, while we were out on a field exercise, I decided to emplace my three machine-gun sections with the three rifle platoons in the company in some manner I thought best. It turned out I had assigned the sections to the wrong platoons, and Bauer, who later served in Vietnam and easily made Sergeant Major, quickly asked me, "Lieutenant, what are you doing?" in a very direct manner. The section leaders, who were all corporals, just looked on waiting to see what would happen. The "Gunny" quickly explained why we did it his way, and adjustments were made. I decided to do it correctly his way, and if I had pulled rank on him, my credibility would have been blown with the troops who were watching this. The valuable lesson learned here was you can't B.S. the troops and don't be afraid to admit—and then correct—a mistake.

The battalion went through an intensive six-week training program at Camp Pendleton in preparation for deployment overseas. Upon completion of the training, we were moved to San Diego to go aboard ship for the eighteen-day journey across the Pacific to Okinawa. The cruise on the USS *Renville* (APA-227) was routine. The major focus was to adjust to life at sea as well as learn to live with the U.S. Navy. Life onboard an amphibious transport in the early 1960s was often cramped and boring for the embarked troops. They were usually stacked four high in the troop compartments with little extra space to move around. If one man got seasick, they all got seasick until they became acclimated to life at sea. The open deck on the first day and night out of San Diego was a dangerous place to be because of the "flying vomit" from seasick Marines. That meant the officers had to come up with plans for classes, exercise and even a boxing tournament for the troops, to retain some semblance of conditioning. All of this was normally held on deck and usually on the hatch covers in various locations around the ship.

We arrived at the port of Naha, Okinawa, in May 1961 and were quickly moved by truck to our new base at Camp Sukiran. Once on Okinawa, our unit designation changed to Alpha Company 1st Battalion, 9th Marine Regiment, 3rd Marine Division. This division was really one of two major organizations on the island responsible for peace and stability in that part of Asia. The other organization was the Army's 173rd Airborne Brigade, which was also based around Camp Sukiran.

The next twelve months saw the battalion participate in several exercises on Okinawa, in Japan and in the Philippines. We always moved from one location to another onboard Navy amphibious transport ships. Most were veterans of World War II in the Pacific. One such ship, the USS *George Clymer* (APA-27). The Greasy George had been captured during the war and converted to a troopship for the U.S. Navy. It still had large bay windows in the officer's mess on the main deck, which was reminiscent of another time in the cruising world. Instead of looking out the windows at the sea, you saw landing craft lashed to davits on the deck of the ship.

The Marine Corps routinely piles extra responsibility on its junior officers with the expectation that the assignment will be carried out successfully. We had been on Okinawa for about four months when I was called in to the battalion commander's office for one of these assignments. He directed me to go to the Philippines and set up arrangements for a Christmas party for the battalion while it was in Manila for the Christmas holidays. That was about the extent of the guidance I received from him. The size of an infantry battalion was around 1,000 troops in those days, and the support for something like this was no small matter, especially in a foreign country. The battalion had not deployed to the Philippines for training as yet, so just getting there was a challenge in its own right. My knowledge of the people, culture, and geography of that country was limited at best.

I was able to catch a flight on a small Navy aircraft that flew from Okinawa to Cubi Point, the Navy air station located in Subic Bay on the island of Luzon. From there, it was a matter of working my way south to Manila. Paying a call at the U.S. embassy in Manila enabled me to receive excellent guidance and assistance about organizations in the city that would host our units. When the details were completed for the visit, I caught another small Marine aircraft at the air station at Sangley Point outside Manila and flew back to Cubi. While waiting for transportation back to Okinawa, I was able to coordinate our visit with the Marine battalion we were to relieve there later in the year. Then it was back to Okinawa on another Marine aircraft. Unfortunately, the party did not come off due to a change in schedule for the battalion. This had been good experience for me, as this sort of tasking came up several times throughout my later career.

During certain times of the year, the Pacific can generate major storms with devastating effects on any country from the Philippines, South China, and Taiwan to Japan. Such was the case in Japan in the fall of 1961. The battalion had deployed by ship to the coast of Japan, landed on the Numazu beaches, and then moved to the Mt Fuji training area for 30 days. The mountain was located in a beautiful region of Japan where the weather was cool at that time of the year. Marine units had been guests of the Japanese government at Fuji for some time and often shared this area with units of the Japanese Self Defense Force (JSDF). The terrain was excellent for all types of small unit tactics and weapons firing on the available ranges. When Marines trained there, they had to build their own tent camps for billeting, storage of weapons and supplies.

The battalion had been in position for about two weeks when we began to get reports of typhoons forming in the South Pacific. We continued to train as planned until one day, we were called in from the field and told to try to tie everything down. A day later, the winds started to blow very hard, and rain began to fall in heavy sheets. Finally, the gale force winds forced the battalion units out of the tents and under our troop trucks that had been drawn up as a buffer for the tents. Captain Pierson was adamant that nobody should leave what cover we had until the storm was over. When the center of the storm hit our camp, tents were shredded and torn to pieces. Sections of Japanese buildings were flying over our camp and out into the training area. The rain poured down for what seemed like hours until the winds finally died down.

When it stopped, we were able to crawl out from under the trucks and survey the damage. The entire camp was destroyed. All the equipment and personal gear were in a huge mess in water and mud. Fortunately, nobody was hurt, but training came to an end, as we had to survey the damage and rebuild some semblance of a camp. That effort took the better part of a week. When we had sufficiently recovered, it was time to go back aboard ship for the trip back to Okinawa. This storm had caused major damage to parts of Japan as well as casualties within the population. I had personally never seen anything like the force of that typhoon.

The cruise back to Okinawa was uneventful. We arrived at White Beach in the center of the island and moved back to our permanent facilities at Camp Hansen. About a week after we were settled in our barracks, the alert sounded again. There was another major typhoon approaching from the south of the island. This time we were ready when it hit. The barracks, armories, and supply facilities were in hardened concrete buildings and somewhat typhoon-proof. The battalion units were again called in from the field and confined to their barracks with supplies of food and water. As in Japan, this storm arrived with extremely high winds for a longer period, and then the rains lashed at everything for hours. When it was over, we did not have much damage, but the small Okinawan villages around the base suffered badly. Fortunately, we did not have to go through another storm like these two for the duration of our year on Okinawa.

For decades up to the present, there has always been a Marine Special Landing Force (SLF) at sea aboard Navy amphibious ships of the 7th Fleet in the Western Pacific. In 1962 this two-month mission was given to my battalion, as we had been training around Subic Bay in the Philippines. This was a deployment normally given to the most experienced unit in training during the twelve-month tour in the Western Pacific. The standing mission was to provide presence and stability, humanitarian operations, or a tactical response to some sort of contingency as directed by the U.S. 7th Fleet. We were embarked on the USS *Princeton*, a World War II aircraft carrier converted to a helicopter carrier. The battalion went on board the Princeton in Subic Bay and joined up with a Marine Medium Helicopter Squadron (HMM-362) known as Archie's Angels. Compared to living on an amphibious transport, the *Princeton* was really comfortable.

The jungles on Luzon provided a very realistic environment for both tactical and survival training for the Marines. The jungle was extremely thick with high humidity and never-ending rain. There were various kinds of snakes and other creatures that could be deadly if a man was bitten. The area around Subic Bay was ideal for patrolling and small unit tactics. One day while we were patrolling through some very thick jungle, I came around a giant Banyan tree and face to face with three Negrito warriors. They were about the same size as pygmies and indigenous to that area of the Philippines. They made no noise when moving through the thick brush and bamboo thickets. This had surprised me because we did not know they were there. All three were armed with blowguns fashioned out of bamboo and wicked-looking jungle knives made from a jeep spring. They were clothed in loincloths and were very dark. The battalion had been briefed on the Negritos, who were considered friendly. After trying to communicate in sign language with them, we moved on. The Negritos were often used to train our pilots in survival techniques and how to stay alive in the jungles if shot down. It was clear we wanted them on our side because they were experts in jungle survival.

One day we were practicing helicopter operations off the *Princeton* when we noticed a World War II Jeep carrier coming into the entrance to Subic Bay. It was the USNS *Breton*, and she was loaded with U.S. Army helicopters (the old H-21 "Banana" Helicopters). The Army birds were to be transferred to our ship for an undisclosed mission. This was accomplished pier side in Subic Bay as the Army pilots eventually got both helicopter companies on board. They were from Fort Devens, Mass., and all the pilots were Army Warrant Officers. They were graduates of one of the best Army Aviation Warrant Officer programs ever, that still exists today. When all of their equipment was safely on the *Princeton*, we sailed for the South China Sea. It was soon announced that we were to provide an escort for them to Vietnam.

The *Princeton* picked up a destroyer escort as we were off the coast of Luzon, which gave us the impression that this deployment was something fairly serious. The cruise across the South China Sea went without incident, although we enjoyed watching the destroyer pitch and plunge through the swells of the sea. It looked to me like the "young man's Navy" as the destroyer was always half underwater. We arrived off the coast of South Vietnam at dawn on the fourth day out of Subic Bay. The plan was to have Archie's Angels H-34 helicopters escort the Army units across the beach and inland to Phu Bai in South Vietnam. This movement took most of the day, but there were no aircraft incidents. HMM-362 helicopters were all back on board the ship by dusk. This operation occurred in March 1962, three years before the Marines landed in Da Nang, South Vietnam, in 1965.

That night and under destroyer escort, the ship turned back east and headed up through the South China Sea toward Hong Kong. At this time in the deployment, the battalion was scheduled for a port call for some liberty ashore. This was special because there were no other ports in the region that were as good for liberty as Hong Kong. It was the only place on the Chinese coast that was open for visits like ours. Hong Kong had been a British Protectorate for years, and it resembled San Francisco in many respects. It also had an excellent harbor that sat between Hong Kong Island and the city of Kowloon, which was the home of major banks, hotels, and businesses. There was a local tradition that when a U. S. Navy ship pulled into the harbor, a contract was issued to a local merchant named "Garbage Mary." She ran a company that would come out in a fleet of sampans and paint the entire hull of a ship below the main deck in a matter of hours just for the garbage that normally came off of the ship. They would turn around and sell the garbage to hungry Chinese in Hong Kong.

While the ship was being painted, we went ashore on Hong Kong Island to see the sights. There was a traditional China Fleet Club where we could go shopping, drinking, and eating. This was also the Wan Chi district, where you could get measured for a suit or shoes within a matter of minutes over a bottle of beer. In any one of several tailor shops, the cost of a suit was roughly $30.00. The tailors would often host a traditional Chinese dinner at one of the restaurants in the district, while other tailors would put together the suit, shoes, or anything else. Usually, they would have the clothes ready the next morning knowing that the fleet's clock for departure was working against them. The quality of the tailoring was excellent and always right to the measured specifications.

The Wan Chi district was famous throughout the 7th Fleet for any number of reasons. Hollywood later made a movie called "The World of Suzie Wong," which was a hit among the troops as it was partially filmed there.

Following the liberty call in Hong Kong, we finished up our training in the jungles around Subic and prepared to move back to Okinawa. The 13-month deployment was almost over, and the battalion prepared to move back to the states. The troops in the weapons platoon had performed well in a variety of situations over the past year. They had come together as a team both in garrison and on numerous exercises in the field. Both machine gunners and rocket men became very proficient with their weapons in support of the rifle platoons. We had relatively few discipline problems throughout the deployment, despite being in some of the seedier locations in the Far East. The troops had gained confidence in themselves. The attitude was that their unit had been successful in almost everything they had accomplished, and now it was time to prepare to leave by ship for home.

In June 1962, the battalion left for the long voyage across the Pacific for California. Before its departure, I received orders for my next duty station, which was to be the Marine Barracks at the San Francisco Naval Shipyard in San Francisco, California. I was sorry to leave the battalion because I had gained much experience in leading Marines and had seen parts of three countries. Leaving a unit that one had molded and cared for was never fun, but necessary. In October 1962, this battalion would become the first one to be airlifted from California to Guantanamo Bay during the Cuban Missile Crisis.

In May 1962, I left Okinawa for the flights back to the states. There was a rousing party at the Kadena Air Force Base Officers Club, where everything sold over the bar went for a penny. This was the famous Copper Night, as I was soon to learn, and it occurred just hours before boarding a DC-7 transport for the flight to California. This event was in the days before jets, so it was to be a long flight. We took off from Kadena and flew all night before landing on Wake Island in the middle of the Pacific. The approach to the island was interesting as we continued to descend but could see no ground. As the plane got lower and lower, the ocean continued to rise toward the aircraft.

Finally, when it looked like we were going to land in the water, we passed over the wreckage of a Japanese transport that had been beached during the battle for the island. Wake had been one of the first locations to be captured by the Japanese at the beginning of World War II. There clearly was not much on the island other than a refueling facility and a compound for flight crews that were staying overnight before moving on. After refueling the aircraft and changing crews, we took off again and flew all day long, landing in the dark at Hickam Air Force Base in Hawaii. Here we had a four-hour layover before taking off for the final night leg of the flight to Travis Air Force Base in California. This brought to end my first of three deployments I would have to the Far East in the years to come.

CHAPTER 4

LIFE IN THE GOLDEN WEST

Arriving in San Francisco was not something new for me, having grown up across the bay in Oakland, and attending school in San José some fifty miles to the south. Getting an assignment there as a reserve officer was considered quite a plum in terms of location. There was a certain amount of luck associated with the whole event; however, I am sure that the assignment officers at Headquarters Marine Corps decided to locate me close to home because as a reserve officer, my normal obligation would be up in two years, and I would get out of the service. That was what effective assignment officers did, and I had given them no indication that I would stay any longer in the Corps. Basically, my plans for any career had not changed much since entering college: Stay active in several things, have fun where possible, and do some traveling. There had not been any negative experiences while on active duty, and we had seen the better part of the Far East. My assignments had required heavy responsibility leading Marines, and I had liked what I was doing.

My arrival in San Francisco was at a good time in the Bay Area. It was a beautiful location with the city sitting between the Bay Bridge and the Golden Gate Bridge. Crossing the Golden Gate and heading north would lead you to the Redwood Empire or the massive winegrowing region between Napa and Sonoma. San Francisco had everything in it as far as entertainment goes. Fisherman's Wharf, Chinatown, and the Cliff House out on the beach were the top tourist spots in the city. At that time, the Presidio was the home of the VI Army Headquarters which overlooked the Golden Gate Bridge as well as the Pacific Ocean. If one were to cross the Bay Bridge toward Oakland, you could drop off on Treasure Island, which sat in the middle of the bay. There was a large contingent of Marines stationed at the barracks there who supported offices of the 12th Marine Corps

District in San Francisco. There was also an old observation tower perched on the very top of Treasure Island that was a relic from World War II. The Navy had converted it into a small club which could accommodate about 20 people, and the views from up there were magnificent. That became the hangout for the officers on Friday afternoons before heading into the city for the evening.

Once we were in the city, we would go to establishments like Carol Doda's on Broadway or nightclubs like the Blackhawk or the Purple Onion. Lefty O'Doul's in Union Square was a great stop for a late-night sandwich. Then there was the world-famous Buena Vista (The BV), the home of world-class Irish coffee, and it is still there today. The San Francisco Naval Shipyard had a history all its own. It had been the anchorage for most of the Pacific Reserve Fleet that were waiting to decommission to a different status following the war. The yard itself was a major repair facility for the Navy and had dry docks that could accommodate ships up to the size of the Kitty Hawk-class carriers. The assignment to the Marine Barracks at the naval shipyard was very different from life in an infantry battalion. We were basically responsible for the security of the shipyard. Like Marines serving at five other Marine Barracks around the Bay Area, we all generally had the same mission as it related to guarding Navy facilities and installations. This called for manning the gates to the shipyard, providing traffic control within the yard, and actually holding a traffic court for speeders. We spent a great deal of time coordinating with the various navy ships in for repair as well as participating in numerous ceremonies in the yard or out in San Francisco. I had been assigned as the executive officer of the barracks and retained the position for the entire length of what was to be my three-year tour.

The requirements associated with my billet were not very taxing, mostly dealing with security issues in the shipyard. My boss was Major Verle Ludwig, who had served in the Corps for many years. He was the quiet type and an avid pipe smoker who pretty much let me run whatever was required. The experience gained at the barracks gave me more insight into another aspect of life in the Marine Corps. The Marine Barracks was a totally self-contained facility that included living areas for the Marines, a mess hall, club, and tailor shop along with the normal office spaces. The average complement for Marines called for sixty-five enlisted men and two officers. The senior enlisted man was the barracks Sergeant Major, and we were blessed with two during my time in the shipyard. Sergeant Major James Jackson had been with the Raider Battalions in the Solomon Islands in the South Pacific during the early stages of World War II. The Raiders were formed to carry out small, highly dangerous operations deep in enemy territory in the beginning, but were later disbanded when amphibious operations grew in scope. Jackson was very effective, and definitely "Old Corps." Duty for the troops was not always challenging, and liberty around San Francisco frequently led to minor infractions. Sergeant Major Jackson had a way of dealing with this so that the first offenders did not want to reappear before him on the second time around.

During my third year at the barracks, he retired and was replaced by Sergeant Major Albert Stuart, who had served for over forty years, starting out as an enlisted man serving in Latin America during the "Banana Wars" in the 1930s. The Banana Wars were occupations, police actions, and interventions by the United States in Central America and the Caribbean. He was a quiet, friendly individual and also one of the "Old Corps" in the way he handled his responsibilities at the barracks. Sergeant Major Stuart had its own unique ways of handling the troops who managed to get out of line. Both of them were solid professionals and institutions in their own right, well respected by the Marines.

One other Marine I would like to mention was a Corporal Lafo Malualu. He was a Samoan Chief who was built like a NFL running back. I had the fortune of pronouncing his name correctly the first time, which he never forgot. Samoans in the Marine Corps were not that unusual, and they all served with distinction. On one occasion, I received an invitation to attend Lafo's wedding. There was a colony of Samoans living a short distance outside the shipyard, and I made plans to attend the wedding. I did not realize I was to be the guest of honor at the ceremony until I arrived there. Lafo, being the chief of that particular clan, had decreed it. It was a very nice traditional Samoan ceremony, and they made me feel like I was one of them. The reception was spectacular but within the traditions of the Samoan culture, which was unique in its own right. This was my first experience with any culture in the South Pacific. The Samoan Marines were absolutely loyal, disciplined, and always stayed out of trouble.

There were few instances when Marines from the barracks would provide honor guards for the commissioning of a new ship that had finished its construction in the shipyard. For one of these events, we were required to participate in the commissioning of the USS *Halsey*, which was a new light missile cruiser. This was a big deal because the ship had been named after Admiral "Bull" Halsey, who was one of the key fleet commanders in the drive across the Pacific during World War II. The ceremony was to be reviewed by retired five-star Admiral Chester Nimitz, who was then living on Treasure Island. Even in his retirement, he was driven around in a big black Cadillac with a Marine Gunnery Sergeant as his personal driver. When the admiral arrived, we rendered honors to him and fired the traditional gun salute from our saluting battery. This was followed by the ceremony that was conducted for such occasions. I remember he was tall and very attentive to what we were doing, although he had probably been through many of these same ceremonies while on active duty. It was a bit of living history for us that nobody had expected.

I lived in the shipyard BOQ, which was only fifteen minutes from downtown San Francisco. That also kept me close to my family, who were living in San José some 50 miles to the south. One surprise I did get was that my mother and father had separated while I was in the Far East, but were still living in the San José area. After a short time, both were remarried and continued to live in the Bay Area.

My grandmother Mimi was still working at the *San Francisco Chronicle,* and we used to get together at Fisherman's Wharf for dinner on several occasions, and then I would drive her home to Oakland across the bay. Her parents had emigrated from Ireland and settled in the Salinas Valley years earlier. She had grown up there, married my grandfather William P. Jenkins in 1914, and lived in the Bay Area in the years following her marriage. She was in excellent health, with a warm personality, and always very supportive of what I was doing in the service.

Most of the junior officers in the various Marine Barracks in the Bay Area were not married. We would get together frequently in any number of settings in Oakland, San Francisco, the actual turtle races at Zack's in Sausalito, or at Lake Tahoe during the winter months. This was where my love of skiing resurfaced. I had not been able to do much of it since my first experiences in high school with the trips to Yosemite. We all went in to rent a large home in the area near the base of the Heavenly Valley ski resort. When not on duty, we would head for the lake on Friday evenings, ski all day on Saturday and Sunday, and then drive back to the Bay Area Sunday evening. Saturday evenings were usually spent in the casinos at Stateline. The rented house became "ground zero" for any number of activities over the next four winters at Lake Tahoe. This was one of those types of duty people read about but rarely get the opportunity to serve in that kind of environment.

The one major event that occurred while I was at the barracks was the assassination of President John F. Kennedy in Dallas on November 22, 1963. I was coming down the stairs at the barracks following an inspection when my administrative chief, Staff Sergeant Bob Dorie, told me Kennedy had been shot. I had an instant flashback to the inauguration ceremony for President Kennedy in Washington and wondered what was coming next. While we were a long way away from that terrible event, the reaction of Marine units around the Bay Area was swift. Not knowing what was coming next, we went to a Defense Condition and locked down the entrance to the shipyard until the situation cleared up. The guard was doubled on each of the two gates, and careful searches were done on all vehicles coming and going as well as around the perimeter of the yard. In hindsight, it seemed like an overreaction, but the contingency plan for such events had worked well, and we were back to normal within a few days.

The arrival of Staff Sergeant Bob Dorie, who was to be the new Administrative Chief for the Barracks, began what was to be called a very colorful time at the Marine Barracks. Between parties and golf, he could handle it all. Bob was one of those interesting characters you often find in the service: a wheeler-dealer if ever there was one, but an extremely capable individual when on duty. He had served in Korea and had risen to the rank of Technical Sergeant before being reduced to the rank of private for flying unauthorized cargo on Marine aircraft. He had worked his way back to Staff Sergeant before arriving at the barracks. He was very popular with the Marines in the barracks, and we would meet again in another assignment in 1971.

One of the tasks we tried to accomplish was to get the Marines out into the field for some tactical training. This was much more difficult than it sounded, being close to downtown San Francisco. Needless to say, one can't run small unit tactical problems in the base housing area. We were able to find some open spaces across the Golden Gate Bridge in Marin County that were better than nothing. Then we got the idea we might be able to exercise on Angel Island, which was located in San Francisco Bay and owned by the state park system. The island sat close to the former federal prison on Alcatraz and was an easy boat trip across the bay. All the coordination was completed, and the necessary support was put in place. It was a beautiful sunny day in May 1964, when the exercise started and the winds were calm, which proved to be a good thing. After about two hours into the exercise, smoke was reported coming up from the brush on one side of the island. It was clear we had started the fire as a result of using pyrotechnics for signaling. Firefighting equipment was brought in to put the fire out. After that, the authorities politely asked us to leave the island and never to return. So ended the tactical training for the troops on Angel Island.

About midway through my time at the shipyard, an announcement came out from Headquarters Marine Corps offering reserve officers an opportunity to apply for augmentation into the regular establishment. In those days, most Marine officers were given reserve commissions unless they were coming out of the Naval Academy. The policy was those reserve officers had three opportunities to apply for augmentation before leaving the Corps at the end of their obligation. As a regular officer, one served as long as he or she desired, providing conduct and proficiency reports were good, appropriate schools were attended, and one could compete successfully with peers during selection for promotion to higher ranks. Applying for augmentation meant that my record would go before a board in Washington. At this point in my short career in the Corps, I had no complaints regarding where I had been and what I had been doing. The selection board recommended me for augmentation into the regulars, and after signing the appropriate papers in San Francisco, I went back to work. I had made no personal commitment to a full career in the Marine Corps at this point. Upon completion of my three years at the Marine Barracks, what came next was something I had wanted to do but did not hold out much hope of getting the assignment. Requesting duty at the Mountain Warfare Training Center (MWTC) on several of my fitness reports at least gave me a chance for the job. It all depended on what the assignment officers at Headquarters Marine Corps needed. Luck played a role along with billet vacancies, I am sure. Staff Sergeant Bob Dorie at the barracks called me one day and announced that I was heading back to the mountains.

I left the barracks just before Christmas 1964 and spent the holiday at home with all the family. Shortly after that, I checked in at the Mountain Warfare Training Center and then went back out to celebrate New Year's in our ski house at Lake Tahoe.

CHAPTER 5
BACK TO THE SIERRAS

The Marine Corps was famous for conducting bloody assaults across the Pacific during World War II. But in the Inchon Landing during the Korean War in 1950, Marine units encountered bitter winter conditions while attacking north toward the Chosin Reservoir in North Korea, and during their fighting withdrawal back through the mountains to the sea. The Corps leadership in Washington soon realized they needed a training facility where Marines could learn to operate successfully in the mountains and during extreme winter conditions.

After a process of evaluation of potential training sites, a decision was made to create such a facility in the mountains, northwest of Bridgeport, California. The site was to be along U.S. Highway 108 in Pickle Meadow and some nine miles east of the Sonora Pass. Elevations ranged from 6,800 feet in the meadow all the way up to 11,000 feet on the peaks north of the pass. The highest peak in that area that overlooked most of the training area was Lost Cannon Peak at 11,099 feet in elevation. Its name came out of a story that when Lieutenant John C. Fremont had explored this region for the Army in the 1840s, one of his detachments had left a small cannon stuck in the deep snow as they fought to survive. It has not been found, but the name was applied to the mountain.

Foliage in most of the training areas ranged from sage and grass in the meadows to thick stands of lodgepole, Aspen, and Ponderosa Pines in the canyons and higher elevations. The snowfall accumulation in the training areas above the base camp could be as much as 10 feet in the canyons and up to 25 feet in the Sonora Pass, which was closed during the winter months. The West Walker River paralleled Highway 108 and would normally freeze over for a portion of the winter. The environment created ideal conditions for winter training as well as exposing the troops to some deadly hazards that they might have to deal with in winter combat operations. This made it the best training environment in the Marine Corps for developing noncommissioned officers as well as young officers into effective leaders. The altitude and steep terrain made any movement difficult and especially during movement through heavy snow. The summer and winter mountain operations courses could put severe pressure on an individual and test his leadership style like nothing else, thanks to the environment.

On December 29, 1964, I reported to the Marine Corps MWTC for duty. Shortly after that, on a very cold and snowy January 6, 1965, I joined the first class for the grueling thirty-day Winter Operations Course. At 0630 in the morning on the first day, we fell out of our World War II Quonset huts for morning physical training. The formation came to order on the snow-covered airstrip. The class commander, Captain Yogi Harden, called the formation to attention and then ordered the class to get down for pushups. That meant plunging into three feet of snow to get in position. As the entire class disappeared in the snow, Captain Harden began to call cadence, and off we went. Upon completion of the various exercises, we were formed up and then jogged down the airstrip and up a snow-covered road to the mess hall for breakfast. This does not seem like much, except we were at 6,800 feet in elevation and definitely not acclimated. Following breakfast, we then jogged back down the snowy road to the Quonset huts to get ready for the day's activities. The snow continued to fall, and we were not sure of what was coming next.

We proceeded through the training syllabus for the course and gradually became acclimated to the harsh conditions and the deep snow. Skiing and snowshoeing were the required methods for moving across snow-covered terrain while carrying heavy loads. Trying to ski in rubber thermal boots ("Mickey Mouse" boots) on old wooden World War II skis created some very interesting experiences.

Captain Harden, who had come in from Guam to attend the course, was a physical fitness horse. He could not master skiing no matter what happened, so he would drop in for ten pushups every time he fell. At the end of the day, he would log in some 250 to 300 pushups as a result of his skiing experiences. Our instructors were good, but they could only do so much with beginners if the equipment was worn and outmoded.

The course covered a myriad of subjects, including survival techniques, tactics, avalanche rescue, cold weather injuries, and cross-country mobility. The final field exercise consisted of a very challenging three-day cross-country movement featuring sleeping in open snow trenches at 8,000 to 9,000 feet while attacking enemy positions both during daylight and darkness. At one point in the exercise, a Marine fell and severely injured an ankle. The man could not walk, so a medevac was requested. Fortunately, we had a detachment of H-34 helicopters at the base camp, one of which responded to the request.

We were in positions overlooking the closed Sonora Pass at an altitude of about 9,500 feet when the helicopter came in to pick up the injured Marine. At that altitude, the H-34 could hardly hover over the side of the slope we were on. After throwing much equipment out in the snow to reduce weight, the pilot was able to lower the bird enough so that we could get the casualty into the helicopter. He then had enough power to ease away from the slope and drift off down the mountainside and out over the canyon.

That was my first experience in the limitations of helicopters in high altitudes. After graduating from the winter course, I was assigned to the staff as an instructor guide for the next twenty-seven months or three winters. One other incident involving the pilot of the H-34 helicopter bears repeating. He was Captain Jim Griego, a pilot with great skills in the cockpit. When things were calm around the training center, he would take-off in the H-34 and look for coyotes while flying up and down some of the cleared areas south of the West

Walker River. I went with him one day to see what we could scare up. When one animal was spotted, the chase was on. The coyote, which had terrific endurance, ran for miles with Griego following it up and over the hills for a while before returning to the base. In those days you could get away with doing things like that because there was nobody anywhere near this area in the national forest. Today that would be grounds for dismissal from the aviation community.

* * *

On completion of the Winter Mountain Operations Course in February 1965, I was promoted to captain and lined up for other courses that I had to finish before taking over a unit at the training center. In those days, one had to complete the Winter Course and the Survival, Escape, Resistance and Evasion (SERE) Course, as well as the Summer Mountain Operations Course before you became a fully qualified military mountaineer. Completing all three without difficulty, I was assigned to take over the Special Training Unit (STU). We were responsible for the unit winter course as well as the summer training of all reserve units that would come in for their two weeks of active duty.

In the fall of 1965, we received word that we would be getting a British Royal Marine on the staff for a two-year tour. This was excellent news because the Royal Marine commando units had a variety of skills that could be integrated into our training program. Captain James Noel Anthony Goldsworthy, RM, arrived one sunny afternoon and reported to the Commanding Officer, Colonel John B. Bristow. Goldsworthy had been briefed by the British Naval Attaché in Washington on how to conduct himself because his record and reputation at that level "was black" with previous incidents. Jim arrived all prim and proper in a way that only British officers can demonstrate. It so happened that we were having a Mess Night that evening in honor of Major General Robert Cushman, who was the commanding general at Camp Pendleton, California. An open bar was followed by wine and toasts to the president, the queen, and numerous others. At 6,800 feet in altitude, that can turn a normally sedate event into a free-for-all, which is what happened. It was a great party, but the last time that Goldsworthy, "the Englishman," was ever really prim and proper. He was an expert climber as well as a skier and added a good deal of expertise to the mountain operations program. He initiated a tactic called the Night Cliff Assault, whereby commandos would scale a cliff face at night when there was no other way around the obstacle. Lead climbers would establish fixed rope anchor points and provide security while other climbers with heavy loads would follow up the fixed ropes. This tactic was put into the mountain operations curriculum as an advanced tactic because it was such a hairy operation at night.

Jim Goldsworthy also instigated several changes to demonstrations we held for new classes or an occasional VIP. The most notable of these was the "Flying Angel." This technique featured Goldsworthy coming off of a cliff head in the commando crawl position on top of a fixed 1-inch cargo rope and descending some 100 feet down the cliff at a 45-degree angle face first, with his arms out for balance. He would grasp the rope with his gloves and apply pressure to slow down before he hit the safety knot at the bottom. His gloves would be smoking by the time he reached the bottom of the rope, which got everyone's attention. This was a technique that would be used if one had to get off a cliff quickly.

It impressed the audience, but Colonel Bristow banned any of our instructors from doing it. John Bristow was a no-nonsense veteran of fighting in the Pacific during World War II. Following the Japanese surrender in 1945, as a Captain, he deployed to north China along with a force of fifty thousand U.S. Marines. The mission was to provide security at various long supply routes and assist the Japanese de facto occupation until Chinese Nationalist troops could move to repatriate thousands of Japanese forces back to Japan. In the spring of 1946, conditions were deteriorating between the Nationalists under Chiang Kai-shek and the communists under Mao Zedong for the control of China. Caught in the middle, Marines became the targets of anti-American incidents.

On one occasion, a Marine supply convoy was ambushed by communists near the village of Anping. In the ensuing battle, four Marines were killed, and a dozen wounded before the column could make it back to its base along the coast. In another incident, a group of seven American Marines out on a hunting party were captured by communists and held for eleven days on charges of spying. Then Captain Bristow was ordered to go into communist territory with a radio operator and negotiate the release of the men. After enduring rough treatment from the Chinese, he eventually succeeded in gaining their release. In 1946 it fell on a Marine captain to go and get them. Today it would probably be the Secretary of State, and God knows who else. Several of the lessons he learned from that incident prompted John Bristow to incorporate some of them into the training scenarios in the courses at MWTC.

The Mountain Warfare Training Center could always be and often was a magnet for colorful characters who served there over the years. One, in particular, was Master Gunnery Sergeant John Marjanov. He had served with the Navy's Seabees in the Pacific in World War II, enlisted in the Army Air Corps in 1946, and then in the Marine Corps in 1949. He served in the Corps for a career as a Marine Combat Engineer for the next 25 years. While in Korea in 1953, he was assigned as a bulldozer operator in support of the British Commonwealth Forces, where he distinguished himself against the Chinese. He was awarded the British Empire Medal for his action and received the medal at the British embassy in Washington in 1955. Although he was never knighted, he was always referred to as Sir John from then on. John served another tour at MWTC in the 1960s, and he retired from the Corps in 1974.

He eventually moved to the Bridgeport area to work as a heavy equipment operator for the state, clearing roads and other assignments. While on that job, he positioned his trailer across the road from the old Staff NCO Club at the dormant training center. When the MWTC was reopened following the Vietnam War, he took over the heavy equipment and repair facility as a civilian, and the legend grew. Operating out of his favorite barber chair down in the motor pool, he would "hold court" with the younger Marines, usually over a beer or cigar, about how to do things in their field. During the driving snowstorms in the winter months, you would often see the lights on one of the snow-clearing machines keeping the only road open at all hours of the day and night. That would normally be Sir John doing what he did best. He later passed away while still in that occupation at the training center.

There were good reasons for the policy of maintaining a cadre of highly qualified military mountaineers on the instructor staff. Military mountain operations, regardless of season, can be inherently dangerous because of the environment, and obstacles that Marines have to be able to negotiate to carry out difficult missions. High altitude, severe weather at any time, and very steep terrain can all combine to disrupt anything a unit might be attempting to accomplish. Mountain operations instructors had to be at the top of their game all the time. That was necessary to effectively teach the various techniques for party climbing, cliff assaults, stream crossing, survival, or cross-compartment maneuvers. Even avalanche and cavass rescue were taught and practiced during the winter months. Safety was always an issue, and instructors had to be alert to reduce the risk of injuries or something worse among the students.

There were two examples of why this policy was so important. In June 1965, Marine Corps reserve units were going through their annual training duty at MWTC. One of the course requirements for them was to learn how to cross rivers utilizing different kinds of rope bridges. One such site was established across the West Walker River in the training area. A single rope bridge was in place, and the students were required to cross this bridge using the commando crawl technique. The event was supervised by Mountain operations instructors who also had a safety swimmer and safety rope line in the water below the bridge in case someone fell in. A Marine got halfway across the bridge, lost his grip, and fell into the water. Another Marine seeing this went into the rushing water to get the man. Both of them were swept down the river and swamped the safety swimmer at the rope. In the ensuing melee with the safety swimmer, both students were swept past the safety rope downriver into a gorge and were lost. We did not find them for the better part of two months.

The second example occurred during a winter operations course in February 1967. In this event, two students were on a night navigation course that crossed a high ridgeline at around 8,000 feet in elevation. It started to snow heavily during the exercise, and it looked like the two Marines had lost their way and had decided to go to ground and wait out the storm. They had been instructed on what to do in such circumstances, which meant digging the snow out from around a tree, creating a shelter, and attempting to get a fire going in the cleared area. What did happen was that they probably went to ground to wait out the storm. Both individuals froze to death. The consensus during the investigation was that they had gone to sleep, which can be deadly in such situations. They were not found until sometime later when the snow started to melt.

I considered myself fortunate to have served at MWTC. It had been a busy time, and I was presented with many challenges. Like so many previous assignments, I was blessed with superb Staff Noncommissioned Officers and Marines who formed the core of the instructors within the Special Training Unit. GySgt Bernard G. Goddard was the NCO in charge, and he was another no-nonsense Marine who took great care of his people. His approach to discipline was to banish a Marine to one of our high-altitude camps for the weekend when the offender was supposed to off on liberty. That way, the infraction never made it into the man's record book. He became famous later as a 1st Sgt in Vietnam. He was shot in the neck in an attack by the North Vietnamese on his combat outpost at Khe Sanh. He continued to fight with a finger in the bullet hole while yelling instructions over the radio until the attack was beaten off. He was another Marine who was easily promoted to Sergeant Major later in his career.

When the Reserves were not at MWTC for training, my instructors in the Special Training Unit would often support the SERE Course on its final field exercise. In late summer of 1966, it consisted of a six-day survival and evasion course that covered a major portion of the training area in altitudes from 6,000 to 9,000 feet. Students would be required to not only escape from an area but also to move in small teams across the country while living off the land. Part of the movement required navigating in areas where they had to check in to a hide site, remain for some time, and then move on for the next leg of the trek. We had set up one of the hide sites on a mountain called Pickle Peak southeast of the base. As the teams would arrive, they were to be hidden for a while before moving further.

I had made the climb to this position the afternoon before the next leg would commence. I had not felt well climbing to the position and told GySgt Goddard that I was going to lie down in one of the shelters we had constructed. My situation got worse throughout the night, and I was curled up in the fetal position to ease the pain. A little after dawn, I told Goddard I had to get back to the base camp to a doctor but was unable to walk. The radios were not working, so we sent Sgt Rocky Hewitt cross-country on foot to alert the medical staff. Goddard organized a party of Marines to carry me off the mountain in a poncho-like stretcher to a point where there would be an ambulance waiting. As we left the camp, I had the impression the students thought this was part of the exercise. Arriving at the base medical facility, Doctor Tom Talley made a quick examination and indicated I had a ruptured appendix. He then ordered an ambulance to move me 110 miles to the Washoe Medical Center in Reno for an operation. I arrived there in time to prevent any further infection in my system but spent two weeks in the hospital recovering before going back to the MWTC.

It would be another three weeks before I was cleared to go back into training. One humorous incident occurred while I was in the last few days in the Washoe Medical Center. Two of my Marine instructors visited me in my hospital room and brought along a pot of flowers. A very nice gesture for sure, but unusual. After they had gone, I noticed the flower pot had some condensation on the outside. Upon further inspection, in the flowers, I uncovered a pint bottle of bourbon packed in crushed ice. Only the troops would come up with something like that.

In the fall, most of the courses were shut down for review and update. We would take some of the instructors down to Yosemite National Park to increase their two-party climbing skills on some of the park's climbing routes. Rock climbing skills were very important in both mountain operations courses, and the instructors had to have a great amount of expertise to work safely with Marines on cliff faces at the training center. Jim Goldsworthy played a key role in coaching instructors when they were either on a cliff face in Yosemite or at the training center. On one occasion in the fall of 1966, we had a climbing party on the face below North Dome in Yosemite when a falling rock hit Staff Sergeant Bruce Threvathin in the shoulder, breaking a bone. Fortunately, he was tied in and did not get knocked off the cliff face. First Lieutenant Ed Means, who was part of the climbing party, worked his way up to where the injured climber was located, secured him on his back, and managed to rappel back down to the bottom of the cliff face without further incidents. Threvathin ended up in the park hospital for a while, but the skill demonstrated by Lieutenant Means was what we had tried to develop in all the mountain operations instructors.

I lived in the BOQ at the base with several other officers who were all single at the time. I had inherited a beautiful black and tan German shepherd by the name of Randy. Randy's original master had been a Marine helicopter pilot who had been shot down on a mission in South Vietnam. His widow had brought the dog to MWTC with the idea of donating him to the training center. Randy ended up in my care as long as I served there. He was a beautiful animal who loved to run all over the training area. However, it did not take him long to develop an intense hatred for porcupines, which were plentiful in those mountains. In his first run-in with a porcupine, he got a face full of quills for his effort. After that incident, Randy would go out of his way to find and attack porcupines. In the three incidents that followed between the dog and porcupines, he came back every time with either a face or mouth full of porcupine quills. Each event required a medevac of the dog out of the mountains and down to the dispensary for treatment. Finally, our Navy doctor, Lieutenant Tom Talley, told me we were going to have to try something else because Randy had gone through all the training center's painkillers and other medicines during treatment. Randy was then confined to the BOQ at the training center for the remainder of my tour there. Randy lived on for many years at MWTC, but to my recollection, he was never allowed to run loose in the training area again.

The married officers lived with their families as far away as Reno or Carson City, Nevada. This involved a very long bus ride from MWTC late in the weekday afternoon and then back on the same bus starting at 5:30 AM each weekday morning. We would spend most weeks in the field with a class of students on mountaineering or survival exercises but would come down to the base for the weekends. In the winter months, we would do more downhill skiing at various locations around Lake Tahoe or socializing in the clubs in Reno. The Sonora Pass would be closed through the winter but available for travel in the summer months to the Bay Area and elsewhere on the western side of the Sierra Nevada range.

This was also a time when my mother, who was divorced from my dad and remarried to a retired police officer in San José, would make frequent trips over the pass to the small lodge in Leavitt Meadows. There they would fish for trout in the West Walker River as well as visit with friends who owned the lodge. This gave me a chance to see them whenever they were in that area as the lodge was only a short distance from the base. On occasion, I would take them up into the training areas or the high lakes around the Sonora Pass. There was one in particular which contained Golden Trout in it. The fishing there provided some fabulous experiences.

At the beginning of 1967, the input of Marine students for instruction began to decrease due to increased combat operations in Vietnam. This trend would continue until the MWTC was put into a cadre status and shut down in the early summer months of that year. In February, I had received orders back to Quantico for the Amphibious Warfare School (AWS), a six-month course of instruction for captains. First, I would spend the late spring and summer months as a staff platoon commander at OCS. This meant spending the better part of six months evaluating candidates in the 44th OC Class, followed by the 45th OC Class. This was a critical period for the Officer Candidate School because we needed the very best we could find who could qualify to be effective Marine officers. This was a hard requirement, as 90 percent of the new graduates would be heading to Vietnam following either Basic School or flight training. An example of the attrition rates in the 44th was that we started with 56 candidates in the class in my platoon but only graduated 19 for the Basic School. Assisting me in this process was Staff Sergeant Dan Mc Fadden, who was both colorful and the consummate professional when it came to evaluating officer candidates. Like so many of his contemporaries at OCS, he was one of the best at knowing when to apply subtle psychological pressure on a candidate who either did not look the part of an officer or was perceived to be weak initially in mannerisms.

On the second day of training with the 44th OCS Class, McFadden spotted a candidate who was slight in appearance and nervous in the ranks. When approaching this candidate, he asked the kid's name. "Gary Soldat" was the response. McFadden asked him what kind of name was that. The response was it was Russian for soldier, after which McFadden exploded, "Russian, you must be a communist!" The answer was, of course, "no." McFadden continued with his tirade "Oh yes you are, and trying to infiltrate my Marine Corps. Russians in my Marine Corps, whoever heard of such a thing!" and stormed off.

Following the noon meal that day, the platoon was in formation and ready to move back to the barracks. McFadden called Soldat out and ordered him to march the platoon back to the barracks. Soldat did not know what to do because the platoon would not move without a correct command. Finally, McFadden, who was now rocking back and forth on his feet with his arms folded, told the candidate in his high South Carolina drawl: "Do something, Soldat, even if it is wrong." The candidate finally got the platoon moving but marched them into the side of a building. Then McFadden said with a deep sigh: "Congratulations, Soldat, it was wrong!" Later that afternoon, Soldat had dropped from the program on his own request (DOR). Subtle applications of psychological pressure determine how the candidate would react to either stand his ground or fold and quit.

Another perfect example of Mc Fadden's growing rapport with some of the candidates was when he would call certain individuals into the office and start playing them to get reactions. In one instance, he asked a candidate positioned in front of his desk what he was going to do that weekend if we were nice enough to let him out. The response was, "the candidate would probably go into Quantico and have one beer." McFadden's retort was that he was going to do the same only it would be "one GI Can full!" Fortunately, the candidate, Mark Rader, did not laugh until well after. He had come up through the Enlisted Commissioning Program (ECP) and had done reasonably well so far in training. He later went on to win a commission and lead an infantry platoon in combat in Vietnam. Seriously wounded and medically retired after a prolonged period in the hospital, he established a very successful career as a lawyer both in the entertainment industry and medical field in Southern California. He is now retired and lives in the state of Washington. We remain good friends.

* * *

One afternoon in late July, we were sitting around the bar in Liversedge Hall at Quantico when another officer, Captain Jerry Bondansa, asked me if I would like to go on a blind date that evening. Not having anything else planned, I agreed. The two of us took off in his car and headed toward Washington. We turned off of what was then Highway 395 and entered the parking lot for Southern Towers, a large apartment complex located on the edge of Alexandria. I had been at Southern Towers the previous weekend for another date, so did not think much about it. We went into the building and took the elevator up to the same floor where I had been previously. As we walked down the hall to an apartment, I thought this was really going to be interesting because it was the same one where the party had been, and I had already dated one of the girls who lived there. Jerry knocked on the door, and Sue, who had not been my previous date, opened the door. Following a few laughs over the coincidence, a relationship began that is still going on some 52 years later at this writing.

We began to frequently date, and the relationship began to grow seriously throughout the fall. I think we enjoyed doing things together and participated in most of the social events that occurred during the AWS curriculum. She was from Southwest Virginia, and we had gone down to meet her parents in Richlands, Virginia. They were really "salt of the earth" mountain folks whom I enjoyed immensely. Her ancestral background can be traced all the way back to France in the late 1600s on her father's side. In 1685 Sue's 8th great-grandfather immigrated out of France to England. Following a short stay there, he immigrated again to the colonies in Baltimore County in what is now Maryland. Her 6th great-grandfather served in the Virginia militia and was with Lieutenant Colonel George Washington at Fort Duquesne during the French and Indian War in 1755. He later served in four Virginia regiments of foot during the Revolutionary War from 1775 to 1780, which included a winter at Valley Forge. He died at the age of 104 in 1814. Sue's Second great-grandfather had enlisted in the 24th Virginia Infantry Regiment in

1862 and fought with the Confederate unit for the better part of the Civil War. I found this part of the family history fascinating.

The specter of the approaching year away in Vietnam had become a consideration we had to address. It had become clear that those of us who had not been to Vietnam were going to go. I think the decision to not wait to get married despite the risks came upon us naturally, and I do not recall any great gnashing of teeth over it. The plan was we would get married upon the completion of AWS in January or February 1968, so planning for the wedding was in high gear. We were married at the base chapel on February 3, 1968, and that was followed by a reception at Waller Hall, one of two officer clubs at Quantico. The groom's party would be in Dress Blues, and some of my classmates would form the traditional sword arch outside the chapel at the end of the ceremony. Several relatives in my family flew back to Washington to attend the ceremony, while several on Sue's side came up from Southwest Virginia. The wedding was a great success, and the reception was a lively event with the assistance of all the normal food and drink to include the keg of beer donated by Diamond Lou. Following the reception, family members gradually moved off for home. Sue and I spent the first day at the Washington DC Hilton finalizing preparations for the drive across country.

I had thirty days following school to report in for duty at Camp Pendleton before shipping out for the Far East. Sue and I had plotted a trip west, which also served as a sort of honeymoon. We took in several sights along the way, but the one that stood out most in our minds was the Grand Canyon. There we decided to charter a small plane with a guide and fly down the canyon following the Colorado River for a distance. That was a thrill because we were flying along 2,500 feet below the South Rim of the canyon while the river was another 2,500 feet below the plane. The flight went off well, but we both decided another flight like this would not be on the agenda in the future. One time was enough.

We traveled through Las Vegas to the Bay Area and San José to meet with my relatives. It was a surreal time for both Sue and me. We did have time to spend with my mother and her new husband, Chad Rolston, in San José. In San Francisco, we were also able to see my grandmother Mimi, who expressed great confidence in my gaining success over the coming year. Shortly after that, I had to take Sue to the airport for her flight back to Virginia for her teaching job. The departure went reasonably well, considering the circumstances, but parting in San Francisco was hard for both of us.

The author's uncle, Harry R. Jenkins, Private U.S. Army, BTRY B, 346th Field Artillery, AEF, France 1917.

The author's grandfather, William P. Jenkins, USN 1910.

The author's grandfather, James W. Finchley 1922.

The author's father, Harry W. Jenkins, PFC U.S. Marine Corps 1944.

The author's sister Susan, mother, father, and Grandmother Mimi, Oakland 1945.

Uncle Fred Wagner, 1st Sgt. U.S. Army, Normandy, France, 1944-1945 with the author's sister, Susan, and a future Marine.

The author's father pinning on the gold bars, San José State 1960. 2nd Lt. Bill McCluskey is on the right.

Gunnery Sergeant Paul Bauer, the author (center) MG and rocket section leaders, Okinawa 1961.

Alpha Company officers meeting during an exercise on Okinawa in 1961. Left to right are Captain Pierson and Lieutenants Kramer, Jenkins, Robinson, and McElroy.

The author's wedding day, Quantico 1968.

PART II: VIETNAM

CHAPTER 6

TO VIETNAM AND THE 26TH MARINES

I want to describe the following year in Southeast Asia to those who are unfamiliar with the chronology and circumstances of the war in Vietnam. In January 1968, the North Vietnamese (NVA), along with the Vietcong (VC) had launched countrywide attacks against both American and South Vietnamese bases in cities and in the field. This was known as the 1968 Tet Offensive. Despite sustaining heavy casualties, the enemy managed to achieve complete surprise across the country. This included the surprise assault on the American embassy in Saigon, which was eventually secured after heavy fighting. The Khe Sanh Combat Base, with its airfield in the northwest corner of South Vietnam, was encircled and placed under siege by at least two NVA Divisions (See Map 1). The NVA 325C division was moving in from the north of the combat base in the vicinity of Hill 881N. To the west, the NVA 304th Division, which had fought at Dien Bien Phu, had crossed into Vietnam from Laos and established positions southwest of the base. The 26th Marine Regiment was in position at the combat base as well as in four combat outposts in the hills north of Khe Sanh. Initially, the Marines continued to fight off small NVA attacks around the base perimeter. Then heavy rocket and artillery fire into the combat base increased over the four-month length of the siege. Further south, the NVA, supported by VC units, captured the ancient imperial capital of Hue City and began the systematic annihilation of its citizens. After recovering from the surprise attacks, American and South Vietnamese units recaptured Hue City after five weeks of heavy fighting. (See Maps 1 and 2).

Politically, in Washington, this was the beginning of the downfall of President Lyndon Johnson, who announced he would not seek another term as the President of the United States. I was an infantry officer who had just graduated from the AWS at Quantico with orders to the 26th Marines in Vietnam. It would certainly be a challenge to lead Marines in combat, but it was also a test one goes through to see if he can measure up to the awesome requirements and responsibilities. I did have some trepidation about what was coming but was more curious initially than anything else.

The Marine Corps had a system that was established to move people from the relaxed environment of Southern California to the conflict in Southeast Asia in a reasonably efficient manner. After years of practice, they had the system down. We reported to Norton Air Force Base in Southern California, where I met my dad for a short period before the long flight that would eventually get us to Kadena Air Force Base, Okinawa. There we would then be transported by truck north on the island to the Marine Corps base at Camp Hansen. You usually spent about ten days at Camp Hansen processing before lining up to fly south to Vietnam. Processing meant you received administrative instructions and a whole host of shots while there. You also packed your seabag for storage and retrieval when you were on your way home. All the required paperwork was accomplished there to include wills and anything else they deemed necessary. The worst part of this was waiting to fly south. The processing did not take ten days, and it became another example of the concept of "hurry up and wait," which was famous throughout the Corps.

We eventually left Okinawa on a Braniff Airlines jet for the flight to Da Nang in northern South Vietnam. The flight was uneventful as the stewardesses, as they were called in those days, tried to make everybody comfortable. The one thing I remember was that the stewardesses were dressed in what looked like space suits, which was the Braniff uniform at the time. Almost everyone onboard the flight was in good spirits upon take-off, but the atmosphere began to subtly change as we neared Vietnam, and the plane began its long approach into Da Nang. People became lost in their own thoughts, and you could feel the tension rise as we descended onto the airport. All of a sudden, you are not bragging anymore because you are about to enter into the reality of a country at war.

The airfield at Da Nang (See Map 1) was a very large complex close to the harbor and port facilities where ships loaded with supplies for the war could discharge their cargos. The airfield was also the home of one U.S. Air Force fighter wing comprised of F-4 Phantom fighters known as the "Gunfighters." Also, there was a Marine Aircraft Group that was also made up of F-4 Phantoms with a call sign of "Ring Neck." Both units had been based at this airfield for some time to conduct a variety of missions in support of both ground operations in South Vietnam, and strike missions over North Vietnam. It was a very busy place with jets coming and going as well as both Air Force and Marine C-130s bringing in loads of personnel and equipment to be transported by helicopters to units operating in the field.

Our plane taxied up to a stop in front of a very nondescript terminal. When the door opened, the overwhelming heat and humidity flowed into the cabin. As we disembarked from the plane, we passed a large fenced-off area that resembled a corral that you would see on a ranch in the west. It was filled with soldiers and Marines who were waiting to board our plane to begin the trip to Rest and Relaxation (R&R) locations or home. The "catcalls" coming from the assembled mass of veterans did not help the morale of the new arrivals as we were moved to waiting trucks for the short ride to a transit center. Along the way, we began to pick up the very pungent smells that permeated from the villages surrounding the airfield as well as throughout Vietnam.

South Vietnam had been divided up into four different geographical areas for purposes of military and some political control. The I Corps Tactical Zone (I CTZ) was in the north and bordered on the Demilitarized Zone with North Vietnam as well as Laos in the west. The South China Sea to the east ran down the coast and paralleled Vietnamese Route One known to Marines as the

"Street without Joy." II Corps Tactical ZONE (IICTZ), III Corps Tactical Zone (IIICTZ), and IV Corps Tactical Zone (IVCTZ) covered the rest of the country all the way south to the border with Cambodia. The Marines, for the most part, operated throughout the I Corps Tactical Zone (ICTZ) area during the war.

The system the Marine Corps used to get personnel to their assigned units in the field defied description, but it worked for the most part. For me, the first task was to find the liaison officer who could assign me transportation to my final destination. This turned out to be a Marine Gunnery Sergeant in a small shack outside the transit center. When I showed him my orders, he told me to wait around the center on the chance there might be a flight north to the Third Marine Division late that afternoon. Observing Marines coming and going through the transit center proved to be another experience. Personnel arriving from units in the north and along the Demilitarized Zone (DMZ) all looked drawn and haggard for the most part. Marines arriving from the ongoing siege at Khe Sanh were all covered with reddish dirt that clearly showed where they had been. There was really nothing like established flight schedules even though aircraft and helicopters were in the air all the time. The nature of the ongoing conflict was such that available air assets could be diverted at any time, which meant you had to rely on opportune airlift when it showed up. It also meant you would be spending a great amount of time getting where you had to go. Marines in Vietnam, as well as members of other services, by the hundreds, were constantly moving around on their own while waiting for flights.

The effort to get to my unit (3rd battalion 26th Marines) was a perfect case in point. Late that afternoon, the Gunnery Sergeant at the shack told me a C-130 was due in and that I could get a ride on it. The plane was going to Dong Ha, which was just south of the DMZ and the location of forward elements of the 3rd Marine Division (See Map 2). The flight north was uneventful until we approached the airfield for landing. The pilot came on the intercom and indicated they had been taking NVA artillery fire from across the DMZ at the airfield. He was going to land and taxi by the large wire gate that led off of the field. He further stated we should grab all of our bags, run off the tail ramp of the plane, and get into the trench, which ran alongside the taxiway. We did that as he slowly rolled by that gate and down the taxiway. When we hit the trench, North Vietnamese artillery rounds were impacting along one end of the runway. The big four-engine C-130 turned around, gunned its engines and flew off without getting hit. With the plane gone, it was deathly quiet for a while. Looking around, the terrain was basically flat and covered with clumps of elephant grass as the road moved away from the runway and west toward a series of Plywood Sea Huts. These were the standard shelters the Marines were working from in what was considered "rear areas." I was trying to get a handle on what might be going on around this area because it was almost silent at the time. It was late afternoon, not overly warm, with no sign of any wind. Then the group of us in the trench picked up our gear, climbed out of the trench, and headed down the dirt road to find the Division headquarters.

When I located the duty officer in one of the huts, he told me the headquarters had moved south to Quang Tri, and it was too late to try to get there that day. Instead, he sent me over to a cluster of sandbagged, general-purpose tents to find a bunk for the night. The first memorable thing I noticed was that everything inside and outside the tents were covered with a layer of reddish dirt. It was now dark, and I attempted to get some sleep, which was not very difficult, considering I had started this trip in Okinawa that morning.

At around 3:00 AM, there were a series of loud explosions that awakened the whole camp. North Vietnamese artillery had struck a Marine ammunition dump about a half-mile from where we were. My initial reaction was: What do I do now? Dust rained down on me from the blast concussions both from inside the tent and in the trench, where I went after gaining my senses following the initial explosions. After determining what the source of the explosions was, we all moved back to the tent for the remainder of the evening. This disruption continued all night, which kept everyone in the tent awake until dawn. Later the next morning, I climbed aboard a truck, which was part of a convoy going south to Quang Tri. Before we could move, the road south had to be swept by engineers for any mines planted the night before by the Viet Cong. When the sweep was accomplished, the convoy proceeded south toward Quang Tri. Even though we—the new guys—had not been issued weapons, we rode on top of the trucks. The movement south gave me a chance to observe the countryside as the trucks moved slowly down the road. We passed small Vietnamese hamlets dotted with rice paddies. Farmers were working in the paddies but paid no attention as we drove by. Judging on what I had experienced in the first twenty-four hours in Vietnam, it looked to me like this was going to be a long tour of duty. I am not sure I really knew what to expect once in-country, but this past series of events gave me an idea of what became a reality when operating in northern I Corps. (See Map 2.)

We arrived at the Headquarters of the 3rd Marine Division without any difficulty, and I checked in with the duty officer. I was told that I was going to the 26th Marine Regiment, which was located at Khe Sanh, but their rear was in Phu Bai, miles to the south of Quang Tri. I was also told that I would have to go there to report in and draw a weapon and the necessary equipment (this was called 782 gear in Marine lingo) to go with it. At the time, going to the 26th Marines at Khe Sanh seemed like a challenge to me. They were currently under constant attacks by fire while encircled and cut off by the NVA in the so-called siege, which had been ongoing since early January. The challenge to me now was how I would do as a commander in that situation. My confidence was such that it was not fear of the unknown but curiosity over what might be coming more than anything else.

I had to spend three days at the Division headquarters, which was not all bad because I had friends there. Captain Bob Johnson, who had led the mountain operations course at MWTC when I was there, was working in the division headquarters at Dong Ha. He was a solid leader and one in whom you could have great confidence in tight situations. It was good to see him, and we spent some time getting up to speed on what was going on within the 3rd Marine Division's zone of operations. The next part of the trip was by air C-130 from Quang Tri to Phu Bai, which was about an hour by air (See Map 2). After checking in to the regiment outside of Phu Bai, I was told that I was going to the 3rd battalion, which was currently at Khe Sanh, but their rear was there in Phu Bai. Finally, arriving at the battalion rear area, I was issued weapons, and the required 782 gear. Three more days were spent there preparing equipment, receiving briefs on the situation, and getting ready to move to Khe Sanh. This did not sound particularly difficult, except the position was located in the mountains in northwest Vietnam near Laos and was cut off from any overland roads thanks to the NVA. The only way to get there was by helicopter, which could be dangerous. The NVA had shot down several in attempts to get in as well as come out of that base. I had already lost one of my classmates from the AWS. Captain Jay Stull was on his way into Khe Sanh when the helicopter he was in was shot down in the mountains with no survivors. He and I were good friends at the school and were in the same study group. We often got together with other officers at the bar in Waller Hall, and he used to remark about how eager he was about getting into Vietnam and leading Marines. There was no question in his mind he would succeed. I did not find out about his loss until sometime later.

It was about this time when I finally had a chance to get a letter off to Sue. Letters were the only way one could communicate with anyone in the outside world, especially if you were operating in the mountains and lowlands in Vietnam. I never saw a phone the whole time that I served in Vietnam. Even mail was sporadic at best, depending on where you were operating. In my initial letters home, I had indicated I would write as often as possible. I had told Sue that she might get a letter one day, hear nothing for two to three weeks, and then get five letters all at once. The same applied for any mail coming into the country for the troops. I had decided to number them all for her to keep track of what I was doing. I had also decided to try to keep her as informed as possible without going into any of the gory details or where we might be operating. She generally knew where I was initially because of all the "blather" in the media regarding the siege at Khe Sanh in 1968. I had told her to not believe much of what was being reported in the papers and on TV because it just was not very factual, especially regarding local operations where we never saw any reporters.

CHAPTER 7
KHE SANH AND HILL 881 SOUTH

Early on the morning on the eighth day since arriving in-country, we boarded CH-46 helicopters for the flight into the Khe Sanh Combat Base. The flight was uneventful, and we arrived high over the runway at the base. The pilot of the 46 began a series of spiraling turns down toward the ground pulling out of the turns at the last moment and flaring out for a landing on the ground. We all piled out of the 46 and ran into the brush while the helicopter pilot revved his engines and was gone. I remember there was an eerie silence on the ground, and I recall that it was cool and damp. Looking around, it seemed like we were in a forest of elephant grass dotted with only a few small trees. The base with its runway sat on a plateau and was surrounded by high jungle-covered mountains to the west, north, and east. From the air, it looked like a giant blister had been carved out of the jungle. The base perimeter ran all around the airstrip and was manned by a series of Marine, Army, and South Vietnamese Army (ARVN) units. The base also sat on Vietnamese Route 9, which, in more peaceful times, was the only road that ran from Laos east to the coast of South Vietnam. It was now blocked by North Vietnamese units both to the east and west of Khe Sanh (See Map 2).

While we were looking around and trying to figure out what to do next, a guide came out to meet us and move everyone to the headquarters area. As we moved quickly across the runway, my initial impression was that of a base that resembled a large garbage dump. Buildings, tents, or bunkers above ground were largely destroyed, and trash was everywhere. There were the remains of at least two helicopters, a twin-engine C-123 transport, and one C-130 that had either crashed or had been hit by NVA fire while on the ground. For three months, the entire combat base had been pummeled by NVA rockets, artillery, and mortars coming from the mountains as far west as Laos. The results were that most personnel were living in bunkers underground, either dug by the occupants or by a team of Navy Seabees that were stationed there. I worked my way to the 3/26 battalion headquarters area past the mess hall, which had been destroyed by fire. I remember seeing pots, pans, and all sorts of cookware scattered in the dirt. The 3/26 headquarters bunker had taken a direct hit from artillery and collapsed a day earlier.

Climbing down into the wreckage of the bunker, I reported in to the battalion commander Lieutenant Colonel John C. Studt, who was actively working in what was left of his office amidst a jumble of 4X4s, paneling, and sandbags. John Studt was the quintessential tactician, thoroughly schooled in the art of combined arms warfare. A disciplinarian but not overbearing, he maintained his battalion area as the only one within the combat base perimeter that did not look like a garbage dump. It was policed, and the bunkers were dug in and camouflaged. That meeting went well, and Lieutenant Colonel Studt told me I was going to command Mike Company. It was currently split with one platoon on the perimeter at the base, and the other two platoons with the rest of the company on the combat outpost located on Hill 881 South. This position was over six thousand meters northwest of the main combat base and one of four combat outposts (881S, 861, 861A, and 558) that were positioned on high peaks to guard the approaches to the main base (See Map 3).

The only way one could get to 881S was by helicopter because it was completely cut off from access from the ground. To get helicopters on and off of 881S in a relatively safe manner, a full air attack had to be staged to suppress NVA mortar and automatic weapons fire. Most of it came from hidden positions all around the outpost and from a large NVA bunker complex on Hill 881 North. (See Map 3) Air attacks usually consisted of fighter bombers dropping bombs and napalm, firing rockets, and even dropping CS gas canisters on certain enemy positions. All of this was called a "Super Gaggle" by the Marines on the hill. Even medevac helicopters had to be escorted by gunships to suppress NVA fire when the helicopters approached the hill.

Nine days after leaving Okinawa, we boarded another CH-46 for the flight out to Hill 881S. This flight was uneventful, and as we approached the hill, I could see Marine positions all around the perimeter, ready to react if necessary. At one point, the entire hill had been covered with 6-8 feet tall elephant grass with a few trees at the western end of the position. Most of it had either been blasted or burned off by constant artillery and mortar attacks. The helicopter landed in a zone that had been scratched out in a shallow saddle between two high points on each end of the position. The bird was on the ground long enough to quickly unload us as well as pick up a few Marines that were going out. He was not on the ground for longer than three minutes. Unloading in that zone meant that we plunged out of the bird and into a trench immediately in case the NVA fired mortars into the position. This did not happen on this particular occasion. The commander of Mike Company, First Lieutenant Tom Esslinger, met me at the trench and guided me to what passed for the company headquarters bunker. It sat on top of our position and would not have taken a direct hit from either artillery or a rocket. Tom was an extremely competent officer with considerable combat experience who would later go on to be a highly successful lawyer in Washington, DC When I assumed command of Mike Company, he became the executive officer and later the Commander of India Company. Tom gave me a briefing on the local situation, our positions around the perimeter, and fire support plans we would use if required to do so. This was followed by a tour in the trenches around the company perimeter that occupied the west end of the combat outpost.

Marines had been on 881 South since early January 1968. The situation was one of intermittent artillery, mortar, and sniper attacks for over three months. This required the troops to improve trenches as well as bunkers to protect themselves from NVA fire. Very slow progress had been made on this because shovels were not available, which dictated that Marines use their entrenching tools to dig in. On my initial tour around Mike Company's perimeter, I met several of the Marines who were living in bunkers of a sort or just in horizontal holes deep enough for them to crawl and sleep. The trench around the perimeter was only deep enough in a few places where a person was able to stand erect without risking getting shot by a sniper. In several locations, it was no deeper than three feet. The troops had jury-rigged overhead cover for their bunkers, but very few of them could withstand a direct hit by either artillery or mortar round. The positions of my machineguns were correctly sited along the most obvious enemy avenues of approach should an attack develop. To date, there had been no organized ground attacks against Mike's position. Very few NVA soldiers had been seen for some time, even though they were all around the outpost. It had been all artillery, mortars, and snipers. The spirit of the Marines seemed to be good even though they had been on reduced water and rations for over three months. This was a good sign in my mind.

I then went to pay a call on the Commander of India Company 3/26, which occupied the east end of 881S. Captain Bill Dabney's headquarters bunker was located on the north side of the position and underground. We moved away from his CP and settled down in an abandoned ammunition bunker toward the top of the hill. He had done an exceptional job while commanding the outpost ever since the siege started in January. Bill was a slow-talking, serious individual, and the son-in-law of a Marine Corps legend, the irascible Lieutenant General "Chesty" Puller, who held five Navy Crosses for bravery throughout his career. The Navy Cross is the second-highest medal awarded for bravery in combat next to the Medal of Honor. On occasion, he would mention General Puller because both of his daughters were married to Marine Captains: Bill to Virginia and Captain Mike Downs, who was also serving in Vietnam and at Hue City, to Martha Puller.

The Dabney name was from an old Virginia family. He was born and raised in the state and a graduate of the Virginia Military

Institute (VMI). In January 1968, he had led India Company on an attack toward 881N at the beginning of the siege. They ran into a significant number of NVA sustaining serious casualties in the process, which forced him to fall back on to his positions on 881S. Mike Company had been lifted by helicopter out to 881S as a reserve to back up India and ended staying there throughout the siege. The relationship between Mike and India Companies was one of the senior dogs on the hill (India) versus the newcomer (Mike) for some time before they got used to each other. This was not a problem with the officers because everyone knew we had to work together. After going over various defensive plans for the outpost, we were about to move back out of the bunker when a loud screech followed by a huge explosion and concussion occurred a short distance from our bunker. This turned out to be an NVA 152mm artillery round fired from some position in Laos. After the dust had cleared, Bill Dabney indicated that this particular gun often fired on his position, but the NVA gunners apparently could not depress the cannon any lower, so any rounds striking the hill never impacted any further west toward Mike's position. This apparently happened often enough that the Marines in India Company would stay away from that particular area on the hill during daylight.

The physical layout of the outpost had Mike Company dug in on the west end of the hill while India Company 3/26 occupied the east end of the hill. The helicopter landing zone sat in the low saddle in the middle. There were the remains of a three-gun battery of 105MM howitzers in India's position that had been shot up and damaged. To the east of India, there was the wreckage of a Marine H-34 helicopter that had been shot down (See Map 4).

The entire position reminded me of what it must have been like in World War I in Europe. All positions on the hill were underground with a continuous trench of sorts that ran all around the outpost perimeter. Everyone lived underground in bunkers because moving around outside in daylight invited 82-mm mortar attacks from Hill 881N along with sniper attacks that caused casualties. One previous

Mike Company commander, Captain John Gilece, had been shot by a sniper in January as he moved around the positions, and he was medevac'd. Even the urinals were constructed out of empty artillery shell canisters and dug in underground. When one of them was full, it would be sealed and thrown down the hill into North Vietnamese positions at the bottom. Any work that had to be done on bunkers or the trench was accomplished at night. Barbed-wire barricades and some minefields surrounded the trenches as added protection against any ground attacks. There was no generated electricity on the hill as we had to rely on candles in the bunkers to work by at night. An eerie silence hung over the entire outpost that could be unnerving when fog or clouds blanketed the position. When it was clear at night, we would often hear NVA soldiers moving around the base of the hill, but if we were encased in fog or clouds, we could not hear or see anything.

Living conditions were primitive at best. Water had to be flown in by helicopters in sealed artillery shell canisters, and there were times when each man on the hill was limited to one heavy C-ration can of water per day. Shaving was not done for the most part unless the Marines had water. The only way to bathe was to stand outside in the trench in what little rain that did fall on the position. Keep in mind many of the Marines in both companies had been on 881S since early January when the siege started, and this was in late March. Resupply of food (C-rations) suffered the same shortages as water. There were periods where each individual would get only one C-ration meal a day. Resupply was limited by the weather (primarily fog and low-hanging clouds), shortage of helicopters, and the need to stage a full-scale air attack on the NVA positions around 881S so the helicopters could make their way in.

The first example of the supply situation I encountered was when I was going around the trench line and bunkers to meet individual Marines. While talking to one man whose breath was really bad, I could see he had serious tooth decay. I asked him why he was not brushing his teeth when they did have water. His answer was that he had been using his toothbrush to clean his rifle, which under the circumstances, was mandatory. There were other examples of the same problem. Here we were in 1968 when the country had astronauts flying around the moon, and we could not get toothbrushes for the troops. I did put in an emergency request for enough dental floss for the entire company, which finally came in by helicopter one week later. This started to cement my relationship with the Marines in Mike Company.

When helicopter resupply missions were scheduled, we could always count on NVA snipers shooting at the helicopters as they let down in the landing zone. Both India and Mike companies had not been able to keep their FAC from getting shot and medevac'd. Normally each company would have a FAC, a Marine pilot doing a two-month tour of duty with an infantry unit on the ground. Bill Dabney came up with a solution that worked wonders for everyone on the hill. He had the remnants of the tactical control party (TACP) commanded by one Corporal Robert J. Arrotta, who was the senior man after his officer had been wounded and medevac'd. Arrotta took over the responsibilities of the officer and became a legend. Over the four months, he was on 881S, he controlled all resupply missions to that position, and was responsible for controlling over 240 airstrikes on NVA positions all around that area. His call sign was "India 14," and Marine, Navy, and Air Force pilots quickly learned who India 14 was and were very quick to rely on him when they checked in on the air request nets.

One day as I was touring our lines, I stopped to talk to a Marine Lance Corporal who was manning a 106 Recoilless Rifle position on the south side of our perimeter (See Map 4). The 106 was a vicious weapon designed to kill tanks and other armored vehicles with high-velocity rounds. He had been watching the ridge to his south and indicated he had spotted an NVA spider hole in the grass that always started to shoot when helicopters were attempting to land. He wanted to use the 106 to take out the position. That sounded excellent except the backblast from a 106 RR was deadly for anyone caught within 35 yards behind the weapon. As the distance from the back of the 106 to the absolute rear of that position was about ten yards. I told him if he could dig a ramp in the ground that would direct the backblast up and away from his position while surrounding himself with a sandbag wall on the side of the gun, I would consider giving approval to try it. He did that while continuing to watch the NVA position for two days until a scheduled resupply mission was inbound to 881S. When the helicopters approached the hill, shooting started from several positions to include the one under observation. The Marine gunner pulled the trigger on the 106, and the round obliterated the NVA position. At the same time, the backblast from the gun created a huge explosion of dirt and rocks, scaring the pilots who waved off from their approach. After explaining that we were firing to protect them, they circled around and came in to the landing zone. All ended well after this incident.

Over the next few weeks, we remained in a stationary defensive position under constant NVA mortar, artillery, and sniper attacks. Hill 881S was chosen as a combat outpost because we had excellent visibility of the mountains to the north, west into Laos, and south overlooking Route 9 and the Special Forces camp at Lang Vei (see Map 3). We would give the main combat base early warning on NVA artillery attacks coming from Co Roc Mountain in Laos, as well as rocket attacks emanating from several canyons southwest of our position. This generally gave the Marines at Khe Sanh time to take cover before the rounds fell on the base. At the same time, the NVA had constructed positions in the mountainous terrain all around 881S for constant attacks by fire on the outpost.

At the beginning of the siege in January, there had been some major battles where 26th Marine units had sustained heavy casualties at the hands of the North Vietnamese. The result was that General William Westmoreland, the Commander, U.S. Forces in Vietnam, believed the NVA were going to try to do the same thing to us that they had accomplished at Dien Bien Phu against the French in 1954. History shows this concern had political reverberations all the way back to the White House in Washington. This included the president and his civilian advisors plotting moves around Khe Sanh from a sand table in the basement of the White House. What Westmoreland really wanted was to use the combat base as bait to draw out large NVA units so that they could be destroyed by overwhelming U.S. firepower.

There were four combat outposts on high ground that functioned as the eyes and ears for the regiment. As previously mentioned, they were hills 881S, 861, 861A, and 558, which guarded the approaches to the airfield at the combat base. We had the observation and fields of fire. This meant that the NVA would have to destroy any or all of these positions before they could launch a major attack against the combat base and its airfield. After those initial bloody fights with the NVA, the 26th Marines policy forbade any unit from proceeding outside the wire for any reason. This kept casualties down, but it also blinded us to what was going on beyond our positions. On 881S, we knew we were completely surrounded to the extent that the NVA had dug positions around the base of the hill for cover from our airstrikes and artillery. By not being able to patrol outside our wire, we could not get a true idea of what they were doing. In addition to this threat, the Marines had been stationary in their positions for over three months without physical activity. The lack of activity, combined with the shortage of food and water, concerned me. I worried the troops were beginning to lose their edge.

There continued to be sporadic NVA artillery and mortar attacks into the second week of April 1968. Both Mike and India Companies suffered casualties primarily when an air attack was in progress in support of helicopter resupply missions. I remember one instance when a CH-46 set down in the landing zone, and the troops poured out the back of the bird. A mortar round landed right near the helicopter, and the explosion caught one Marine in mid-air with shrapnel as he rolled into the trench. Wounded badly, he was picked up and tossed back into the helicopter as it was lifting off. That was probably the shortest tour in combat anybody could have had and survive.

There was another incident where the last forward air control officer (Marine pilots doing a tour on the ground) on 881S was in the same trench directing helicopter resupply operations. He was hit by shrapnel from a mortar blast at the edge of the landing zone. He was quickly treated and moved to another CH-46 just before it took off for the combat base. After that incident, it was all up to Corporal Arrotta to carry the load, which he did without breaking stride. In still another case, a CH-46 had come in with an external load slung under the bird. It hovered just off the landing zone and discharged the cargo net full of ammunition. As the pilot started to pull up, the helicopter was hit by sniper fire and started to lose what little altitude he had. He managed to limp around the other side of the position before crash landing hard outside India's eastern perimeter. The crew was picked up by another Marine helicopter and flown back to the combat base. The downed CH-46 sat there for another two weeks before they were able to bring in a CH-53 heavy helicopter and lift the wrecked helicopter off of the hill.

If a Marine was wounded and required an emergency medevac, we were usually able to get a medevac helicopter with an escort of gunships to pick him up. He still had to get to the medical facilities at the combat base for further treatment. Getting off of 881 in a medevac bird was a step in the right direction but no guarantee that he would make it for treatment. One night I had a Marine who was digging in the trench line when we heard an explosion. There had been no sound of either artillery or mortar round coming in, so we were not sure what caused it. The Marine had lost both feet, so it was either a mine or an artillery round that had buried itself at some point in the past. An emergency medevac was requested, and soon an escorted H-34 helicopter arrived over the landing zone. The casualty was quickly put on board, and the helicopter lifted off. Later we heard that somewhere between 881S and the combat base, there was a mid-air collision and the H-34 with the casualty as well as the crew had crashed. We received no definitive word as to the casualties in this incident.

One of the major differences between what the Marines had for support at Khe Sanh, and what the French had at Dien Bien Phu, was airpower. The French had very few attack aircraft, and we had Marine, Navy, and Air Force assets up to and including B-52 bombers. The result was that the NVA avoided massing their troops for fear of the overwhelming air attacks that could be called down on them. Instead, they continued both artillery and rocket attacks on the combat base and, to a lesser degree, on the combat outposts. We got used to seeing American fighter bombers attacking one artillery or rocket position daily in areas west of the combat base. On occasion, B-52 strikes were called in when intelligence indicated a build-up of NVA units in Laos or closer to Khe Sanh itself. The call sign for such an attack was "ARC LIGHT." When we were warned that an ARC LIGHT mission was inbound, everyone went to ground until after the attack.

The area covered by the bomb pattern, along with the utter destruction, as a result, was frightening in its proximity. Debris from the explosions would sail over our positions as the ground shook violently. Normally such strikes would not be conducted less than a half-mile from our positions, but they always felt like we were right under them. B-52 strikes were a source of entertainment for the Marines on the hill. I had told Sue how they would yell obscenities in the direction of the NVA positions every time a strike would occur on the surrounding ridges. The troops knew that the NVA were reeling from these strikes, but it was a way of releasing tension after being cooped up for almost four months in those trenches.

The restrictions against staying inside the wire were finally relaxed around the end of the second week in April. Units could then patrol for short distances outside the wire to probe for NVA activity. Shortly after that, orders came down that the battalion was to conduct another attack on NVA positions on Hill 881 North. This complex of bunkers had been bombed and strafed for the better part of three and a half months. The NVA still occupied that area, and we knew they were dug in. The battalion command group arrived by helicopter to plan out the attack on 881North. This was the first time that I had a chance to meet and coordinate an attack with John Studt or Major Matt Caulfield, the operations officer for 3/26. Matt had been in Vietnam for about eight months and had gone through some very heavy fighting with the NVA along the DMZ and around Con Thien. It was clear that he knew what he was doing and was not afraid to think out of the box, as we discussed how the battalion was going to go after the NVA. The nature of the terrain on the approaches to 881N and the condition of our troops dictated a night movement to attack positions to try to achieve some surprise on the enemy. Shortly after midnight on Easter Sunday, April 14, 1968, we moved off from our positions in the combat outpost. Mike Company was in the lead and followed by Lima and Kilo Companies in a column downhill to the bottom of 881S (See Map 5). Still undetected, we began the long climb in the dark over intermediate hills toward the objective. Lima Company veered off to my left, and Kilo moved to my right flank. Most of the area we had to climb over was open with little cover and few trees.

I had scout dogs with the lead elements. They proved to be very effective at picking up scents from enemy positions to the extent we were not detected until after dawn. When the shooting started, our supporting arms opened up with artillery, mortars, and 106 Recoilless Rifles from our positions on 881S. All of this was under the control of Captain Bill Dabney, who had relinquished his command of India and was now acting as a fire support coordinator for the attack. The 106 was supposed to be used primarily on tanks, but it worked wonders on detected NVA bunkers in front of the attacking companies. Mike Company advanced by fire and maneuver up to the assigned intermediate objectives. They were occupied by NVA soldiers who, after several grenade exchanges, were either killed or driven off toward the main positions on 881N. That skirmish cost us one death and a few wounded.

Lima Company on our left flank was engaged in a major firefight, with the NVA and inflicted over 30 enemy casualties. The enemy in front of them broke contact and fell back toward 881N. Then Lima, Mike, and Kilo Companies continued the coordinated attack under heavy supporting arms fire from 881S for the next couple of hours (See Map 5). Kilo Company was pushing toward 881N from the east when aerial observers indicated that the NVA were running off of that position. Airstrikes were called in to deal with what appeared to be a retreat. When we approached the now abandoned enemy positions, the attack was stopped. We were lucky to be able to drive the NVA off of 881N because they had been in positions with interlocking bunkers and fields of fire that could have caused severe casualties in the attacking Marine units. After accounting for everyone on the ground, the companies were ordered to return to our original positions on 881S. It had been a long day, and everyone was dog-tired. The battalion did achieve some success despite the casualties (10 killed and several wounded) sustained in the attack. This was often a typical day in the war in Vietnam. We rarely ever stayed on the objectives that we had captured for very long. What usually happened was that NVA elements would sneak back into their original positions at some point after our departure.

The mail situation never really improved while we were on 881S. If we had mail to go out, it would be given to a Marine who was awaiting a helicopter back to the combat base. When this did occur, he would usually be dragging a mailbag with all the letters going off the hill along with all of his normal equipment. The same situation occurred for incoming mail, which often depended on when there was a helicopter coming in to the hill that could take mail out. I thought that Sue held up pretty well under this very erratic flow of information. It was frustrating, but nothing could be done about it, as the helicopter assets were just not available. There were instances when small observation planes or even helicopters would pass over the hill, and the crews would toss out packages of one thing or another for the troops. It could be anything from cigars, magazines, and candy to an occasional case of soda or even C-Rations. That is what happens when there is a strong sense of brotherhood in combat units in some very tight situations.

To try to ease concerns at home, I resorted to making tape recordings of my daily activities on a small recorder that I carried with me to Vietnam. I had it stored in a relatively safe place in our command bunker so that it would not get fouled with all the dirt and grit that existed in our position. It would normally take a few days to fill a cassette with what was going on. I sealed it in a plastic container, addressed it to Sue, and then waited to get it out in a mailbag along with everyone's letters. Hearing my voice on these tapes helped ease the tension I was sure had built with her as time went on. I still have some of them in a footlocker in our home.

CHAPTER 8
LEAVING KHE SANH AND THE DMZ

One week later, the higher headquarters believed that the siege at Khe Sanh had been lifted. It was announced that the First Air Cavalry Division was coming in to relieve the 26th Marines on Operation Pegasus. This meant that the regiment would be leaving Khe Sanh for operations in other parts of I Corps. Mike and India Companies were lifted by helicopter off 881S, and back to the combat base in preparation for further movement out of the mountains. The North Vietnamese had not gone away. They continued to pound the combat base with artillery and rockets from Co Rock Mountain in Laos.

On April 16th Mike Company was scheduled to leave the combat base. We had moved across the runway and into a trench that paralleled the main runway where we waited for the helicopters to lift us out. NVA spotters in the hills had seen an ARVN Ranger unit walking up the runway *en masse*. NVA artillery fire commenced to rain down on the ARVN, as well as where we were located. We could hear the guns firing off from Co Roc in Laos, which meant that we had about 10 seconds to find cover before the rounds hit. The trench in our area was not more than three feet deep, and it gave me the feeling I had to go deeper into the ground to escape the fire. This was impossible as I just cringed while the incoming rounds fell and exploded all around us. It went on for about 90 minutes before it was over.

The result of these attacks was that I had one platoon commander, Second Lieutenant Ken Ammon, who was killed by an almost direct artillery hit on his position. His platoon sergeant and several other Marines were wounded. The next senior man in the platoon was Corporal Terry Stewart, and I called for him to come up and take over what was left of the platoon. He had great difficulty reaching me because of the impacting NVA artillery rounds that continued to fall in our area. Terry was a very experienced noncommissioned officer (NCO) whose skills had quickly come to my attention back on Hill 881. By the time he finally reached me, he had been in and out of the shallow trench a half-dozen times thanks to the NVA artillery. All helicopter activity was canceled, and Mike Company had to move back across the airfield to find empty bunkers for the night.

The next day we were finally picked up by CH-53 helicopters and flown out of the mountains to a new base near Quang Tri City. This was supposed to be a quiet area, but the location where the battalion was concentrated was rocketed the night before, resulting in the deaths of three more Marines.

Upon my arrival at a tent near the runway, I was introduced to several replacements, including two new Marine fighter pilots, who were coming in as replacements for the FACs that we had lost on 881 South. Both of them had already spent part of their tour in Vietnam in F-4 fighter squadrons based in Da Nang. This was an abrupt change in environment for them, so it would take a little time to adjust to the way we lived. Captain Dave Gould was the senior of the two. He was an aggressive, outgoing aviator who went on to do very well in the two months he served with 3/26, and specifically on Operation Mameluke Thrust. This was to be another operation that the battalion would be engaged in later in the spring.

One day after the beginning of Mameluke Thrust, we had been probing for NVA in the steep mountainous terrain for over a week. I spotted Dave coming up a narrow trail carrying the 65-pound air-ground radio. He was beet-red, soaked with sweat, and not happy. I smiled and asked, "How's it going?" knowing what the answer might be. He glared at me and swore that if he ever got out of 3/26 alive, he would get even and come back to haunt us. I laughed and said, "Welcome to 3/26". More to follow on Dave Gould later.

My first task upon our arrival in Quang Tri was to get the troops cleaned up and into new uniforms. Field showers had been set up in a dried rice paddy, and everyone went there first. Once dried, each Marine was issued a new set of jungle utilities and fed a hot meal. Old uniforms were thrown in a pile to be burned, and each individual went for the showers. In many cases, this would be the first shower a man had in three months. In mine, it was the first shower or the first washing of any kind in over thirty days and the first haircut in six weeks. I had also lost some weight, and the new uniform kind of hung on me.

After the initial orientation in the area, the next thirty days would be spent operating west of Quang Tri City (See Map 2). Marines were engaged with two different threats in I Corps at the time. The first was with the North Vietnamese, mostly in conventional combat. This is what we faced when up against the NVA, whether it was in the mountains or along the DMZ. It was characterized by the use of artillery, rockets, and mortars along with combat between large units and occasional armored vehicles. In early February, an NVA attack utilizing Russian PT-76 armored amphibian vehicles had overrun the Lang Vie Special Forces Camp southwest of Khe Sanh. This was the first indication they had that kind of capability. The PT-76's came out of the jungle in Laos and attacked along Route 9 into the camp. After a night of heavy combat, they were finally driven off. The second threat was with the Viet Cong, normally along the coastal plains and low lands. This featured the VC's use of mines, booby-traps, and ambushes with small mortars, B-40 rockets, and machine guns. They would use hit-and-run attacks and then melt back into the population. Operations around Quang Tri meant that Mike Company would be up against the VC for the most part, and tactics had to be adjusted.

3/26 had been tasked to provide security for one of the First Cavalry Division's helicopter bases near the city. The mission was to protect the base as well as disrupt VC infiltration into the local hamlets around Quang Tri. To accomplish the mission, a concept was developed whereby Marines in four-man fire teams would saturate a particular area in late afternoon and set up small unit ambushes at dark. The terrain was generally flat and covered with tall elephant grass, which made movement difficult. We knew that the VC were coming in at night to get to the hamlets for support. This employment of what were called "killer teams" proved to be highly successful. The areas to be saturated with the killer teams were moved every night as the VC continued to blunder into them with regularity.

We inflicted heavy casualties on the Viet Cong, but it was not without cost. On May 9, 1968, we had an engagement in the tall elephant grass that covered the area. In the ensuing battle with the VC, we sustained two Marines killed and eight more wounded as both sides were mixed up together and firing blindly into the brush. On another occasion, a report came in that there appeared to be a small concentration of VC in an overgrown canyon to the west of Quang Tri. Lieutenant Colonel Studt directed Mike Company to move toward the area to flush any VC out of hiding. At the same time, he organized his "Jump Command Post" and moved into the area where we were operating. The search did not turn up anything. His command group was returning to the base camp when we heard a loud explosion. Later it was determined that the battalion executive officer, Major Joe Loughran, had stepped on a mine, killing him as well as one radio operator. That stunned us because the executive officer was rarely allowed in the field at the same time with the battalion commander. The loss of the senior leadership of the battalion could be devastating to the organization, especially in combat. A very good reason why only one of the two were normally in the field together. This had been a really hard lesson learned.

The North Vietnamese often staged heavy attacks out of the DMZ and into the area around Dong Ha, known as the Leatherneck Square. It was bordered by positions at Dong Ha, Gio Linh, Con Thien, and Cam Lo (See Map 2). In late May, there had been a major battle in and around the hamlet of Dai Do. Casualties had been heavy on both the 4th Marines units and the NVA. 3/26 was alerted to be prepared to move back north to relieve one of the battalions that had been in support of the battle. Up to this point, Mike Company had been doing nothing but saturation patrolling and killer team ambushes for a month when the alert came in. Preparations were made, and the battalion was staged the night before we were to go back north. The idea of returning to the DMZ area, and going up against the NVA again, was not really appealing to anyone. I remember a full moon was out that night, and it was actually peaceful. I had written another letter to Sue and had polished off a few cans of beer at our club. I went to sleep on top of one of the bunkers we had constructed as there was a cool breeze blowing at the time. Sometime after 3:00 AM, the word came down that the movement had been canceled, and the battalion ordered to move by air to Da Nang. Upon arrival, we were to be ready for further employment into the mountains southwest of the city. On May 17, 1968, Mike Company was to be at the Quang Tri airfield at 8:00 AM for movement by C-130 to Da Nang. It required most of that day to fly the battalion south, but it was accomplished without incident. This was the last time in the war that 3/26 ever served or operated around the DMZ.

CHAPTER 9

MAMELUKE THRUST: FIFTY DAYS IN THE JUNGLE

Arrival at the big airbase in Da Nang was like most moves at the time. We were herded off to one side of the field to a holding area to wait for trucks that were late in getting there. There was a Pan American 707 sitting next to our area with both pilots standing there in amazement, watching our unit armed to the teeth and milling around them. Many of the Marines were covered with festering sores on their arms as a result of cuts from elephant grass sustained during patrols outside of Quang Tri. Infection thrived in the dirt, heat, and humidity, and the sores took weeks to heal. Nobody had been in a shower for a couple of weeks and was emaciated from the lack of a balanced diet and constant operations for the better part of four months. Appearance-wise I was in the same shape, except I also had an infected cut under my nose, thanks to having run into some low hanging barbed-wire earlier at Khe Sanh.

I remember picking up my shotgun and then going over to talk to two guys who were clearly not sure of what to say. Curiosity finally got the best of them, and they began to ask where we had been. When the trucks finally showed up, we went on our way to the new location. What impressed me with that conversation was it was a great example of two clean, good looking, and well-fed Pan Am pilots from some other world mingling with warriors coming out of the jungles of what looked like the "lost world."

The battalion was transported out of the city to a firebase on Hill 10 southwest of Da Nang. This position was manned by the First Battalion Seventh Marines, and it was an "eye-opener." There were fixed positions, showers, and hot chow to start with, something we had not seen up north. The Marines there looked reasonably healthy and well-fed. Individual flak jackets were not worn on the firebase unless they were under attack or out operating. There was even a small Post Exchange, which was something our Marines had not seen in over four months. The differences between operations in the Da Nang and Hill 10 area, as compared to operations up along the DMZ, were striking. Large unit conventional combat operations with the NVA did not occur very often, and no NVA artillery or heavy rocket attacks were sustained around Hill 10. Here it was all about saturation patrolling and ambushes with the VC. When the Marines from 3/26 mingled with Marines from 1/7, there was no question of who had been where just by appearance.

We were now no longer a unit in the 3rd Marine Division but under the operational control of the 1st Marine Division. This sort of changing parent higher headquarters was normal for Vietnam. It usually occurred when additional assets were necessary for an operation to get the required combat power to meet the mission. It worked reasonably well, thanks to the flexibility of the planning staffs and the resilience of the superb troops. The huge drawback to this approach was the unfamiliarity of a specific area by an incoming unit, which could and did lead to enemy action with disastrous consequences on occasion.

3/26 was on Hill 10 for about three days when I received my first "care package" from Sue. I had asked her to get things like powdered drink mix, and purification tablets that did not taste like chlorine when mixed with the local water. I had also requested contact paper to waterproof our maps because we could not get any. She included several other things not available that really made the difference for me, as we were still basically on C-Rations. About this time, there was an incident whereby the troops had torn up the First Division Club after a night of heavy drinking, which was the first in four months for some of them. This required the battalion commander John Studt to report to the Commanding General of the 1st Marine Division for an explanation. Afterward, the battalion moved off Hill 10 early on a new mission, which would eventually have the Marines operating in the mountains west of Da Nang for fifty-six days. This operation, called Mameluke Thrust, was to go after NVA base areas used to stage attacks against Da Nang and surrounding areas during the 1968 Tet Offensive.

The mountains southwest of Da Nang were similar to what we experienced all along the border with Laos that ran the length of the country. The terrain was steep and covered by dense triple canopy jungle featuring large stands of Teak, Mahogany, and Monkey pod timber, surrounded by thick growth on the ground. Water in those mountains was plentiful, as steams were everywhere at the bottom of canyons. Leeches and various kinds of insects were also prevalent everywhere, which caused great discomfort among the troops. It was extremely difficult to cut and work through as foot movement on the ground could take hours just to go a quarter to a half-mile. Any trails that we followed were invitations for ambushes by either VC or occasional NVA, and visibility was not more than 10-20 meters in most instances. In these situations, scout dogs at the front of a column were invaluable at alerting and smelling out the enemy. This often enabled my lead units to attack and disrupt enemy positions by surprise instead of the other way around. An untold number of lives were saved due to the exceptional work of our dogs. To this day, they still do not have a technical capability better than the nose and instinct of a German shepherd scout dog. The dogs were so valuable they rated an emergency medevac by helicopter along with the handler if they were wounded. One day after we were allowed to patrol off of 881S, I had a reconnaissance team working off to the northwest of our positions when they were hit by mortar fire. They had a big beautiful silver German shepherd named "Nick" who was wounded by the impact and blast of a round. He was injured badly enough the handler recommended that he be evacuated for treatment. A request for an emergency medevac was called, and within a short period, an H-34 helicopter arrived to pick up both the dog and his handler. They were subsequently flown back to the main base for treatment. This was indicative of just how important those dogs were to us.

On May 18, 1968, we kicked off the operation by moving off of Hill 10 and advancing west and up one ridgeline into the higher mountains. This piece of terrain was known as "Charlie Ridge" by local Marine units that had fought over it on several occasions. 3/26 was used to employing massive amounts of supporting artillery and airstrikes while operating around Khe Sanh. Our initial movements were to be no different this time. We pounded Charlie Ridge with artillery, mortars, and several airstrikes to the extent that we were able to move through the elephant grass and up ridge against very little resistance by the end of the first day. What followed were days of patrolling over ridges and into canyons without much contact with the enemy. Movement was extremely difficult due to the steep terrain, thick jungle, and very high humidity. To be resupplied by helicopter, it became necessary for the battalion to clear landing zones big enough to permit the helicopters to land. At each location, this required a major effort to blow down large trees as well as clear out the undergrowth. Usually, a company would move onto some high ground and establish a perimeter where the LZ (landing zone) was to be built. Then engineers would move in on foot and start to clear out the jungle using explosives and chain saws as long as they lasted. After about two weeks of this kind of activity, the battalion became rather proficient at clearing LZs, getting resupplied, and then moving further west to establish another position for more patrolling in search of the NVA base camps.

The standing operational procedure for any security around one of these LZs was to put out small unit ambushes along trails or crossing points over streams that might be used by the NVA. The teams would go out right at dusk to set in the ambush site before it got really dark. After establishing fields of fire, each unit would place claymore mines on the flanks of the position. They were to be fired only if enemy troops wandered onto the established kill zone of the ambush site. The claymore was a vicious mine that could be command-detonated by the team leader at the site. Upon detonation, it would spray dozens of steel balls that would spread out and shred anything caught in the blast pattern.

One very dark night, I was monitoring the buzz on the radio nets for our ambush teams when I heard a click on the handset coming from one of the teams. I responded in a low voice by asking what they wanted. The Marine on the other end of the net was whispering that they had a large tiger sitting in the kill zone and looking toward them while sniffing the air. It was obvious that the kid was scared and did not know what to do. Now tigers in the mountains of Vietnam were not unusual, but they were normally seen only by reconnaissance units patrolling deep in the jungle. I asked the Marine what was the cat doing, and was it showing any signs of aggression? The response came back; it was just looking right at the team but not moving. I did not want to give away the ambush position in the middle of the night, but I did not want anybody to get hurt either if the cat charged into their position. Finally, I instructed him to not move but carefully watch for any movement on the part of the tiger. If it started to lunge toward the team, then they should fire one of the claymores and kill the cat. This back and forth went on for about an hour when another click came in over the handset. The Marine whispered the tiger had slowly turned around and moved away from the ambush site. That ended a scary night for the team, but they were greeted warmly by other members of other teams upon returning to our company position at dawn the next morning.

We were getting used to operating in that environment, but things did not always go smoothly. On May 29th, 1968, a new LZ was in place, but it offered a narrow approach for any helicopter coming in to the site. An inbound CH-46 was approaching this makeshift LZ when the pilot lost power and started to drift toward the trees. The blades struck one of the trees, the helicopter rolled over and struck the ground upside down and started to burn. We were fortunate to get the crew and eleven Marines led by Staff Sergeant Ron Echols out of the wreckage before it exploded. Staff Sergeant Echols was the commander of the 1st platoon and a superb combat leader who was a veteran of the vicious battles late in 1967 around Con Thien. He had been elevated to platoon commander at Khe Sanh and continued in that capacity until the end of his tour in-country. He had also been recommended for a battlefield commission to lieutenant but later turned it back in, as one tour in Vietnam had been enough for him. Fortunately, nobody on board the helicopter was injured, but we had a Marine in a nearby mortar pit killed by flying pieces of one of the helicopter blades. The wreckage burned all night while the crew spent the night in foxholes with the rest of us. They were picked up the next day by another CH-46 that landed in the zone, which had been expanded considerably by the explosions and fire of the previous night.

Moving up and downhill in the jungle was extremely difficult, even for Marines that were in excellent condition. Unfortunately, many of my Marines were not in the best of condition due to being worn down by so many operations in the field. We would often move slowly along small trails with a scout dog on the point, frequently stopping to give the troops a rest but to listen for any movement up ahead. The procedure was for everyone to drop just off the trail and face outboard alternately into the jungle. I was reading my map when I heard a gasp from my radio operator who was just off the trail behind me. He had been lying back on his pack listening to the radio while staring out into the jungle. Turning around, I saw that he was frozen in place, and a deadly green Bamboo Viper snake was slowly crawling across the front of his flak jacket and on to the ground. Fortunately, he did not move, and the snake moved off into the jungle. We had been briefed on several species of snakes before jumping off on operations in the mountains, but this was the only time we had encountered one. My radio operator was as white as a sheet but unharmed.

One another day shortly after that, it came to my attention that one of the junior enlisted was having a very tough time making the hills and had taken to falling out of the movement. On two occasions, it required requesting a helicopter medevac to lift him back to the rear for treatment. When he recovered, he was lifted back to the battalion to rejoin his platoon. The troops were beginning to get down on him because he still had trouble keeping up. One of my staff NCOs asked what we should do because Private First Class James Charles Middleton was a good Marine. I decided to bring him up and into the Mike Company command group, where he became one of my security guards. There he could function but not at the frenetic pace required in the rifle platoons. What happened next became somewhat of a legend within 3/26. The Marines had given him the nickname "the Mouse" because he only weighed one hundred pounds. We gave him a captured AK-47 assault rifle complete with an NVA vest with pockets for three banana magazines for the AK. We also supplied him with plenty of the required ammunition. This was probably illegal, but it achieved its purpose, which was to elevate the Mouse to star status among the troops. This worked really well as the word spread rapidly that Middleton was now the captain's bodyguard and carrying an AK-47. Both the battalion commander Lieutenant Colonel John Studt and the regimental commander Colonel Bruce Meyers approved of the move as long as the AK was put away when we were ever back in a base camp. On a couple of occasions, we got into a firefight with the NVA while moving through the jungle. We had to be careful because whenever the Mouse opened up with his AK, it could cause confusion on both sides as to who was firing the weapon. Looking back on all of that, I think he had the symptoms of Sickle-cell Anemia, but we did not know what that was at the time. There will be more on the Mouse later.

3/26 was now deep in the mountainous terrain with no sign of relief from any other Marine units. Up to now, the NVA had generally stayed out of our path except for occasional probing and sniper attacks when we were in a fixed position around a LZ. The pattern would change whenever we got too close to one of their base camps, and then the resistance would increase. Gradually the battalion began to see how the NVA operated and where they almost always positioned their base camps. There were certain characteristics that we always found in these areas. Each camp was always near water and at the bottom of a canyon or on the lee side of a mountain. This puts them away from any direct or indirect fire from artillery or mortars. Each camp had several caves dug back into the mountain where they lived and worked. Now and then, we would find small huts where they lived but always on water and well camouflaged. There were a series of these camps that ran all along the mountain chain, which could house units of varying sizes and generally be safe from attack. They were all linked in some manner to the famous Ho Chi Minh Trail, which ran the entire length of the country. It was in these base areas where North Vietnamese Army units staged before coming out of the mountains to attack various cities during Tet in January 1968.

Mike Company had discovered several of these sites along with large supply dumps of weapons and ammunition. In one location, the NVA had hidden it on platforms camouflaged over a streambed with the water running under the stash. In another site, we discovered a cache of Soviet RPD automatic weapons—similar to our Browning Automatic Rifle (BAR)—that had been abandoned. Most of these weapons had been originally transported by porters south down the Ho Chi Minh Trail from North Vietnam. We also found significant amounts of rice in the caves, much of which was in the traditional United States Agency for International Development (USAID) sacks donated to South Vietnam. This also included cans of U.S. soybean oil as well as corn and beans. The American people were feeding the NVA and didn't even know it. One of the largest sites discovered had a field hospital dug in caves with running water constructed out of bamboo pipes along with bamboo racks for casualties. It looked like it was capable of supporting a company-size unit, albeit in a fairly primitive way.

NVA resistance in these sites varied with what was to be discovered in each one. Occasionally they would make a hasty defense of the site and then move out to other areas. Here again, the use of scout dogs by my Marines was invaluable. There was never a time when one of my units walked into an ambush during the entire operation, thanks to the dogs. Once inside a site, the dog handlers would turn the dogs loose into the caves. Any NVA soldier that confronted one of our German shepherds usually surrendered without a fight. We did take prisoners in those sites and discovered some of them had been there for over well over a year. The one thing that struck me was any NVA prisoner we captured was always clean, had a good haircut, and a carefully maintained uniform. At the same time, we looked like something else with dirty uniforms in need of haircuts and a bath. Some of my troops were even wearing North Vietnamese packs and ponchos because we could not get any from our own supply system.

I have been asked many times of my opinion of the North Vietnamese soldier. He or she was totally dedicated to their cause. They were tough and resilient troops and well-trained. Their innate ability to suffer hardship for long periods had been clearly established. Tactical flexibility was not a strong suit with the NVA. They would stick to a plan right down to the point of annihilation before adjusting to circumstances. This was a weakness that we often exploited. The bottom line, though, was the North Vietnamese were good soldiers, knew how to use their supporting arms, and were far superior to any conventional force the U.S. encountered in later conflicts in the Middle East.

On June 2, 1968, Mike Company had been patrolling in steep, jungle-covered mountainous terrain for almost two weeks. We were slowly moving through thick foliage in overwhelming heat and humidity while climbing up a sharp razorback ridge. The 1st platoon with a scout dog team was on the point, followed by the 2nd Platoon. The 3rd platoon was bringing up the rear. When they reached the top of the ridge, Echols called back on the radio that they had come across a small trail that moved along the ridge through thick jungle. I gave him instructions to carefully follow the trail but to make no noise.

As the company moved along the ridge, the scout dog on the point froze in place, a sure sign that he had detected something. The column halted and went to ground strung out along the narrow trail. In the silence, the point could hear sounds of someone talking in Vietnamese and someone cutting wood or bamboo in the canyon below. I told my radio operator to call back to battalion and request an airstrike on whatever was in that canyon. After a short pause, the battalion air officer came up on the net and indicated a strike had been requested, and two aircraft were inbound to the target area. When the pilots acknowledged the brief on the target, they were cleared to roll in on it.

What happened next was something I never thought would ever happen to me. We were all kind of relaxed along that trail, and I was standing behind a very large boulder taller than I was. The 3rd platoon under Second LT Dennis Andrews was strung out along the trail on the other side of the boulder. The first Marine plane rolled in and dropped two 250-pound Snake-Eye bombs that went into the canyon and exploded with a thunderous crash. A few minutes later, the second plane came in and dropped two more Snake-eyes as he roared over our position. The next thing I knew, a huge explosion occurred with massive overpressure that really stunned me. For a short moment, I lost my sense as to where I was. It felt like I had been caught in a giant cymbal. The second two bombs had gone off in the treetops right over the 3rd platoon's position.

What happened next almost defied description? Echols remembers being tossed in the air with the concussion, as were other members of the 2nd Platoon. When I peered around the boulder, the sight was almost unimaginable. Bodies, body parts, and smashed equipment were everywhere. Lieutenant Andrews had recovered enough to start to render aid to the seriously wounded and to try to get a count of all the casualties.

Following the bomb strike, my company executive officer, First Lieutenant Bill Hutsler, had been in the very rear of the column. He was stunned and disoriented but otherwise not badly hurt. He moved quickly to get control of the situation and tried to get an accurate count of the casualties, but the site was a mess. Eight Marines were dead, and five more were seriously wounded. The other 18 members of the platoon were either stunned or in shock. Hutsler was a decisive, gruff Marine who was a Gunnery Sergeant when he was elevated to 1st Lieutenant. This process occurred when the Corps was critically short of platoon commanders as the war ground on. He had a sixth sense in situations where we came into contact with the enemy and always responded aggressively and correctly. In this case, he was at his best, even though dizzy from the overpressure of the blast.

The first thing I did was to call off the jets and request an immediate emergency medevac for mass casualties. We brought most of the Navy corpsman from the other platoons on the ridge to the site to render as much aid as possible. The next challenge was to get both the wounded and the dead out of the position and back to the rear. This was almost impossible because there was no LZ within a thousand meters from our location, and the trees all around our position were 75 to 100 feet high.

We had requested CH-46s, and the response from the air wing was good. The plan was to have one CH-46 come in to hover in the treetops, while the seriously wounded were hoisted up through the trees using both jungle penetrators and Neil Robinson slings. The severity of the injury determined which device would be used to get the casualty some 90 feet through the canopy to the hovering helicopter. The CH-46 could handle a half-dozen casualties if it could hover in the treetops for that amount of time. This required great skill on the part of the pilots. When the wounded had finally been medevacked, the removal of the dead became another matter. We could not carry the remains from where we were located to include the equipment they had been carrying. The solution was to bring in another CH-46 with an external cargo net slung under the bird. The helicopter again hovered in the treetops over our position, and the net was lowered and dropped to the ground. It was then spread out, and the dead were carefully placed within the net along with body parts, weapons, and equipment. When the remains were all secured in place, the 46 carefully retracted the net back up through the trees and secured it to the bottom of the helicopter. It then flew off toward the rear with the net and its contents swinging slowly under the machine.

That was one sight I never wanted to see again.

After the medevacs were completed, I had gone around the position to make sure that we had gathered everything up. It was very quiet within the Mike Company perimeter that night as the troops on watch were reflecting on the day's events while the others were trying to sleep. We had also been lucky in that the NVA had stayed away from our position while the medevacs were being processed.

After this incident, we were called back to the 3/26 battalion position on Hill 1235 for some rest and reorganization. The ensuing investigation conducted by the First Marine Aircraft Wing found that the pilot of the second aircraft had been off some ten degrees in his run-in heading as he approached the target. At high-speed moving cross-compartment over the terrain, coupled with the difficulty in recognizing the target, he had been too low when the bombs were dropped. This was before the days of GPS, smart munitions, and target acquisition. The lieutenant colonel from the wing who was in charge of the investigation questioned me carefully about the circumstances of the incident. When he was finished, I asked him if the pilot had been told about the results on the ground. He said that he had not. My response: "Don't tell him."

Three days after the "friendly airstrike," Mike Company moved off of Hill 1235 and continued to hunt for more NVA base camps. I had mentioned earlier that NVA resistance would increase when we were getting close to one of their sites. On the fourth day, we had a meeting engagement with a small NVA unit that developed into a solid firefight lasting into the night. I now had several wounded that could not be moved on the ground after dark in the jungle. Our corpsman was working on the most seriously wounded man whose veins were beginning to shut down and were not accepting an IV solution. We ended up drawing a perimeter around some old bomb craters, the results of an earlier B-52 strike.

I had called for an emergency medevac for the severely wounded Marine, but the fog had grounded all helicopters early in the evening. In the meantime, the battalion had 106 Recoilless Rifles on Hill 1235 that kept up regular fire into where we thought the NVA were located. This tended to keep them away from our positions. Around midnight an escorted Ch-46 attempted to try to get the casualties out. This meant coming in and hovering over our positions in the dark, basically in the treetops again some 75 to 100 feet above the ground. In another example of superb airmanship, the pilot lowered a Neil Robinson sling 100 feet into the crater where the casualty was located. There, a corpsman and Marines secured him into the device. The helicopter then began to retract the sling and raise the casualty up through the trees until they could get him into the bird. The effort on the part of that helicopter crew saved the Marine's life.

The other three casualties (one of which was Lance Corporal David Muller, my radio operator) were extracted by jungle penetrators all in the same manner. Muller was a hard-nosed Marine from Pikeville, Kentucky, and that was the last time I ever saw him. There was no more contact with the NVA that night. The next day we moved back through the jungle with the walking wounded to the battalion position on Hill 1235.

One day some thirty-five years later, I received a call at our home in Virginia. It was David Muller calling to see if I was the same Captain Jenkins that he had served with in Vietnam. He was in El Paso, Texas, and was taking a long shot to see if it was the same commander of Mike Company. We had a great conversation over the phone and maintained contact over the next couple of years. There have been several instances like that for me, as Marines tend to stay in contact if it is possible after numerous experiences together in the Corps. It is almost like one giant fraternity.

Around the middle of June, Mike Company was moved by helicopter off of Hill 1235 to Hill 55 in the flatlands for a day's rest, showers, and decent food. Even one day was better than nothing, and I did manage to get another small pile of letters from Sue along with another care package with all kinds of treats in it. The mail situation had been reversed back to what it was at Khe Sanh. We were so far back in the mountains that the only chance of getting regular mail required having helicopters readily available, which was not the case. This short period of rest followed 35 days of continuous operations in the mountains. Hill 55 was south of Da Nang and the headquarters for the 7th Marine Regiment. It overlooked a large flatland of paddies and growth called Dodge City by virtually every Marine unit that had fought there. This area had been used as an infiltration route for NVA units moving toward Da Nang, and it was infested with Viet Cong. A dirt road ran west of Hill 55 for about six miles that was used as the main supply route to a Civilian Irregular Defense Force (CIDG) camp occupied and run by Army Special Forces. The camp was located at the end of this road and in the mountains above a small hamlet called Thuong Duc. Their only means of resupply was over this road.

Shortly after our return to Hill 1235, I received an order to move overland and down to the dirt airstrip at Thuong Duc. On June 17, Mike and India Companies were to provide security for a scheduled resupply convoy bound for the CIDG camp. The positions along the road gave one the impression that we were at the bottom of a bowl surrounded by mountains on three sides and all covered with thick jungle canopy. I vividly remember June 18 and 19 as I employed Mike Company on small hills out in the open just north of a dirt airstrip. Almost immediately, we were hit with NVA mortars from within the jungle canopy that lasted all day long on the 18th. We had to sit there partially out in the open and take the mortar attacks until the convoy finally passed through. Marine artillery counter-battery fire from Hill 55 never did silence the enemy fire, which lasted into the early evening. Casualties sustained were two killed and five wounded. This was one occasion when I talked about sustaining those casualties in the next letter to Sue, as my frustration with being unable to strike back and not knowing for sure of getting any results really grew on me. This particular mission turned out to be a very expensive waste of time.

The only somewhat positive thing occurring on the 19th was that someone in the rear decided we needed a resupply of ice cream. Mike Company Marines had not seen ice cream in over five months. Sure enough, a CH-46 helicopter came in about mid-day with a jeep trailer full of ice cream and packed in ice slung under the bird. He landed near the airstrip and dropped off the trailer. The troops, not being shy, took more than their share and left the rest for India Company. India was now commanded by Tom Esslinger, who had done an exceptional job as the company commander. Now I had numerous sick Marines with the runs later in the day as a result of eating too much rich ice cream. It was a nice gesture, but nobody had thought of the consequences.

On June 19th, Phase II of Mameluke Thrust went into effect. We were lifted back into the mountains to a location known as Happy Valley, a place where many units before our arrival had met more than their share of grief. The terrain was just like every area we had seen since the initial attack up Charlie Ridge. I remember moving through swampy areas with water up to my waist and being bothered by jungle rot that would not heal on my back. This was also when we began to deal with leeches coming out of the trees. There was one night when we were deep in the jungle, and leeches were everywhere. I spread out a plastic sheet and poured mosquito repellent around the edges of the sheet. This worked and kept leeches from crawling on to your body while sleeping. It did not cure the problem, but it helped. Our corpsmen were kept busy removing these nasty little creatures from various locations on our troops every morning. The one bright spot at this point was that Matt Caulfield had just returned to the battalion after being off on R&R for ten days. He had brought in one bottle of Irish whiskey, which was passed around that night. After the whiskey, we all slept well despite the leeches.

Happy Valley was also an area honeycombed with NVA base camps that still contained numerous supply sites with all kinds of weapons and munitions. The resistance encountered around these areas increased as well. All four rifle companies in the battalion were finding new NVA base camps as well as meeting daily contact with North Vietnamese soldiers. Mike Company sustained two more killed in action along with nine wounded as we pressed deeper into the mountains capturing another NVA base camp and more weapons and ammunition.

On July 9th, the battalion was airlifted out of the Happy Valley area and back to Hill 55. There we immediately launched another search and destroy operation, this time under the control of the 7th Marines. This would be the battalion's first operation in the Dodge City area, and it was an education. Extreme heat and humidity in the flatlands, coupled with Viet Cong hideouts, bunkers, and underground billeting areas laced with mines and booby-traps, created significant problems for the troops. Heat casualties were now a major problem, and we had to ensure the troops were hydrated and supplied with clean water. On occasion, we would stop and draw water from local streams when we could not get a helicopter resupply of freshwater. It had to be purified. We had discovered some troops avoided that, which increased their chances of coming down with various diseases like malaria so they would be medevac'd out of the field. So I directed our Navy corpsmen to stage themselves at the water's edge and personally put purification tablets into each mans' canteen.

This operation continued until 18 July and consisted of saturation patrolling with an occasional firefight with VC and NVA elements. One night I had sent Lieutenant Hutsler, who was still the executive officer of the company, out on a reconnaissance patrol. They got into a firefight, almost immediately killing two NVA soldiers. One of the dead was an NVA officer loaded with documents. Hutsler gathered up the documents and proceeded to move quickly back to Mike Company's position. What he had found was an attack plan for another major NVA attack on Danang that included maps and the objectives. This was quickly passed on to higher headquarters, which had no prior knowledge of what was coming. For his effort, Bill Hutsler received the Bronze Star. In addition to firefights, the mine problem was worse than anything the VC could throw at Mike Company.

In three days, I lost Second Lieutenant Andrews and two other Marines killed by mines. Five more were wounded, including a highly decorated Navy corpsman. I can still see the huge explosion that killed the 3rd platoon commander. On one miserable night, we were in a perimeter defense in the rice paddies. We could hear VC or NVA moving all around our perimeter, coupled with sounds coming from a small hill complex to our west. The company was close to the coast where U.S. Navy ships were standing by to back up Marines on the ground with naval gunfire support. This particular night the battleship USS *New Jersey* was on station for such missions. I requested naval gunfire be placed against a small hill, not knowing New Jersey was out there. What followed was a quick response whereby she hurled 2400-pound rounds over our position and into the hill. We could hear the report of the sixteen-inch guns going off, and then what sounded like freight trains passing overhead as the shells slammed into the target. After a half-dozen rounds were fired, all was quiet for the rest of the night. An aerial spotter over the target the next morning reported that the entire hill was cleaned of any natural or manmade growth.

We continued to move south the next day to link up with some Marine M-48 tanks that were sitting on Vietnamese Highway 4. This very rough road ran from the intersection with the National Highway I west toward the mountains. Route 4 was more like a dirt track splitting the area known as Dodge City to the north and Go Noi Island to the south. Go Noi was poison for any Marine unit that had to go in there after the VC. We managed to link up with the tanks but discovered they would not move down the road without infantry security and support. This led to a confrontation between the tank unit and myself, which was finally resolved when 3/26 modified its plan of attack to escort the tanks back toward Hill 55. My initial experience in Dodge City was not pleasant, and it would not be the last time we operated there.

CHAPTER 10
DODGE CITY, DA NANG AND THE HAI VAN PASS

On July 20th, the entire battalion was pulled out of Dodge City and moved by truck to a new location in Dai La Pass. There we became the 1st Marine Division reserve. Our camp was in an old quarry site on the edge of Da Nang, known as the Rock Crusher, and behind the 1st Division's headquarters on Hill 327. It was also a time where various changes in commanders were to take place. This started when Lieutenant Colonel Studt was relieved by Major Dick Blair as the battalion commander at the end of his tour. John Studt was an extremely effective, tactical commander and very well read in how to conduct operations. He had been an exceptional leader and was respected by the troops. Major Matt Caulfield then moved up from being the S-3 Operations Officer to the position of executive officer of 3/26. I turned Mike Company over to First Lieutenant Bill Hutsler and moved up to become the S-3 of the battalion. This did not come as a surprise and was the natural flow of officers from commands to different staff positions in the battalion. I did not want to leave the company and the superb Marines that were in it but also knew they would be in great shape with Bill Hutsler. He was a proven natural leader and a superb tactician in the field.

My tour as the commander of Mike Company had been one of the most rewarding experiences in my life, and it was everything I had hoped it would be. The huge responsibility of leading Marines in combat effectively cannot be matched by any other military or civilian occupation. It is really the last level of command where you have direct control over your men and their welfare. Marines will do whatever is asked of them and do it well, but they deserve the best leadership they can get to be successful and survive.

Losing Marines in combat is painful, but at times it is unavoidable because the other side has a vote. Mike Company had sustained 21 killed and over 71 wounded in five and a half months of operations that I was in command. Several of the wounded returned to the company following their recovery, while many others were medevac'd out of the country to hospitals in the region or back to the states. Combat is a gory business with steep costs, and I learned combat leaders must retain their cool when under fire, and do everything possible to provide for the health and welfare of their Marines. If they don't, the troops will begin to doubt their leadership and lose confidence, which can lead to disaster.

The S-3 of the battalion is responsible for the operations and training of the various units in the organization. I would now be drawing up plans for coming operations as well as drafting tactical orders when required by the battalion commander. Instead of planning and moving one rifle company tactically, it was now my responsibility to plan for the employment of the four rifle companies in 3/26. That also included planning for the employment of appropriate mortar, artillery, and aviation assets, depending on the mission. We never went light in the use of supporting arms assets, and I was not hesitant at all to bring down the roof on some target even if it was overkill. One learns this quickly to save the lives of your men. The troops understood someone was watching their backs, and it gave them more confidence to go out and do what was required.

In early August, some of the senior billets in the battalion changed again. Lieutenant Colonel J. W. P. Robertson became the new commander of 3/26. Dick Blair reverted to the executive officer's billet, and Matt Caulfield rotated home after a long tour with the battalion. What was to follow was a colorful tour with the new battalion commander, which was both fun and frustrating at the same time.

This was also the best time for me to take my ten days of R&R that everyone rated. Sue and I had thoughts about this almost from the beginning of my tour in Vietnam. The services had good programs in place with paid for travel to locations stretching from Korea to Australia. Our plan was to meet in Hawaii for ten days and spend the time relaxing and enjoying life. She had to do most of the planning because I had no access to anything from where I was at the time. This was pretty much the way things worked out, though it never was a sure thing until we saw each other at Hickam Air Force Base (AFB) near Honolulu. Those of us going to Hawaii would fly from Da Nang to Guam for a brief stop. There several of the Marines on our flight raided the Package Store at Anderson AFB for all kinds of spirits in preparation for their R&R in Hawaii. Then it was on to Hawaii, where we would meet up with our wives and families.

On numerous occasions, guys who had signed up to go to Hawaii would be wounded or killed in combat before it was time to leave. The wives or other family members would come out to Hawaii only to find out that he had not made it. I can remember getting off the plane at Hickam and being herded into a large briefing room for a quick review of policies regarding R&R. Then they would open the large doors, and we went out to the wives and families. I noted a few chaplains were standing around on the sidelines, ready to deal with someone whose husband or other relative had not made the plane for whatever reason. If she had not received any word on him, they were there to assist. Not pleasant, to say the least.

Sue had made most of the plans, and the time there was really nice. I had lost over 45 pounds in six months, thanks to constant operations in the field. I had not seen a tall building since leaving the states and quickly noted everything was so clean along the beaches in Honolulu. We had no difficulty in making the most out of the time spent there. We had a great hotel, ate plenty, and toured over part of the island. We also managed to take in a couple of shows in the Honolulu area. It was all very enjoyable, and just as we were getting used to the routine, it was time to depart. This time the departure was more difficult because, unlike my earlier departure for Vietnam, this time, I knew what I was getting into. For Sue, it was back to Virginia and school, and for me, it was back to Da Nang and the war.

In late August, 3/26 was moved out of the Rock Crusher in Da Nang and north over the Hai Van Pass to a new position near the village of Phu Loc (See Map 6). We were actually sitting in an old French fort in the shallow Phu Gia Pass overlooking Vietnamese National Route One. The mission was to provide security for U.S. and RVN units and convoys all along Route One. We had units in the battalion strung out along the road for over ten miles that stretched north from the Hai Van Pass all the way to Phu Loc. As was often the case in Vietnam, they would take a really tight battalion off of the line and break it up its integrity to cover wide swaths of territory for security missions. When the battalion was operating as an integral unit, and the Marines were relying on each other for survival, the discipline problems were generally few. When the unit was spread out over great distances for security duty, trouble would start. If the troops did not have much to do or even have contact with the enemy, discipline problems would climb for all sorts of infractions. This time it was no different for 3/26.

The static positions 3/26 and its rifle companies occupied did not require any major planning for large unit operations on my part as the S-3. Our mission was to try to provide security all along that road, or Main Supply Route (MSR) as it was called. This meant patrols, ambushes, and mine clearance in each company area of operations. In the flatlands north of the Hai Van Pass, and along the coast from Lang Co to Phu Loc, there were small Vietnamese villages all along the road. We knew there were VC in some of those locations. Whenever possible, Marine patrols would move through them looking for hidden caches of weapons and mines and especially large quantities of rice. Booby-traps were a major threat in these areas, and we did sustain casualties as a result.

On one occasion, our forward air controller was working some airstrikes on a series of small hamlets that were out close to the ocean.

This sort of activity was generally routine when VC units were spotted moving around in what was then a designated "free-fire zone." A Marine F-4 Phantom fighter checked in with our FAC and acknowledged the target. I was watching when the pilot rolled in to hit it but instead continued to fly into the ground. That was a shock because we had heard no enemy fire in the area. The crew was killed, and the only explanation we had was the pilot may have had target fixation and didn't pull out when he should have. I learned later this was a fairly common occurrence in Vietnam.

This was also that point in time when Captain Dave Gould, who had left the battalion, decided to get even with the "grunts" (a term applied to Marine infantrymen). One afternoon we were sitting outside the command bunker on top of the Phu Gia Pass when our FAC indicated that an F-4 Phantom fighter was inbound, but would not give his call sign. I looked south and saw the fighter bearing down on our position low and at a very high rate of speed. As the jet roared over us, the pilot kicked in both afterburners on the plane and peeled back on a high rate of climb. In addition to the noise, the shock of the afterburners so close to the ground caused one of our tents to come unhinged from its anchor points and flutter in the air. That was Gould, but he never admitted it. I did see Dave at a pool party after the war in Virginia. He was then out of the service and flying for Eastern Airlines. We had many laughs, but he never did own up to that high-speed pass over our position on Phu Gia Pass.

One final word regarding Private First Class James Charles Middleton (the "Mouse"). He had survived all the remaining operations in the mountains after I left Mike Company. He continued to perform well in the company command group under now Captain Bill Hutsler. One day I was out visiting the companies that were strung out along Route One when I ran into the Mouse. He looked good, although he had a sizable cut that was not quite healed on his forehead. It turned out that he had tripped over some wire and cracked his head on the sharp edge of an engineer stake. That required another medevac to get him sewn back up. He had not lost any of his smile when he saw me. It was a chance meeting with a fine Marine who, I believe, managed to survive the war.

There was a hard requirement to sweep the National Route One every day for mines that had been planted the night before, primarily by the VC. Vehicles and convoys were not allowed to pass over the road in our sector until it was cleared. Our Marine engineer teams would go out each morning with security to make sure the road was clear. Of course, the local Vietnamese did not always pay attention to that, and one morning we saw a small civilian vehicle moving down the road with five or six villagers in it. Just below our position, it hit a mine that blew it to pieces, killing all the people in the vehicle.

Occasionally a request would come in that asked for fire support for a particular search operation that was to be conducted in some of the villages. One day I was informed that there was a civilian vehicle coming in through the gate with what appeared to be heavily armed occupants. I went out to meet the vehicle and the leader of this group. He was an American who identified himself as Rollo and nothing else. His guards turned out to be Nungs, who were known as ethnic Chinese mercenaries that worked for the CIA and Special Forces. This was a team that was going after VC infrastructure in some of the villages in our area, and what they wanted was artillery and mortar support if they needed it. The request was approved and coordinated. It was some time after they had left our area that it became clear they were part of the Phoenix Program that was designed to root out Viet Cong political organizations among the population. This was part of the shadow war going on while conventional American and ARVN units engaged in combat operations with the VC or NVA.

When 3/26 headquarters was in the old French fort in the Phu Gia Pass, Lieutenant Colonel J.W.P. Robertson was determined to put his stamp on the battalion. He was a Virginian who claimed to be a distant relative of Powhatan, an early American Indian who had lived in what became Virginia when the colonies were established. Boisterous, very outgoing, and domineering, Robertson's ego was such that he could not stand the fact he was the new boy in the battalion. JWP continued to reinforce this as time went on. Initially, it started with morning physical training within the compound, followed by one ceremonial shot fired from a 106 Recoilless Rifle into the mountains daily. The next event was a required small happy hour in the late afternoon among the senior officers in the battalion. This was followed by another requirement for a formal Mess Night within the compound for the officers. This tradition goes way back to the days of the Royal Marines and is normally conducted as a formal affair with toasts, food, and music. Needless to say, that was not possible where we were, and the uniform was not evening dress but combat utilities. As well-meaning as these initiatives were, they became distractions from what we were trying to accomplish in our area of operations.

On a more personal note, the mail service was getting much better. I was now getting mail from Sue and my family on a fairly regular basis. At the same time, my outgoing letters and tapes were getting to Virginia generally within ten days of when I produced them. Sue had also purchased a small tape recorder, so we were now getting cassettes to each other. Also, I had picked up a fan club when I was in command of Mike Company at Khe Sanh. They were dependents of Navy families in Coronado who knew my parents, and most were in school in the San Diego area. This relationship had led to a series of care packages being sent to me for distribution to the Marines in the company. The boxes would arrive about every ten days and would be full of snacks, cookies, lemonade powder, and numerous other things to eat. The troops would always make very short work of the contents in those care packages.

Marine commanders are never really amazed at some of the things the troops will do. One morning the battalion Sergeant Major came in to say that there was a Lance Corporal Sullivan outside the tent requesting to see the battalion commander. This was unusual because Sullivan did not belong in 3/26 but was a member of a Combined Action Platoon (CAP) unit located about one mile north of our position. A normal CAP unit consisted of a squad of Marines assigned to a Vietnamese hamlet or village. They lived with and provided protection to the villagers as well as teaching them how to defend themselves. This was a major initiative that the Marines had instituted at the beginning of the war, and it had proven to be quite successful throughout I Corps. So successful that the majority of the CAP units were targeted and overrun by NVA attacks at the beginning of Tet in January 1968.

Sullivan was there as his unit's representative to forcefully request we give him some uniforms. He claimed they were in rags and had not had any support from his own senior organization. Sullivan was about five feet two inches tall while Lieutenant Colonel Robertson was over six feet in height. When asked how he had got to our position, he stated he had come cross-country through VC territory on foot. Armed with only his weapon, he clearly advocated his need for uniforms for his troops in the village where they were living. JWP stated that we could not turn down such a request from such an aggressive leader. The picture of the two of them standing toe to toe and negotiating was something to see. Lance Corporal Sullivan got his uniforms along with several other items and was provided an armed escort back to his unit.

One day we received word a large convoy was scheduled to make the run up National Route One to Camp Eagle, which belonged to the 101st Airborne Division near Hue City (See Map 6). Due to the size of this movement, it was necessary to put all units along the road on high alert. All superfluous activities within the headquarters were suspended to support this movement. Late that afternoon, we could see the dust coming from the convoy of trucks as they made their way down from the Hai Van Pass and out into the flatlands. When the convoy reached and passed our position, over forty semi-trucks were moving at a high rate of speed and escorted by helicopter gunships. What we did not know until the convoy had passed through, was they were hauling beer for the troops of the 101st Airborne. The Army certainly had its priorities straight in this instance.

Following more convoy security drills and the mission at hand, activities within the headquarters gradually settled down. The battalion commander wanted to conduct a sweep through some of the villages and out to the coast. The plan was briefed, and the battalion moved out toward the coast. We knew there were VC elements in some of the hamlets, but they had generally stayed out of our way. The search and destroy movement lasted for most of the day while we lost a few Marines wounded by booby-traps along the axis of advance. Returning to the base camp that evening, the operation was considered marginally successful. After this experience, we were down to just the happy hour.

Toward the middle of October, Dick Blair rotated out of the battalion, and I moved up again to become the executive officer of the battalion. This was highly unusual for me as a captain, but I had no complaints. Captain Jess Bennett moved out of Lima Company to become the S-3. Jess was ex-enlisted (a Mustang: the name for an enlisted man who rose to become an officer) from Arkansas and a terrific officer. He was another natural in that environment and a tremendous combat leader who was also a thorough planner with exceptional common sense. Jess stayed with the battalion long after I had moved up to the Division and finished out his tour. We really worked well together, and he was totally reliable. The battalion had also been alerted for another move back to the Rock Crusher in Da Nang as soon as we could be relieved by some other unit. What occurred next was another unexpected experience. I was sitting in my tent when I noticed a Jeep come wheeling into our compound with the white letters "All The Way" painted across the front bumper. The driver had a helmet on but no shirt or flak jacket. Two other men were in the back seat, fully armed and dressed. This became the official arrival of Lieutenant Colonel Charlie Beckwith, U.S. Army, and the commander of the Second Battalion, 327th airborne infantry. He was driving the Jeep, and the driver and Sergeant Major were in the back seat. The 2/327th was there to relieve 3/26.

What followed after his arrival was a contest between Beckwith and Peyton Robertson as to who could outdo the other, primarily during the happy hour. Fortunately, this went on for only a week, as we were relieved and, on our way, back to Da Nang. Beckwith was an interesting character. A really solid combat leader and a Special Forces officer, he had served a tour with the British Special Air Service (SAS). In the years following Vietnam, he became one of the founders of the Army's DELTA Force in 1977 and stayed with that elite organization as it developed. Later he was one of the commanders on the ill-fated Desert One rescue operation in 1980 that attempted to free the American embassy hostages in Tehran.

It did not take very long to get settled back in the Rock Crusher before the battalion was ordered out on another operation. This time it was in the mountainous area north of Da Nang and west of the Hai Van Pass in what was to be some of the toughest terrain the battalion had encountered since Khe Sanh (See Map 6). My responsibility as the second in command in the battalion was to direct the activities of the staff as well as provide any support that was needed in the field. In several instances, the executive officer can be the one who would replace the commander due to casualties, his rotation, or his fleeting up based on seniority and experience. That was never going to happen with me, due to rank and experience at the time. If the commander was wounded and medevacked out of the country, I could serve for a short time in that capacity but would be relieved by a more senior lieutenant colonel, which was appropriate.

During this operation, 3/26 was operating out of a firebase on the southwest side of the Hai Van Pass. The mission was to conduct patrols in very steep terrain to gain contact with NVA units reported to be operating in that area. One day, while rifle companies rotated in and out of the firebase, both Jess Bennett and I were promoted to major. Lieutenant Colonel Robertson conducted the ceremony in front of a formation of Marines. A great day to be sure, and it means more if such an event occurs in combat.

Chapter 11
Operation Meade River and Pacification

My tenure as the executive officer of the battalion lasted until January 1969. During this period and in between operations, I had the unenviable task of trying to sort out the records and equipment we had on the books and in our table of equipment. What the battalion had in its possession versus what was required by tables of organization was vastly different. This was not unusual for units had been operating for months in various parts of I Corps because there was little time to keep adequate records on what we owned, and especially when a battalion was separated by miles from its administrative rear. When 3/26 came out of Khe Sanh, most of its vehicles (Mighty Mites and Mechanical Mules) had been destroyed.

I remember a day when the battalion staff officers rode to the headquarters of the 1st Marine Division in borrowed Mighty Mites because we had none left at the time. Most of the mess equipment for feeding the troops hot meals had been destroyed. A majority of the battalion's tents had been either lost or destroyed. Also, we had over 500 weapons of different calibers that were missing. Some of the latter could be explained by the fact weapons were destroyed in combat, while many others went out with Marines who were casualties and medevacked to the rear. Some weapons found their way back to the battalion, but many did not. At the same time, Marines would pick up weapons that had been discarded along the way that were not on the battalion's books. Fifty-caliber machine guns and an extra 106 Recoilless rifle were two examples among many.

Captured enemy weapons were another issue. 3/26 had been capturing weapons of all infantry calibers for over five months. Many of them were turned in to the proper authorities at the time of capture during an operation, but there were several occasions where there was never enough time to turn in weapons due to the battalion's constant movement. The result was that there was a significant stash of enemy weapons that had been left in the rear to be disposed of. When we finally got an accurate count, most of the NVA weapons (but not all) were turned in to the appropriate units in Da Nang.

The posting to the Rock Crusher in Da Nang was helpful because we could get some stability before going out on another big operation. From the middle of September to late December, the staff and I had worked diligently to bring some semblance of order to the battalion's property and records. After trying to get an accurate account of the weapons issue, the 1st Marine Division finally agreed to let us write off the missing weapons. Also, turn in those that we had but did not rate on the table of equipment. Other improvements were being made to bring the battalion back to the level of equipment it needed. New jeep-like vehicles were being introduced to replace the destroyed Mighty Mites. Mess hall equipment that had been destroyed at Khe Sanh was replaced. New jungle utilities were issued to the troops, and damaged 782 gear was either repaired or replaced.

Life in the Rock Crusher was much better than what we had experienced in the previous six months, but it could be improved. The first challenge was to find enough adequate shelter for the troops. Our battalion units were still operating locally for security purposes but were coming back to the camp and living on the ground in some instances. Here is where the famous scrounging capability of the troops went into effect. I had indicated that we had turned in most of the captured enemy weapons. Some of our staff ranged all over Da Nang looking for materials to construct Southeast Asia Sea Huts to match some of which we had already inherited when arriving at the Rock Crusher. The goal was to get the troops off the ground while they were in camp. The best example of scrounging occurred when we were able to get two truckloads of lumber and building materials delivered by the Seabees for the price of two AK-47 assault rifles. NVA weapons were a hot item around Da Nang and excellent bargaining tools. It was surprising just how many people serving in the combat zone had never seen an AK-47. Other trades, including RPD machine guns, were made, bringing in even more materials until we had accomplished our objective. At least the troops could stay dry when it rained, as these huts were primarily constructed out of plywood but held up pretty well.

The constant operations along the DMZ and areas around Khe Sanh had precluded 3/26 from getting involved with any of the ongoing pacification programs sponsored by the government. Pacification is vital in this kind of conflict if the government is going to hold the loyalty of the civilian population. We discovered that the national level pacification programs did not work very well, due in large part to the weakness and corruption of the South Vietnamese government. The security of the population is the first priority in any kind of insurgency. Until then, any number of pacification programs from secure hamlets, economic improvement, better schools, and medical facilities will not be successful without effective security and good local governance.

In late October, the Government of Vietnam announced the start of a countrywide "Accelerated Pacification Campaign" intending to extend the legitimate government influence into many hamlets in I Corps. The effects of Tet 1968 had severely disrupted major pacification efforts throughout northern South Vietnam. Following the new government pacification strategy, the 1st Marine Division had planned for a major cordon and search operation to support the pacification campaign. Rather than surround and search each hamlet or village, the plan was to put in a cordon around some 36 square kilometers of territory in the region south of Da Nang. The specific location was to be in the Dodge City area between Hill 55 and Go Noi Island. This operation was called Meade River and was the largest cordon and search operation of the war. Once the cordon was in place, the plan called for the 51st ARVN Regiment to begin security checks and registration of all the Vietnamese civilians caught inside the cordon. This would be followed by a series of pacification programs to bring the population under the control of the government.

The area where Operation Meade River was to take place was infested with communist units, both VC and NVA. This area is mostly flat and intersected by small waterways bordering on numerous rice paddies. Hamlets and small villages dotted the landscape and patches of heavy growth; tree lines and deep elephant grass were everywhere. It had a specific potential as a source of food, security, and training for recruits for VC units. The area was considered a staging area for attacks on villages and urban areas around Da Nang along with the ARVN District headquarters in the town of Hoi An. Intelligence indicated the area was also infested with bunker complexes, especially along a railroad berm and the approaches to the river Song La Tho on the north side of the cordon. The zone of the operation was bordered on the south by Go Noi Island and Route Four. The National Route One would be the east border, while the Song La Tho River would bound the area in the north. This area was also bisected in the west by the Vietnamese National Railroad, which ran north to south on a previously mentioned high berm (See Map 7).

On November 20, 1968, seven Marine battalions began to move into assigned positions along the cordon either by helicopter, truck, or on foot. Four battalions, including 3/26, moved in quickly by helicopter, and two others came in by truck. The goal was to completely secure the perimeter around the established boundaries so that there would be no escape by VC/NVA units trapped inside the cordon.

The initial goal was accomplished against light resistance from the enemy. We landed in what was a very wet and muddy area covered with elephant grass and an occasional rice paddy. After securing our portion of the cordon at the railroad berm to our left, we moved to tie in with the 3rd battalion 5th Marines (3/5), which had landed by helicopter on our right flank. We had sustained no major casualties at this point, which was good. Shortly after arriving on the ground, I noticed a Marine Ch-46 helicopter descending at a very rapid rate toward another unit on our right flank. I kept thinking he should be pulling out of the dive, but that never happened. The helicopter flew straight into the ground, and what followed was a huge explosion. I learned later that there had been a company command group of six Marines on the bird, but nobody survived.

When all the assigned units were in place, the plan was to gradually shrink the perimeter in certain sectors of the cordon (See Map 7). This would force the enemy units into an ever-shrinking area to operate. When the 2nd Battalion 7th Marines (2/7) units attacked on the west side, the NVA/VC were pushed back to prepared positions dug in along the railroad berm. That culminated in the battle of the Horse Shoe. 3/26 then began an attack north along the berm that met heavy resistance, which lasted for a few days. This effort on the part of 3/26 and 3/5 ended up with the Battle of the Hook. This was to be the pattern for every Marine battalion in the cordon as they began to shrink the perimeter. Heavy combat from entrenched NVA and VC units in the battle of the Bunker Complex on the northern boundary of the cordon continued until the operation was secured on December 9, 1968 (See Map 7). Casualties on both sides had been heavy with the enemy losing over 1,000 dead while the Marines suffered 108 dead and over 500 wounded.

One of the better stories to come out of Meade River involved the Chaplain for 3/26, Lieutenant Ralph Hensley USN. He was a veteran of World War II in the Pacific, had gotten out of the Navy at the end of the war, and become a circuit preacher based in the Silver City area in New Mexico. He wanted to serve the troops, so he came back on active duty and was assigned to 3/26. I had briefed him early on in the operation and left to go back to the Rock Crusher after four days in the field. I began to hear stories of Ralph's exploits in the field during the numerous attacks on the enemy positions. When he tended to disappear for short periods, they found him accompanying combat patrols with cookies for the troops. This carried on throughout the entire operation until he was told to not do that because we could not afford to lose him. His bravery and perseverance were amazing, and the troops loved it, finally giving him the title "Muddy Boots." He stayed with the battalion for several months, went home and out of the Navy. He continued his preaching responsibilities in Silver City, New Mexico, until his death in 2017.

3/26 sustained moderate casualties but had done well in this operation. When they returned to the Rock Crusher, the emphasis turned to integrating new replacements, cleaning up the troops and the equipment, and getting some rest. We held a very moving memorial service in our camp for those Marines who had been lost on Meade River. Then we prepared for whatever we could in the way of a celebration for Christmas. Here again, Ralph Hensley went out of his way to bring in gifts and other items that might give the troops some feel for the holiday and home. Shortly after Christmas, we received notification from the 1st Marine Division that all Marine units participating in Meade River were to receive a Presidential Unit Citation (the third one for the battalion in 1968) for the success achieved on the operation. That was a big deal.

In January 1969, another major upheaval occurred in the battalion. Higher headquarters had designated 3/26 as the next SLF that would go aboard amphibious ships for two months. This was the same kind of mission that I had experienced as a 1st Lieutenant with 1/9 way back in 1962 in the Philippines. The mission of this SLF was to be ready to be employed as reinforcement for other Marine units operating anywhere along the coast of South Vietnam. What it meant was that they would be sent in to support ongoing operations, which inevitably involved more heavy combat. The personal policy for the SLF was that any Marine with less than 90 days to go before he rotated home would be pulled out of the battalion and assigned elsewhere for the remainder of his tour. That was good for the individuals affected, including me, but it decimated the battalion as far as combat experience went because many of the replacements were brand-new. The end result of this standing policy was the SLF was always employed ashore, and the casualties were always high initially. 3/26 fared no better than any other battalion in that regard.

In mid-January 1969, I was transferred out of the battalion and assigned to the 1st Marine Division headquarters as the Division Civil Affairs officer. What that meant was that I was responsible for the myriad of civil affairs and pacification programs ongoing within the Division's area of operations. I had a staff that really managed all of our programs, and most of our activities were within a 20-mile radius of Da Nang. As stated earlier, civil affairs and pacification were critical if the government wanted to assist the population and gain loyalty from its people. The problem was you had to have a measure of security in the countryside if you wanted to be successful.

An example of what happens when you clear an area but do not stay and hold it occurred in Dodge City. By the end of December, the 1st Marine Division reported the area that had been cleared in Operation Meade River was being reoccupied by VC and NVA. Their objective was to prepare for more attacks around Da Nang. Any pacification efforts in the Dodge City area had failed due to the lack of security and effective host-government support, and corruption. It is ironic that fifty years later, we still have not learned that lesson in Afghanistan.

I was now living inside the Division compound on Hill 327, which was a generally secure area on the edge of Da Nang city. This was a far cry from the camp at the Rock Crusher on the other side and west of Hill 327. Moving around the Da Nang area during night or day was a fairly safe activity. Consequently, most of the civil affairs programs we were working within the Da Nang area went on without much interference from the VC. The security levels went down the further away one traveled from the Division headquarters and out into the countryside. This impacted on the progress that we were trying to make with our pacification efforts. The security had been an ongoing problem since the start of the war, and it usually improved only where the government had a substantial number of troops and advisors occupying broad areas of control.

Despite the relative stability in and around Da Nang, there were instances where the enemy could slip into the city and stage attacks on the large airstrip and the port area. One night after I had been in the new job for about five weeks, the Division headquarters was alerted to new local attacks. The NVA had infiltrated a rocket team into the outskirts of Da Nang and launched a barrage of rockets into the airfield, hitting one of the major ammunition dumps. I can still see the huge initial explosions that went on for three days. The result was everything around that facility was decimated. Flight operations round the major airfield were severely disrupted as a result of flying debris. I do not believe the perpetrators were ever caught.

Often, I would accompany my staff members into the local countryside to visit and inspect some of the ongoing projects. In this instance, I was accompanied by First Lieutenant Nick Shore, a native of Tennessee and a Marine officer who had extensive experience in agriculture before coming into the Marine Corps. He really was one of our experts on a variety of programs we were managing in the Da Nang area. One day we stopped at a small hamlet south of Da Nang to observe how one of the local pig-raising programs was progressing. You found pigs all over the country, but we were in the process of trying to get the Vietnamese better breeding habits to give the villagers bigger pigs for food and sales purposes. The protocols for one of these visits required we pay a call on the village or hamlet chief first. This allowed him to show us what they were doing. Next, we were usually invited to have lunch with the chief and hamlet elders. It was no different in this instance. To turn the invitation down would have caused the chief to lose face, and that was a clear insult to be avoided. We all sat down around a table outside with our weapons in our laps and had lunch. The food was surprisingly good as they had prepared roast duck, French fries RVN style, green beans, and Tiger beer. After comments through an interpreter and examining his flock of pigs, we thanked the chief and left. These activities were being conducted regularly between my staff and the village and hamlet chiefs. This was necessary to demonstrate that we supported their efforts while measuring the progress they were making. Results were important in the short-term, depending on the security issues locally. However, nobody had any idea as to how long it would take for the culture to sustain long-term improvement, which depended on the effectiveness of the South Vietnamese government.

In addition to various poultry and animal raising programs, there was a major effort to improve the local rice production. Until the beginning of the war, South Vietnam had been a rice-exporting nation to various other countries. Major combat operations against the VC and NVA in the Mekong Delta, along with government incompetence and corruption, had disrupted much of the rice-growing in the country. This was especially true in the vast regions in the Delta. Over time Vietnam was forced to import rice from elsewhere in Asia to feed its own people.

USAID had been experimenting with new strains of rice that would increase crop yield annually. It was an attempt to give both the local and national economy a boost in rice productivity within Vietnam. There had been a new strand of rice developed in the Philippines called IR-8 or "Miracle Rice." Attempting to get the Vietnamese to adopt this strand that could give them more than one crop a year became a challenge. It is hard to change a culture in existence for hundreds of years when security is the dominant issue in the countryside. Although we observed the local farmers understood the financial advantages of this new rice, they were reluctant to change the status quo. Making more money with the new rice crops meant higher taxes from both sides, and a danger to the farmers if they showed loyalty to the government. For survival purposes, they tried to stay neutral.

This had been an interesting three months, but I was ready to head home. While it was clear that in fights with the NVA and VC, the

Marines were mostly successful, U.S. firepower proved the NVA could not sustain themselves under constant attacks. It was also clear that no matter how tactically successful we had been, the NVA were in it for the duration despite the losses they sustained. The South Vietnamese government was weak and did not exercise effective economic and political control in support of the Vietnamese people. This had been obvious from watching the pacification programs. At the same time, our leadership all the way back to Washington was at a loss as to how to achieve any kind of long-term success. This could be attributed to ignorance of the Vietnamese culture, political games in the Congress, a lack of moral leadership, and poor strategic planning at the highest levels of our government. Much has been written about this, and I will not dwell on it but contend that successive administrations have not learned much from our experience there.

When I was still with the battalion in the jungle west of Charlie Ridge, Sue had been contacted by Major Bill Keys at Headquarters Marine Corps regarding my next assignment. Bill Keys was a Naval Academy graduate and a Navy Cross winner among other awards on his first tour as an infantry company commander in Vietnam. We had grown to know each other while students at the AWS. An exceptional combat leader, he was well known in the Corps for taking great care of his Marines. Bill would often have few words to say unless addressed directly, but when he did open up, the smart officers would sit up and listen. He possessed an outstanding personal reputation and could be extremely accurate when sizing up individuals quickly. He later went on to retire as a three-star general and become the CEO of Colt Industries. He is now living in full retirement on a farm in the Virginia horse country and has always been a loyal friend.

Bill had told Sue that we would be going to NROTC duty upon my return. The choices were either the University of Wisconsin or Illinois. We chose Wisconsin, as we had never been there. It turned out to be a good decision, and it was a rewarding experience, despite the demonstrations and upheaval on campus due to the war. About mid-March 1968, I received word that the university wanted me to be there by early May so that I could go through one of their graduation ceremonies. I thought this was strange going direct from the combat zone and back to the world to college graduation in one hop.

My tour was up in early April, and I flew back to Okinawa and Camp Hansen. I went through a period of processing before flying back across the Pacific to California. We took off from Kadena AFB in a jet and landed at El Toro Marine Air Station in a driving rainstorm at around 2:00 AM. My dad met me, and we then visited with my ailing grandmother Mimi for a day in Oceanside, California. Then it was off an all-night flight to Washington to meet up with Sue. Following a brief period around northern Virginia, we flew off to San Juan, Puerto Rico, for time on the beach and then over to St. Thomas for a few days of rest and relaxation. We had been planning this trip to Puerto Rico and the Virgin Islands for the better part of the previous ten months. As I entered my last three months in Vietnam, the planning had picked up momentum. The trip was a success, and after arriving back in northern Virginia, we prepared to drive to Madison, Wisconsin, for my next tour of duty at the university. We arrived in Madison in mid-July 1969 and had moved into our rented apartment in Middleton on the day that Neil Armstrong landed on the moon.

CHAPTER 12
ON TO WISCONSIN

Much had changed in the year I had been in Vietnam. The anti-war movement on college campuses across the country was in full swing, along with the anti-draft demonstrations. The University of Wisconsin in Madison was no exception in both cases. The university sits on the shores of Lake Mendota, a beautiful location. In the fall, the colors are spectacular, and in the winter, the ice on the lake can be up to four feet thick. That made ice fishing or ice sailing with specially designed boats the sports of choice. The university was one of the early land-grant colleges, and the campus was spread out around the western part of Madison with a population of around 35,000 students. On my first day on campus, I witnessed a student demonstration that was marching down University Avenue carrying both Viet Cong and North Vietnamese flags and chanting "Ho, Ho, Ho Chi Minh." They were heading past the Navy ROTC building on the way to the Selective Service office that was a block and a half away. This was the normal thing in those days where demonstrations would be held to protest the war, but also the draft, which was in full effect at that time. The crowd of about 1,000 marchers was met head-on by both the Madison police and units from Dane County. The marchers were dispersed with tear gas and a lot of pushing and shoving on the part of the police.

On the way back past our building, the protesters trashed our windows and doors with bricks and rocks. The Naval armory had been an old garage many years before but had been converted into the headquarters for the Navy ROTC program on campus. Inside, it housed an old 5-inch 38 caliber naval cannon that had been taken off of a ship decades earlier. It did nothing but sit there and remind old sailors of times in the past. One of the Navy security officers made a big deal about how secure the armory was and noted particularly the reinforced windows in my office that faced the street. It sounded good until one of the bricks hurled by a demonstrator came through the window, crossed the office, and bounced off the wall. This particular event was mild compared to what was to come over the next three years we were there.

We worked closely with a Marine Corps reserve unit stationed in Madison, regarding any civic relations activities in which they were engaged. The instructor-inspector who commanded the unit was Major George Hemple, an artillery officer who functioned as an advisor to the reserve artillery battery that was stationed in Madison. One day in 1971, my telephone rang, and the caller was none other than Staff Sergeant Bob Dorie. He had just reported in for duty at the reserve unit as the administrative chief under George Hemple. This led to two years of social activities, primarily over golf and pheasant feeds that he and his wife Charlotte would put on for his guests. Bob was an ardent pheasant hunter, and the farm areas around Madison were ideal for hunting. He was also an excellent golfer who always knew how to have a good time. The odds of the two of us coming together on independent duty away from any major Marine Corps commands were really long. What it really demonstrated was that the Corps is not that big, and everyone knew Bob Dorie.

Campus life was not all bad despite the environment at the time. The Naval ROTC unit was commanded by Colonel Bill Dyroff, a Marine on his last tour of duty. He served as the Professor of Naval Science at the University and was a member of the faculty. He was a quick-witted, articulate individual who was perfect for the assignment of dealing with the midshipmen in the unit. Upon retirement, he moved to Albuquerque, New Mexico, and began a second career as a farrier in the horse business.

All the Navy and Marine Corps officers served in the same capacity on that staff and were responsible for instruction in a myriad of subjects related to naval science. Midshipmen in the NROTC unit were really high-quality young men who had to put up with much harassment on the part of certain elements of the student body. At Wisconsin, all freshmen had to live in the dormitories provided by the school. The dorms were organized by groups like the Young Maoists, who made it their business to harass ROTC students who were associated with the military. Most of this was harmless, but the psychological and peer pressure did not make it easy for the midshipmen. Uniforms were required for drill days only, and most of the leadership activities were conducted either in the Navy Armory or the campus field house. Demonstrations on campus were regular events, and crowds would soar into the hundreds if the police became involved, which they usually did. Dane County police were all decked out in black jumpsuits with black helmets as well as all kinds of riot gear. They would move in with specially converted cars with window screens and other additions. The police would use large amounts of tear gas to break up demonstrations. Then the gas usually worked its way into the buildings on Bascom Hill, where classes would be disrupted or canceled in some instances.

The Wisconsin faculty generally went along with these disruptions until an incident occurred on August 24, 1970, that began to change the outlook on what was going on. A small group of radicals had driven a van loaded with manure and diesel fuel into a narrow alley between Sterling Hall, a building that housed an Army Math Research Center, and the Chemical Science building across from it. When the makeshift bomb was detonated, the explosion tore a hole in the building two stories high, destroying the facility and killing one civilian researcher. The power of the blast also destroyed life research in cancer located in the Chemical Science building across the alley. The cost of damages was over three million dollars. The FBI descended on the campus to get to the bottom of this incident, but it was months and in two cases years before the perpetrators were brought to justice. It was also during this period that a demonstration was going on in town when the protesters stormed the state capital building and took over the legislative chambers. The authorities finally got them removed by the police, citing a Civil War-era statute that forbade the occupation of the state building.

The major incident which touched off numerous riots and fire bombings nationwide was the Kent State shootings in Ohio. Four students were killed, and several were wounded when Ohio National Guard troops opened fire on what had been a relatively peaceful demonstration on that campus. The result was upheaval on several college campuses around the country, as well as in Washington. At Wisconsin, someone tried to firebomb the Navy ROTC building, but this proved to be unsuccessful. A major fire was started in a Civil War-era building in the middle of the campus that housed the Army ROTC offices. The fire gutted most of the old brick Camp Randall building, including student athletic facilities, but did not destroy the Army offices.

I was standing near Army Colonel Edwin Pike, the Professor of Military Science for Army ROTC on the campus who was soaking wet from water from the fire hoses. He was rocking back and forth with his cover tilted back on his head and saying, "They got everything but my offices," with a large smile on his face. It had been really cold that night, and there was ice everywhere, including on Colonel Pike. Those two events, along with really nasty demonstrations later in Madison, brought two battalions of the Wisconsin National Guard to the campus to restore order. The Guard stayed on campus for about two weeks before deploying back to their respective armories. It was during this period that Sue was taking classes toward gaining a Master of Science degree in Curriculum and Instruction. There were times when she would have to wade through tear gas and student demonstrators to get to class on Bascom Hill. She finished her requirements for the degree later at Virginia Tech after we had left Wisconsin.

That show of force by the Guard plus a more aggressive faculty started to turn things around on campus, but it took months before relative peace returned. The staff normally did not go through the campus in uniform unless it was necessary or for faculty meetings. I remember the first time I attended one of these events, I was met by a retired Army brigadier general who was in charge of the Agricultural School on campus. He welcomed me to the gathering with the comment "Welcome to the great one-act play," and proceeded to rip the faculty apart for demanding their perks and seat assignments. That situation beat anything I had ever seen while on active duty. We did have a Marine recruiter from Milwaukee who would visit the campus in uniform on occasion looking for potential recruits. He was about 6'4" and had been shot in the nose in Vietnam so that it pointed off in an odd direction. This made him look fierce. Nobody harassed him for any reason, which was kind of comical. Enrollments in ROTC had declined significantly during this period, but those students who stuck with the program turned out to be first-rate officers in both the Navy and Marine Corps following graduation.

I had begun to work on an advanced degree during my second year and managed to complete requirements for a master's degree in Curriculum in 1972. In the meantime, I had received orders for my next duty station, which would be Headquarters Marine Corps in Washington, DC Despite all the trouble created as a result of the war and the draft, life at the university was like being in Paradise when compared to Vietnam. One thing about the demonstrators at that time: They were dedicated to their issues but never demonstrated during meal hours or in inclement weather. I always thought this was interesting considering what the troops were going through in Vietnam. The local citizens were hard-working, conservative, and friendly for the most part. We had excellent support locally, and the people were proud of their beautiful state. Sue and I participated in several of the campus activities to include football games as well as hockey. At the time, the football team was not very good, but the hockey team was terrific. The Badger hockey team was always in the hunt for the annual NCAA national championships.

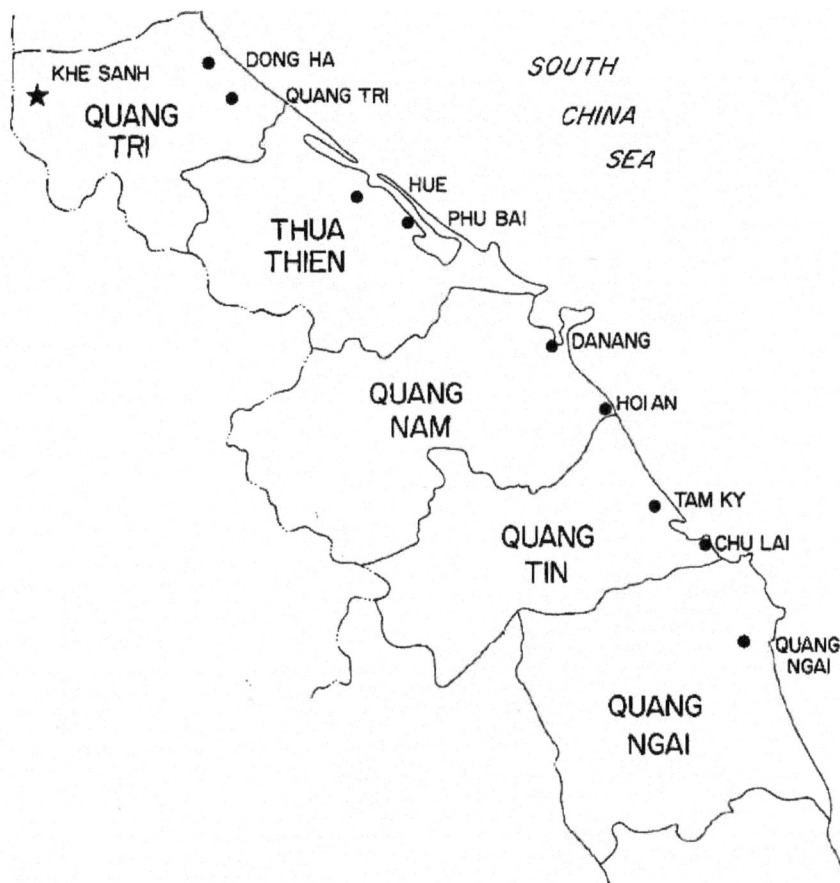

Map 1 I Corps Tactical Zone.

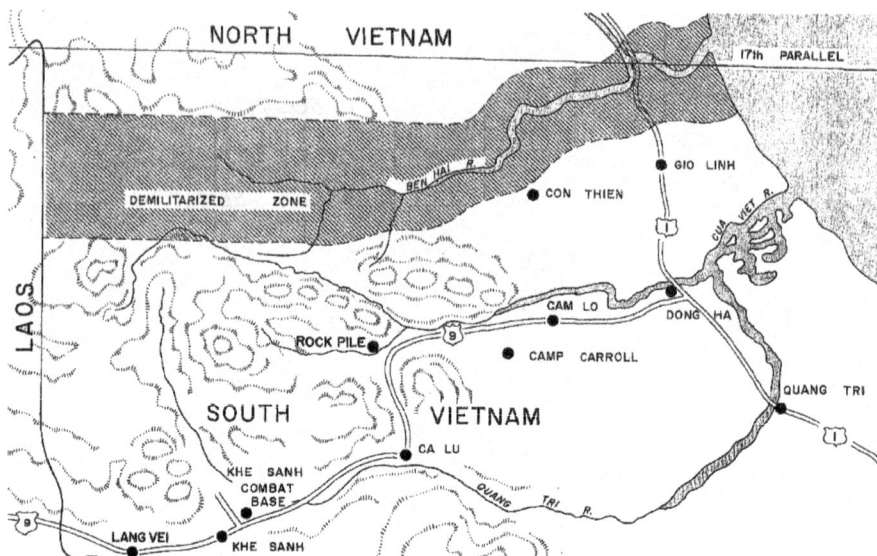

Map 2 Northern Quang Tri Province.

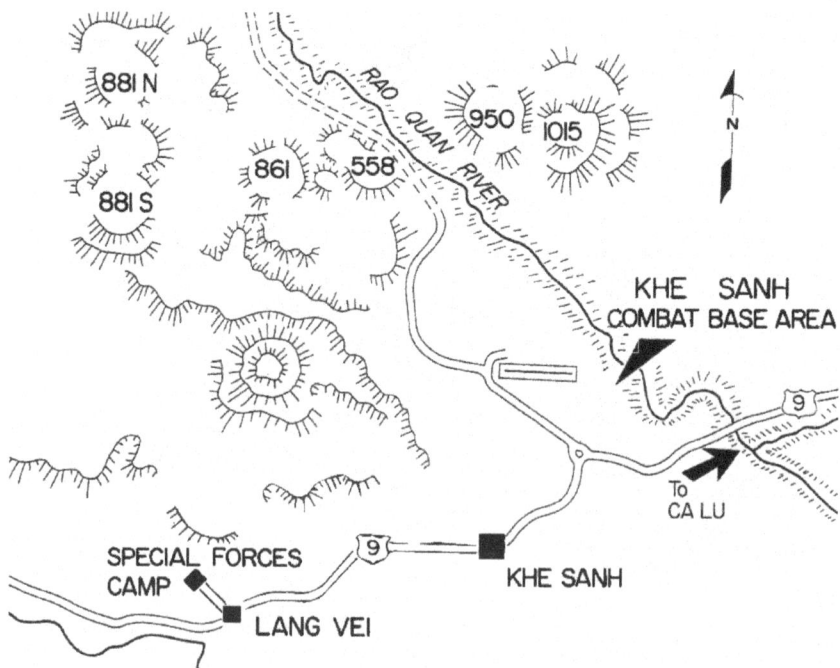

Map 3 Khe Sanh Valley and Hill 881 North.

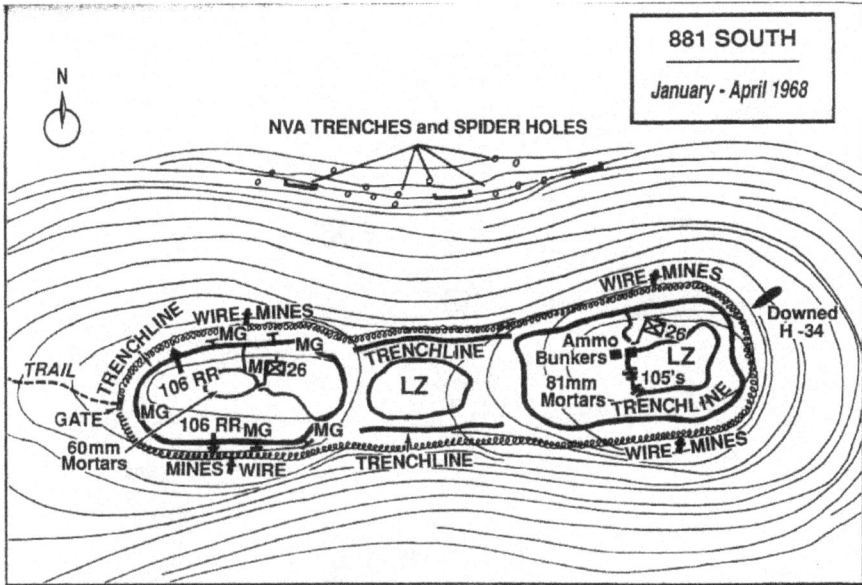

Map 4 Hill 881 South - January to April 1968.

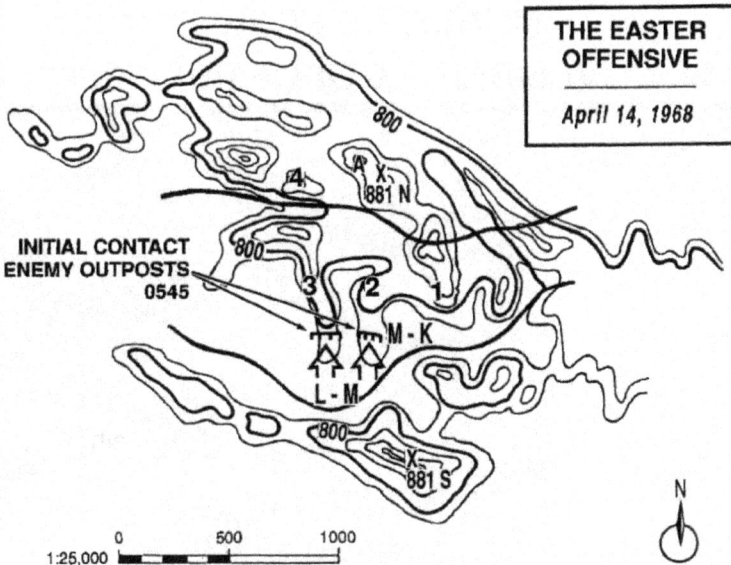

Map 5 3/26 Easter Attack April 14, 1968.

139

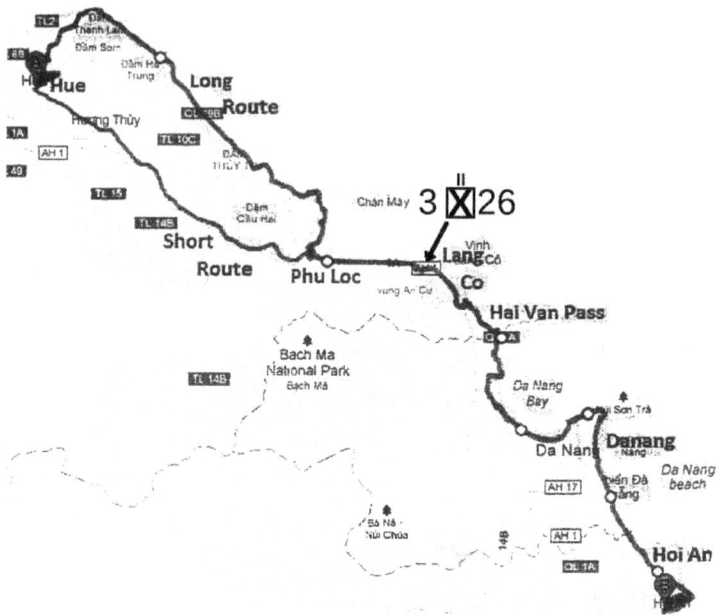

Map 6 The Hai Van Pass to Hue.

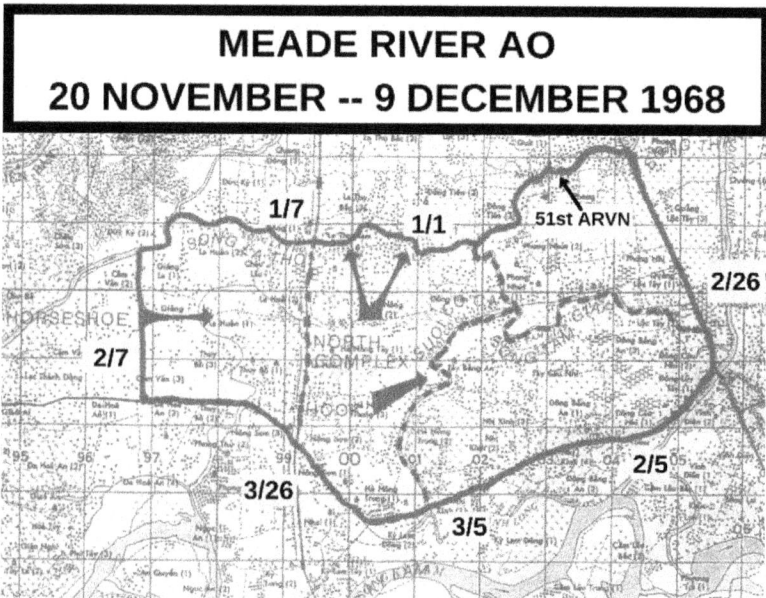

MEADE RIVER AO
20 NOVEMBER -- 9 DECEMBER 1968

Map 7 Meade River Cordon Operation.

Helicopter Resupply Hill 881 South Khe Sanh.

Staff Sergeant Ron Echols, Hill 881 South.

Corporal Robert J. Arrotta (India -14), Hill 881 South.

The author devouring a CARE package Hill 10
Southwest of Da Nang.

The author briefing First Lieutenant Bill Hutsler, Operation Mameluke
Thrust May 1968.

Private First Class James C. Middleton (the Mouse)
with his AK-47 and the author.

The author with First Lieutenant Bill Hutsler Mike Company XO
deep in the jungle.

The author's promotion to major at a firebase in the Hai Van Pass.

Two new majors: The author, Lieutenant Colonel JWP Robertson, and Jess Bennett.

The author, XO 3/26, and Lieutenant Ralph Hensley USN (Muddy Boots), with his NCM w/ Combat V, Da Nang 1968.

Awards and memorial service for Operation Meade River, Da Nang 1968.

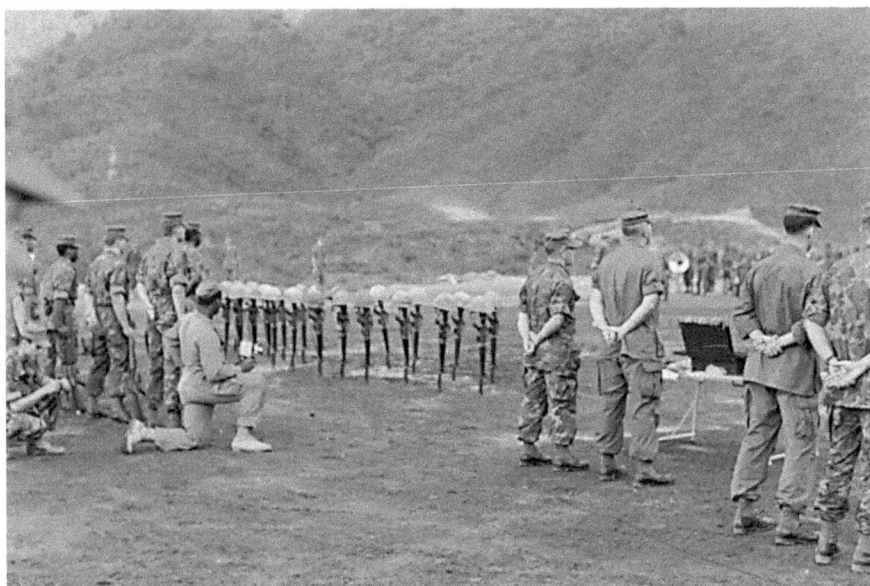

Marines lost on Meade River November 1968.

PART III: WASHINGTON & PERSIAN GULF

CHAPTER 13
WELCOME TO WASHINGTON

We departed the University of Wisconsin in June 1972 for the first of what would be five different tours of duty in Washington, DC, over the years. Sue went there early to find and purchase a townhouse for what was our first real home in Woodbridge, Virginia. Going to and from the headquarters was usually done by carpooling with other officers who lived in the same area. At the time, going up and down Highway 95 was not the trauma in commuting it is today. One can look at serving in the nation's capital as something to be avoided at all costs, or face it as the price for learning how the various parts of the government actually work. Like any assignment in the military, it can have its advantages as well as its disadvantages.

Officers who generally want to be effective at the higher levels of their respective services have to understand "how the sausage is made." This means individuals coming into Washington have to learn how to work within numerous government bureaucracies if they want to get anything accomplished. It is totally different from working in commands across the services or in the operating forces where issues are much more black or white. In Washington, everything is gray and heavily nuanced. Nothing ever happens quickly unless there has been a disaster of some sort, and even then, getting to a solution can be frustrating. There is a saying that the real wars are in Washington because it is about money and the budgeting process. Some observers would go further and say that it is all about the money as well as influence where appropriate. The services have to compete for funding for everything they desire, and all of it comes from Congress through a very laborious process. Service credibility is vital when dealing with Congress to fund various initiatives. Lose it for whatever reason, and programs can be at risk very quickly.

Headquarters Marine Corps was at that time a very drab place. Located on some high ground in what was called the Navy Annex, it sat on the east side of the Arlington National Cemetery overlooking the Pentagon. The Annex was one structure of old World War II buildings, all joined by long passageways that connected each one of several wings that made up the building. Most of the Marine Corps leadership was located there and not in the Pentagon. The Navy also occupied a large portion of the Annex because there was no room for them elsewhere. On the top floor of the wing, where my office was located along with several others, was actually one large open room with cubicles that occupied about one-third of the wing. There was no acoustical tile in the ceilings, and the floors were made up of a wine-colored tile that had been in place so long that it was beginning to decay. The whole place smelled of old papers, even if it was air-conditioned. Computers had not arrived on scene as yet; consequently, there were piles of reports, papers, and fitness reports (a semi-annual report on each officer that describes and evaluates his or her service for that period) stacked everywhere.

After a day in our wing, the dress shoes were covered with a reddish film. I remember one incident where I had complained about why someone could not get up there and at least swab the floors to get rid of the dust. Shortly following my complaint, I was visited by a member of the civilian staff responsible for maintaining the internal part of the building. I was told, "They swab the floors whether they needed it or not," and to stay in my lane. I never did see a maintenance team up on our level, cleaning the floors.

Working there was grim, but what made it acceptable was the quality of Marine officers and enlisted who worked together. Most of them were Vietnam veterans, and we had all seen much worse conditions. There was a sense of purpose in achieving the mission assigned to that part of the Officer Assignment Branch. Physical training was what everyone did at lunchtime. We all ran or jogged daily all over part of northern Virginia to work off the frustration of the duty.

There were some moments where light-hearted behavior was acceptable. Major Mike Sweeney arrived there about the same time I did. He was a solid infantry officer who had commanded a rifle company in Vietnam and was an expert outdoorsman of the highest order. He had been a Marine Officer Instructor in the NROTC Unit at Oregon State before arriving in Washington DC Built like a linebacker with an exceptional sense of humor, he would arrive at the door of our wing every morning and periodically announce in a very high and strong voice: "I hate this GD'd place." This generally got everyone who was there off on the right foot with a few chuckles. During a break from duty there in 1974, Mike and I participated in a couple of fishing trips that took us to two of his favorite locations in Northern Nevada. The first location was Wild Horse Reservoir, some 90 miles north of Elko, and in the middle of nowhere.

The fishing was terrific. We would float around in inner tubes and cast for big trout, which would fight like the devil when hooked. Some of what we caught were packed in ice for the trip back to Washington and distributed to our friends. A second trip a year later found us in the Ruby Marshes 60 miles southeast of Elko. There fishing was done from levees, and the trout were even bigger. One humorous incident occurred on this trip that led to an amazing story. One of our party had been fishing further down one of the levees when we heard him start to yell. We watched as Doc Arch was being attacked by a bald eagle that was after his fish. Watching him swing at the eagle with his fishing pole was worth the price of admission. I do not remember if the bird ever did get one of his fish, but it was not for lack of trying.

The story of this eagle, Silver, started when he was shot in the wing by a hunter in Alaska in 1970. Trying to save the bird federal officials sent him to the San Francisco Zoo for recuperation. Over four years, he was brought back to health, issued an ID tag, taught to fly, and trained to hunt all over again. Released into the wilds of the Ruby Lake National Wildlife Refuge with a mate, Silver often badgered fisherman in the marshes until he obtained one of their catch. In the summer of 1975, Silver was mistakenly shot by a retired

California police officer who thought it was a buzzard in the sagebrush. The officer was apprehended and fined by law enforcement officers in Nevada. What followed was a year of planning for a display featuring Silver in the Northeastern Nevada Museum in Elko. This beautiful bird is now stuffed and in residence in the Elko museum.

I spent my first two years at Headquarters Marine Corps learning the finer points of officer management, the augmentation process I had applied for back in San Francisco, and trying to figure how to try to make things better. This latter point was the most difficult as it became obvious you are expected to stay in your lane and not cause problems for those civilians who have spent careers in that environment. The approach for decision-making in the Fleet Marine Force did not work at headquarters. One had to learn how to outmaneuver some of the entrenched interests to achieve some success for the good of the officer population, primarily at the lieutenant and captain level. That meant doing your homework, establishing relationships, and learning what buttons to push with the staffs to gain some support for your initiatives. Over time some success was achieved, and several changes to the process were improved, but cracking the bureaucracy was hard. In my final year, I was assigned to work in a special projects staff for the Commandant of the Marine Corps. The Commandant is a four-star general who serves in that top position for four years. That experience gave me some insight as to how senior general officers worked: what they needed to do to meet everyday challenges and what they required for support from civilian leadership as well as the Congress.

This third year also provided me with some real insight as to how service secretaries have to work on behalf of the Administration when supporting international programs and issues. In the spring of 1974, the Assistant Commandant of the Marine Corps, General Earl Anderson, an aviator, assigned me to a special staff that would accompany the Secretary of the Navy J. William Middendorf on an inspection trip to countries in the Middle East and Europe. The

Secretary was well connected in Republican circles in Washington and was an active proponent of the arts. Friendly, outgoing, and approachable, he took full advantage of the various ceremonial events that both the Navy and the Marine Corps staged annually around town. The two-week trip had scheduled visits to Spain, Saudi Arabia, Iran, Bahrain, Italy, the Netherlands, and the United Kingdom (UK). The subject of the visit to Saudi Arabia involved paying a call on the king as well as getting an update on how the construction of U.S.-sponsored desalination plants was proceeding in various locations in that country. In Iran, the issue involved negotiations with the Shah regarding the sale of 80 F-14 fighters to the Iranian Air Force. This later came to pass before the Shah fell from power. The last night in Tehran, the Iranian Navy staged a very nice reception in honor of the Secretary at the Tehran Hilton. I have often wondered how many of those senior officers and wives survived the purge that was to come in Iran. After a quick stop in Bahrain to examine an old British base, the U.S. was going to inherit, we flew to Naples, Italy. Here was the first chance for the Secretary to visit the Headquarters, 6th Fleet, for a series of briefings. It was also the beginning of the famous (depending on one's perspective) "Golden Snipe Award."

The Secretary of the Navy had been a junior naval officer during World War II, and I believe he was an engineer who served in the engine spaces in the bowels of Navy ships, primarily in the Pacific. He had established this award (a well-decorated plaque) to be given to the top engineering teams serving in fire rooms of various ships in the fleets. The Navy leadership generally went along with the program, although the feeling was this was much ado about nothing. Upon our arrival on the waterfront in Naples, there were two or three designated ships the Secretary would visit and present the award. He accomplished the mission in three ships and kept going. I believe that he eventually boarded six ships, the latter three unannounced, and went straight down to the engine spaces to personally hand out the Golden Snipe Award to the various crews (or "snipes" as they were affectionately called). Needless to say, people were surprised, schedules were thrown off, and the Navy Brass was not happy. The sailors who accepted the awards, however, were impressed that the Secretary of the Navy would take the time to go to the engine spaces of the ship to visit them. I believe that this was an excellent example of leadership on the part of the Secretary. Very few officers, and especially senior admirals and ship commanders, ever took the time to visit the fire rooms in a ship. They were unbelievably hot, humid, and dirty for the sailors who had to work in those spaces.

After leaving Naples, we went to Amsterdam so that the Secretary could pay a call on the queen, and visit with Dutch government officials. This was a carryover from the days when he was the U.S. Ambassador to the Netherlands. From there, it was a flight to the UK for meetings with several British officials, followed by a visit to Holly Loch in Scotland. There the Secretary was to check on the U.S. ballistic missile submarines based at that location. When we arrived back in Washington, the details of the trip were reported to the Assistant Commandant, General Earl Anderson. Much was learned from this experience that gave me real insight into how relationships with our allies are maintained.

Two weeks following our arrival back in Washington, I was again detailed to accompany Secretary Middendorf on his trip to the Pacific. The itinerary was similar to the one we had completed in Europe and the Middle East, only there would obviously be different countries in Asia, different issues, and more ship visits. The first stop on the Pacific trip was Pearl Harbor in Hawaii. Following the normal briefings and social events with the Navy leadership, there were more Golden Snipe Awards to be handed out. It appeared that the Pacific Fleet had heard about those experiences in the Mediterranean as they tried mightily to control the situation. In one incident, we were proceeding along the waterfront when the Secretary told the driver to stop the car. He opened the door and bounded toward a ship that was tied up and proceeded up the ramp to the officer of the deck. I believe that the individual was a Navy Lieutenant JG (junior grade) who had this stunned look on his face. The Secretary said that he wanted to go below and inspect the engineering spaces. He proceeded to head down the ladder into the ship, closely followed but the Commander of the Pacific Fleet and a few other senior officers. Arriving in the engineering spaces, the Secretary met the "snipes" who worked in those spaces. One of the ship's boilers was cold and being maintained on the inside. The Secretary proceeded to climb into the boiler to have his picture taken with the sailors working there. In this case, the "snipes" just ate it up and were left with the impression that someone cared. Leadership again at a level that was rarely seen by enlisted sailors.

Meanwhile, the ship's captain, who was initially unaware that the official party was in his engine spaces, sort of launched down the ladders to catch up with the Secretary before he left the ship to find another one. It ended well for the ship, but people were jumping all over the place. Several more Golden Snipe Awards were handed out to various ships that we encountered on this trip.

From Hawaii, we proceeded across the Pacific to Guam in the Mariana Islands. The Marianas had been the scene of severe battles between the U.S. and Japan on Guam, Saipan, and Tinian during World War II. The Secretary wanted to go there to see the island, meet the few sailors and Marines stationed on the island, and get an inspection of the potential for port facilities in the Agana Harbor. We then proceeded off the island to visit Saipan, which had been the scene of a terrific battle with the Japanese. To get there, the Commander of the Pacific Fleet had to send his four-engine prop aircraft out to Guam so that the Secretary could go and land on Saipan's airstrip. We had a normal Special Air Mission Jet from Andrews AFB dedicated to the Secretary, but the airstrip on Saipan could not take a jet of this size. The purpose of this stop was to give the Secretary, who had been on Saipan as a junior officer during the war, the opportunity to go back and visit some of the locals. The aides to the Secretary had the opportunity to tour the island. At the north end of Saipan, in a spot known as the Suicide Cliffs, there were numerous Japanese memorials dedicated to the hundreds of soldiers and civilians who committed suicide rather than be captured by Marines in the final stages of that battle. What impressed me was the dozens of Japanese memorials that were everywhere along those cliffs.

We flew back to Guam and then were off to Hong Kong to visit some U.S. Navy ships that were in the harbor, and to see the sights. The Secretary had meetings scheduled with senior British officials in Hong Kong, as it was still a British Protectorate. It many respects, Hong Kong reminded me of San Francisco in terms of the bay and hills that surround the harbor. One night the U.S. Consulate staged a lavish reception for the Secretary high on one of the hills overlooking the city and Kowloon. It turned out to be an excellent event, and it was a beautiful sight at night.

The next leg of the trip was to the Philippines and Subic Bay in particular. During the Vietnam War, aircraft carriers coming off of Yankee Station in the South China Sea would get time off to give pilots a break after staging strikes against targets in North and South Vietnam. Carriers would come in and tie up at the carrier pier at Cubi Point. The aviators had their club on a high hill overlooking Subic Bay. The only way to describe the club at Cubi Point when a carrier air wing was in was "wild." The authorities generally let the boys blow off much steam until things started to get out of hand before they would close it down. They even constructed a separate building where the pilots could play all of their games, such as "Carrier Quals," to save the club from too much damage.

The surface Navy had its own club across the bay in a beautiful location, but it was much more sedate. The Secretary had several meetings scheduled with fleet and ship commanders, as well as checking in with the local politicians from Olongapo, a city that sits on the edge of the naval base. When the United States closed down Subic Bay at the request of the Philippine government, certain enterprising individuals in the naval aviation community managed to box up the famous Cubi bar. This included dozens of plaques from all the squadrons and ships that had been in the Cubi Club. It was all shipped to Pensacola, Florida, and is now part of the active Cubi Club in the Naval Aviation Museum in Pensacola.

The final leg of our journey was to Vietnam. The plane landed at the big Ton Son Nhut airbase outside of Saigon. From there, we went by an Air America helicopter to the embassy in the city. The purpose of this stop was to get the Secretary an assessment of the latest events occurring in South Vietnam. We had extensive briefings on the situation, as well as an extended luncheon with the U.S. Ambassador Graham Martin.

We were not on the ground in Saigon more than one day before taking off for Clark Field in the Philippines. There the plane was refueled and readied for the long flight back to Hawaii. While in Honolulu for a short layover, the Secretary debriefed the naval leadership in Pearl Harbor and then went to pay a call on the Commander of U.S. Marine forces in the Pacific, Lieutenant General Louis H. Wilson. He had won the Medal of Honor as a captain on Guam during World War II. General Wilson was known as a very hard taskmaster with a solid vision for the Marine Corps. This was at a time when discipline and race relations were not good in the ranks. He would live up to his reputation when he became the Commandant of the Marine Corps a short time later.

After our visits to the Marine Headquarters, the Secretary and party moved back to Hickam AFB to meet our plane for the flight back to Washington. These two trips with Secretary Middendorf had been a valuable experience considering the several countries we had visited, and the programs and issues we had faced along the way. There was really no other way an officer at my level at the time could gain as much exposure to so many subjects, cultures, and personalities. When it was over, it was back to the mundane reality as a junior field grade officer in the bureaucracy at headquarters.

The academic year 1975-1976 was spent as a student at the Command and Staff College at Quantico. The base at Quantico, Virginia, had been established by the Commandant of the Marine Corps in May 1917, when he directed that a Marine Barracks be constructed there. In the following years, it had been used for training as well as conducting experiments in amphibious warfare. It was an ideal location because of its location on the Potomac River, where small ships could navigate up the river to participate in different exercises. Several schools would eventually be established there primarily for Marine officers at different stages in their careers. This has since been changed to include several schools for Marine enlisted. When I arrived back at Quantico in 1975, it was the home of OCS, the Basic School (TBS), AWS, and the Command and Staff College (C&SC).

The C&CS was another one of those requirements officers had to get through as they climbed further up the ladder. It was a good year because we had several allied officers in the class who brought different perspectives on issues and exercises that varied from some of our beliefs. Relationships established with allied members of that class were important because there were a few who rose to high ranks of service in their own countries in later years. One of my classmates was a major in the Israel Defense Force (IDF), who later rose to be the Chief of the IDF in the 1990s. Amnon, an Israeli commando early in his career, was a really sharp individual who would always give the Israeli perspective to any map exercises we would be doing on issues in the Middle East. This was extremely valuable when it came to real-world issues much later in my career. Relationships established earlier often paid great dividends when we were operating together in counties overseas.

All my classmates were also involved in the running program, as well as in academic exercises. Physical exercise has always been part of the normal training routine within the Marine Corps, and it was no different in the staff college. On occasion, it can get carried away to the extreme, as you will see in my next tour of duty on Okinawa. At

Quantico, we were required to go out and run every day while we were in school. Then we were to record the daily mileage on a large board located in the basement of the staff college. That was alright, but what occurred was some individuals would go many miles further than some of the other classmates. That tended to make people feel they had to do the same if possible. This became a competition that went way beyond what was required by any Marine Corps order. It almost turned into a fetish. Nobody wanted to look bad because he only had forty-five miles per month on the board, whereas somebody else had logged one hundred and fifty over the same period. The school leadership generally encouraged the physical activity. When we graduated from the C&SC in June 1976, that board in the basement seemed Pavlov's bell, and we were the dogs.

CHAPTER 14
THE "STRIKING NINTH"

My next set of orders had me going back to Okinawa for my third unaccompanied tour in the Far East. I had delayed my departure for Okinawa because we were blessed with the birth of our first child, Anne Elizabeth, in June 1976. That was a very short thirty-day period for me, but thoroughly enjoyable before I had to leave for Okinawa. This time communications would be better during the twelve-month tour on the island. In addition to letters between Sue and me, there was adequate access to operating telephones on the island. I was to be assigned as the S-3 or operations officer for the 9th Marine Regiment, an organization that normally consists of 3,000 Marines and sailors. At this point in my career, I was enjoying what I was doing and liked the responsibility but did not enjoy being away from home with Sue and our new daughter.

The 9th Marine Regiment was one of two infantry regiments that belonged to the 3rd Marine Division on Okinawa. The regiment had a storied history dating back to the campaigns in the Pacific in World War II, as well as combat during the Vietnam War. The regimental patch featured a lightning bolt striking across a background of a number nine in different colors. Hence the label "Striking Ninth."

The regiment was located at Camp Schwab on the northern end of the island. It was somewhat isolated from any of the other Marine camps further south toward the central part of Okinawa. It really was a beautiful location that overlooked Ora Wan Bay with great beaches. It was also close to the Northern Training Area, which made it easy for units to get jungle training there. The island had been the scene of a vicious battle between the Japanese and American soldiers and Marines in 1945 and had remained under American administration for several years following the war. Okinawa had reverted back to

Japanese control in 1972, and several major changes had occurred under Japanese jurisdiction. The result of population growth and farming on the island had reduced the number of available live-fire ranges, which meant units had to go off-island to conduct realistic training.

This tour of duty would provide some colorful experiences over the coming year. Due to the personalities among the commanders, events would resemble elements of something like "Catch-22" at times. The regiment was initially under the command of Colonel William ("Wild Bill") Weise, who had been the commander of 2/4 in the brutal battle of Dai Do in Vietnam in May 1968. For his actions, he had been awarded the Navy Cross, among other decorations. He had about a month to go in his tour when I arrived at Camp Schwab. A very colorful and open individual, he would do things like go to the tank park, check out an M-48 tank, and proceed to drive it around the camp by himself to impress the troops. Social activities at the club on base were always lively, as well. He was also determined to show how the 9th Marines headquarters functioned in the field when his replacement arrived to relieve him. He placed the camouflaged tactical command post deep into a jungle-covered canyon in the Northern Training Area. He wanted to make sure the new guy on the block knew how the "Striking Ninth" operated. It also meant we would be doing a command post exercise (CPX) in full battle dress with everyone decked out with greasepaint, something rarely done at the regimental level short of combat.

Two days into the CPX, with the miserable conditions of heat, humidity and no wind at our site, our new Air Liaison Officer (ALO) asked me if it "was always like this?" He was just coming off of watch, and I was outside the operations tent lying under a tree at 2:00 AM. My answer was, "It can be worse, and welcome to the Grunts." Major Tom Conley, an F-4 Phantom pilot from Colorado and a really good officer, just shook his head. The next day the incoming regimental commander made his appearance, observed what we were doing, conducted a quick inspection, and was gone. Shortly after that, the

CPX was concluded, and the command post was broken down and moved back to the base camp.

The new commander of the 9th Marines was Colonel Robert Thompson, a Navy Cross winner in the battle for Hue, one of the longest and bloodiest battles of the Vietnam War. He was a tall, rigid individual from the state of Tennessee, who had been an instructor at the Basic School while I was there. He taught military law, among other subjects. Thompson was best remembered for yelling to the class in military law to "shut up and pay attention" when two lieutenants were caught talking in the back of the class. That stuck with me for several years until we met up again in Okinawa. His reputation arrived ahead of him at Camp Schwab, where he was now known as "Starch." He was well-grounded tactically and had excellent ideas for training the regimental units, but could be inflexible in the extreme when it came to execution. In August 1976, during his first two months in command, he fired the commander of 1/9 over differences in how the battalion was going to be run. Some issues were over the regimental physical fitness programs that were being dictated by the colonel. This was unusual because the battalion commander had an excellent reputation and was well thought of by the troops.

More fallout on this came when the S-3 of the battalion, Major Mike Sweeney, my fishing partner while at HQMC, also had his differences with the regimental commander over the physical training program. The result was that he was able to wrangle a set of orders for another assignment in the G-3 Section of the 3rd Marine Division headquarters. Mike then was selected to be a liaison officer to the Australian Army for a major exercise slated for later in the fall. He sailed south on the USS *Blue Ridge* (LCC-19), the flagship for the amphibious force for the exercise in Australia. During the long voyage south, they stopped in the waters off of Guadalcanal, the site of the first amphibious landing in the South Pacific during World War II. The ship stood off the shores of that island and conducted a sunset memorial and wreath-laying service in memory of those sailors and

Marines who died in battles at sea and on Guadalcanal. Following the exercise in Australia, Mike moved back to Okinawa and finished out his tour in the Division. He went on to serve out his time in the Marine Corps, eventually retiring as a lieutenant colonel. He purchased forty acres of lovely ground overlooking the Snake River in Central Idaho. He is still there.

Four months after reliving the commander of 1/9, Colonel Thompson fired the second commander of the battalion for a variety of reasons, not the least of which was getting his battalion lost on an exercise. This started rumors about what was really going on at Camp Schwab. The third battalion commander in 1/9 managed to serve out his tour without crossing the colonel. Both of the previous two commanders were assigned elsewhere on the island.

Meanwhile, the commanders of both 2/9 and 3/9 were still on the island and pushing to deploy. 2/9 was scheduled to go to the Mt. Fuji training area in Japan, and its commander wanted to go early. A capable individual who believed in absolute order and discipline was a perfectionist almost to a fault. He became affectionately known as "the Fuhrer" by his officers. Lieutenant Colonel Jim McWilliams, the battalion commander of 3/9, was a combat veteran and a very capable officer. A tough Marine, he would do things in his own way and was strong enough to stand up to "Starch" and get away with it.

My responsibilities as the S-3 for the regiment involved planning all the off-island deployments as well as the on-island training requirements. I also had to coordinate the physical training programs established and dictated by Colonel Thompson. The requirement was all Marines had to take the Physical Fitness Test semiannually and pass it. At Camp Schwab, we ran it five days a week when in garrison. Also, he established a regimental run program that started at five miles the first month and then would be increased one more mile each month. I can still remember watching the 2,000 Marines in the stands at the football field when he made the announcement. You could feel the wheels turning in their heads at facing 9-11 mile runs before they got off the island to go home. Juice stands were also required at certain points along the route through the mountains so the troops could get a drink if necessary. It was not uncommon for the colonel to approach you, usually at dinner in the club, and "request the pleasure of having you accompany him on a long run early the next morning." That generally struck fear in those who were not great runners. Consequently, they would avoid the officers' club during dinner hours.

I actually received my invitation at the ice cream machine one night at the club. We started at 5:30 the next morning and proceeded out the main gate and down the road. He would usually quiz you on a variety of things as you were jogging down the road to find out more about you. On this particular occasion, we were under Typhoon Condition Three as a major storm was bearing down on the island. On the way back, it started to pour rain as only it can in the Far East. We came back through the main gate in sheets of rain, and I am sure that the sentry on duty though we had lost our minds. Thompson actually believed that if he ran the troops long enough, they would be less inclined to go out and raise the devil on liberty. That was simply ludicrous because the 18-20-year-old Marines always had enough in reserve to go on liberty and blow off steam. Finally, and after all the rumors on what was going on at Schwab reached the Commanding General of the 3rd Marine Division, he directed that his Marines were only required to abide by the Marine Corps order and nothing more. This put an end to the regimental runs, much to the chagrin of the regimental commander.

The 9th Marines headquarters did deploy off-island to the Fuji training area in Japan in October, as well as in the Philippines for jungle training on Luzon in November 1976. A third deployment saw the headquarters go to Korea in February 1977 to participate in a joint exercise with the South Koreans, as well as observe 3/9 in training there. The purpose for all three was to join up with one of our battalions in each location and run a command post exercise with them while we were acting as the higher headquarters with different scenarios.

I had not been back in the Fuji training area since my first tour as a second lieutenant in 1961 when we were hit by that large typhoon. The quarters were a little better this time around. Upon arrival, we were invited to a small reception hosted by the officers of the JSDF at Fuji. This was in honor of Colonel Thompson, who was the senior officer in the camp. I had learned before if you get invited to one of their events, be prepared to go low and slow when it came to the drinks. The Japanese were very hospitable and really fond of Johnny Walker Red bourbon, which they would drink like water. The usual result was that after about two hours, they would be rip-roaring drunk, and some would be passed out on the furniture or the floor. This time was no different, and getting completely smashed out at the party was always part of the approach. We were careful not to insult anyone, but that was a challenge before the Japanese were gone for the evening. The next morning, we were up on one of the firing ranges when one of the Japanese colonels came up to see how we were doing. He looked like "death warmed over" and clearly felt the same way. I asked him how he was getting along, and the response was "number hucking ten" (in their language number one was always the best while number ten was the worst and F was hard to pronounce).

We continued with training in the Fuji area while observing the activities of 2/9, which had been up there for almost a month. The battalion headquarters for 2/9 covered several acres of ground. In preparation for our arrival, the battalion commander directed that the entire area be raked off with all the rows in the volcanic ash created by the prongs of the rakes going in one direction. They did not have enough rakes to do the job in time, so Marines had to go out a get more from the Japanese. He had also directed the communications officer to hang loudspeakers on poles at various locations around their camp so that he could address the troops on any number of issues from his tent. That was highly unusual and reminded me of scenes right out of the TV series "M.A.S.H."

It was also about this time that Tom Conley had called to my attention 2/9's air officer and some of the challenges he was facing within the battalion. While Tom was the senior air officer in the regiment, he maintained close ties with the junior aviators who were ALOs in each of the three infantry battalions. The word was that the colonel had driven the 2/9 commander almost over the top by digging into the battalion's affairs. I had not known Captain Mike Hough before his arrival in Okinawa. Mike was a Naval Academy graduate with a razor-sharp mind who had initially served in the aviation training command under Lieutenant Colonel Don Conroy. Conroy was a wild and domineering fighter pilot who was the subject of a not-too-complimentary novel, The Great Santini, by his son Pat Conroy. This was also the title of a movie starring Robert Duvall. Mike flew F-4 Phantom fighters, F-18s, and helicopters over his long career. A very outgoing individual, Mike's call sign was "HAWG," but was frequently called "Mikey" by his battalion commander. Never by his rank, was which also strange. He carried out his tour with 2/9 functioning both as the S-3 Operations Officer and ALO but had been tasked to carry out several requirements on the staff that went well beyond his original assignment.

One of the events battalions tried to accomplish while there was to climb Mt. Fuji itself. This was sort of a ritual and a good experience for the troops, depending on the climbing season. Fuji is an active 12,388-foot volcano that has been sacred to the Japanese for centuries. Pilgrimage to the summit of the mountain has been a popular activity for the Japanese and almost everyone else who favors mountain climbing. 2/9 had planned on climbing the mountain after we had departed for Okinawa. Colonel Thompson got the idea that it would good for the headquarters to do the same thing before we left for home. The problem for me was we were in the winter months when most hiking activities had ceased among the Japanese due to unstable weather and snow conditions on the mountain.

At the time when he wanted to do this, there was a band of clouds at about the 9,000-foot level that blocked any vision to the top. My recommendation to the colonel was that we not try it, and this was based on my experience at the Mountain Warfare Training Center over three winters in the Sierras. We did not have the proper clothing and equipment to deal with snow and winter conditions at high altitude. This did not stop him, so after a rather heated discussion, we started up one of the trails that led toward the top. We had been on the route for about an hour on a trail crossing back and forth as we continued to climb. It was slow going due to the wet and soggy volcanic ash we were moving on. At one point, I heard a "wumph" sound from above and turned to see a boulder about half the size of a Volkswagen Beetle bounding down the mountain and right at us. I yelled out a warning as the rock bolted right through the center of our column that was zigzagged across the mountain. Our 150 troops scattered as best they could, and fortunately, nobody was hit. The boulder kept going and disappeared down the mountain. When I got back down to the rear of the column, the colonel asked me if I was "now happy we were going back down?" This led to another heated exchange before we moved down to the trucks.

Despite the weather conditions on the mountain, 2/9 did try to make an attempt to climb Fuji after we had departed for Okinawa. The battalion managed to get to the 7,500-foot level before running into a thick cloud bank that continued up the mountain for another 1,500 feet. At one point in that cloud bank Marines in the lead slipped on the icy terrain and caused several others to roll back down the mountain. Three were injured, and two sustained broken bones, which required a helicopter medevac. Mike Hough requested helicopters from the Naval Air Station in Atsugi, Japan, which was about an hour away. Upon arrival over Fuji, the two CH-46s had to be talked into the mountain by Captain Hough, who was located on the fringes of the cloud bank at about 9,000 feet. At that altitude, the helicopters did not have the power to lift out all the casualties, so one of the crewmen had to be left with the battalion to be picked up later.

The casualties were then flown to Atsugi for medical treatment before returning to their units. The battalion commander then elected to turn the battalion unit around and make the difficult descent back down the mountain. To illustrate the dangers of climbing Fuji at that time of year, three experienced climbers were later caught in a storm at the top and died of exposure and hyperthermia.

The next deployment off the island was to Subic Bay in the Philippines. There we were going to conduct jungle training as well as run a CPX, this time with 1/9 in the hills behind the naval base. The CPX went off reasonably well, although the staff in 1/9 was still "gun shy" of the regimental commander. At the end of the exercise, we were sitting in a tent camp on the shore of Subic Bay and directly across from the end of the runway at Cubi Point. There had been a squadron of Marine F-4 Phantom fighters based there while doing some air-to-ground training at the excellent Crow Valley ranges in the center of Luzon. It was in the early evening with a slow breeze coming in from the bay when we noticed activity building up on the runways. Tom Conley was sitting on a box smoking a cigarette and watching F-4s lining up for take-off. The first two jets started their take-off roll coming right at us. The squadron knew we were in the small cluster of tents serving as our headquarters, so when the first two closed on us, the pilots kicked in their afterburners as they passed right over where we were sitting. Of course, the noise was deafening, but this was another one of their ways of acknowledging the "Grunts." Tom Looked up, smiled, and said, "There goes the sound of freedom."

Colonel Thompson had indicated he wanted to go north to Baguio in the mountains in northern Luzon. Our transportation back to Okinawa was not due to pick us up for another four days, so the plan was to fly up there for about 24 hours. Baguio had been a vacation and R&R site for years. It was high in rough mountains and had been the center for silver mining in the Philippines for decades. There were several hotels and restaurants, along with numerous shops that sold all kinds of silver filigree jewelry. The air was usually cool and fresh, which was a relief from the intense heat and humidity of the tropical lowlands. Major Conley had requested the helicopter for the flight to Baguio, and the wing had responded with a Vietnam vintage CH-46. That is where the fun began! The colonel and six of his staff were ready to go at the designated pickup site in Subic Bay. For whatever reason, the helicopter was late getting there, which irritated the colonel. When it did show up, it clearly was in sad shape, just in appearance. All the Plexiglas windows were missing, although not unusual because of the way they had operated in Vietnam. We took off and headed up the coast to make another unplanned stop at a communications station along the way. The colonel had not been aware of the stop, which irritated him even more because we were now cutting into the amount of time, we could spend at Baguio. When we were high over the mountains, he noticed the crew chief was wiping oil leaking from somewhere near the rear transmission of the helicopter as he moved around the cabin. He asked the kid what he was doing, and the response was, "No sweat, colonel, this was only a one-ragger. We don't get concerned until it becomes a two-ragger." That response did not help the situation as Thompson was now really bent out of shape.

We made the approach into the runway at Baguio, landed, and taxied up to the control tower. The routine was for the pilot to shut down the helicopter before the party would debark on to the concrete pad. The pilot was having some sort of problem trying to shut the bird down and kept spending more time revving up the engines. Now "Starch" was out of patience, so he proceeded to put the entire crew on report to the wing headquarters back on Okinawa. This created another explosion there because they were all aware of Colonel Thompson. Our abbreviated overnight stay in Baguio went off very well as I did get a decent night's sleep. In the meantime, Tom Conley, who had been sweating blood over this whole episode, managed to get a different helicopter to pick us up late the following afternoon for the trip back to Subic.

The regimental headquarters deployed to Korea for the winter exercise in February. These annual exercises usually started with an amphibious landing at a location on the east coast of Korea by the Republic of Korea (ROK) Marines. Then forces would move inland into the mountains against opposition. 3/9 had been in Korea for a couple of weeks before we arrived and had been conducting mountain training. Our plan was to conduct our own training as well as observe the landing. We would then conduct another CPX with 3/9. Our arrival in Pohang, the site of the headquarters for the ROK 1st Marine Division, was greeted with another reception in honor of Colonel Thompson. Of course, we attended, but the results were the same as the event we had participated in while at Fuji. The Koreas were serving only Johnny Walker Red, and the event ended up in a complete drunk-out. More for them than us, as the colonel had passed the word to not overindulge.

This was my first experience in Korea, and it had been an eye-opener. Very rough mountainous terrain that tested everyone. The ROK Marines were extremely professional, well-trained, and ready to go to war tomorrow if necessary. Their Blue Dragon Brigade had established itself as a superb warfighting organization during years of combat in South Vietnam. They understood the VC/NVA better than any other military organization, including the U.S., and had the patience and perseverance to play the game to outwit the adversary most of the time. In Korea in the 1970s, it was now all about potential combat with the North Koreans, and they were very serious about the mission.

Colonel Thompson had deployed into Korea with two stress fractures in his legs from running back on Okinawa. Unfortunately, he was somewhat confined to his vehicle and could not move over the mountains on foot. This led to some limitations as well as frustrations regarding what he could do in the exercise. 3/9 had been working already in the mountains, and the only way to get to them was by helicopter. He already had one confrontation with Lieutenant Colonel Jim McWilliams, the battalion commander, over some issue that I was not aware of. As I had mentioned earlier, McWilliams was a very independent individual with a solid combat record, which usually kept him in reasonable graces with the regimental commander. In this instance, Thompson wanted to go out and talk to McWilliams on the ground. Tom Conley had requested another CH-46 to pick us up and visit with 3/9 at their location. What I had suspected was that McWilliams had deliberately set his command post in a location not accessible by helicopter.

We took off and did a general airborne orientation over the exercise area. A request had come in for a medevac for a Marine who had fallen and twisted his leg. We were the only available aircraft, so we diverted to go get him. This was accomplished, but it required the pilot to essentially hover along the side of a very steep hill and slowly back the bird close enough to get the casualty up the rear ramp without having the blades strike the hillside—a very nice piece of flying on the part of the crew. After dropping the casualty off at a treatment center, we proceeded to go locate the 3/9 position as Thompson was determined to find him. We arrived over their position, which was located on a very steep pine-covered ridge with little room for anything but foot troops. To land required the approval of the unit on the ground for safety reasons. We circled the position several times, trying to contact the unit on the radio. That failed, and the colonel was not happy. Finally, it was time to return to base as fuel was running low. McWilliams had turned off his radios, so contact with the helicopter would be impossible. Such were the relations between the commanders in the Striking Ninth.

The regimental headquarters site had been established in a large steep bowl with a few trees and plenty of tall grass. The responsibility for setting it in fell to the Headquarters Commandant, Captain Zack Johnson. He was a lively and energetic officer who had done a reasonably good job of staying within the good graces of the regimental commander. Zack had placed the colonel's CP tent (living tent) in the middle of the bowl with all the other headquarters tents organized and spread out around it. He had even placed wooden pallets on the ground in the colonel's tent to keep the dust down. That night we received a terrific downpour of rain, which flooded the bottom of the bowl. This included the regimental commander's tent with him in it. The next morning the "air was both wet and blue." The colonel was wading around in the water and mud with a cane because of the stress fractures. Zack couldn't get the vehicle into the position to get the colonel because of the mud. Zack paid for that one as he looked like he was in shock after confronting "Starch." Following the episode, it was time to get ready to fly back to Okinawa. When we were dried out and packed up to go, the next step was a road march to the big airbase at Taegu in preparation for the Air Force airlift home. I had been having spasms in my lower back but had thrown it off on the motor march to Taegu.

Upon arrival at Camp Schwab, it was back to business as usual in garrison. In one of the very first, early morning runs, I had managed to get a severe spasm in my lower back and had to walk back a good distance to reach Schwab. I checked in with the dispensary on the base to get some assistance with my back but quickly found out the x-ray machine was broken. The fallout from that got me transferred to the Camp Kue Hospital in the central part of the island. I was destined for a short stay there until things improved. I remember the doctor telling me I was too old (49 to be exact) to be doing things like this. My response to him was, "You don't understand the conditions at Camp Schwab." I eventually returned to duty, but the back problem was to be with me for another six years. My tour was about over in the regiment when I was promoted to lieutenant colonel in the spring of 1977. Shortly after that, a message came in, notifying me the next duty station would be back again in the nation's capital, this time in the Pentagon. The twelve-month tour in the 9th Marines was exceptional despite the variety of crazy incidents and the peculiarities of the commanders. Looking back on it, you just can't make this stuff up.

CHAPTER 15

THE PENTAGON AND THE NATIONAL MILITARY COMMAND CENTER

In July 1977, I flew back through Japan on commercial flights, arriving in Washington to meet Sue and our one-year-old daughter. Anne was a joy to be with, as she seemed to be very curious about me. That transition was easy for all three of us.

Following my return to Washington, I was assigned to the Pentagon and the National Military Command Center (NMCC) as a watch officer. In assignment language, this meant I would satisfy my first joint tour requirement required by officer assignment policy. The Pentagon was constructed during World War II to house and support the services in their efforts to fight the war. Working in the bowels of the Pentagon can be a surreal experience not found in many other places. First of all, the place is gigantic, and it takes a good period just to figure out where you are and how to get around. Working with representatives from all of the services was not bad, as long as you realized they had their priorities that very often were different from those of the Marine Corps. This is where the effective officer reestablishes relations with the peers from the other services and learns to negotiate where it is feasible. Even as an NMCC watch officer, where we were monitoring military activities around the world, one had to learn to give a little when working various issues involved with the other service representatives.

After a year of this kind of shift-work, I was moved up to the staff of the Assistant Secretary of Defense for Public Affairs to work Defense Department community affairs assignments for the equivalent of one year. Luck intervened again as I was selected to attend Top Level School, which for me would be the Naval War

College in Newport, Rhode Island. Newport is a great place in which to live and work. Situated on the shores of beautiful Narragansett Bay, it had been the site of the development of Naval Strategies as well as tactics that proved so successful in both World Wars and the Cold War. It was also the home of several Navy schools in addition to the War College. We had decided that Sue and Anne would stay in our home in Fairfax Station for the year, and I would commute to Virginia when it was possible. This was another one-year assignment in a purely academic environment that concentrated on strategy and policy, naval operations, and defense procurement and financing issues. The War College had a very strong faculty, and we would often go out in town to one of the famous restaurants for the strategy and policy classes. The weekly reading assignments were huge, but we had the time do get the assignments done. This provided me with opportunities to commute between Virginia and Newport. It worked out pretty well, as I could read the assignments there as well as in Rhode Island. Small exercises were conducted occasionally to reinforce what was being presented to us in class.

Our class's final project in the Defense Procurement and Financing course was to manage certain aspects of the overhaul of a *Forrestal* class aircraft carrier. This project tested everyone. When the project was completed, it left us with the impression this was no easy task, starting with obtaining the funding and then working the issues with the carrier. It was another good year, and one could learn a lot from the difficult courses of study. The further up an officer advances in rank, the more likely he will become more involved in utilizing elements of what was presented at all three courses at Newport. The best event for us in August 1980 was the birth of our son Thomas Jonathon. Sue and Anne were already living in our home in Virginia, so there was no requirement to move as I was destined for Washington again.

I thought my chances of getting back to the Fleet Marine Force were pretty good following school. That proved to be wrong, as it was back to Headquarters Marine Corps for my third tour in town. This time the assignment would again be the manpower world and in the Officer Assignment Branch, starting in July 1980. We had a saying about doing duty at Headquarters Marine Corps. In the first year in an assignment there, one is trying to figure out how to survive and be successful. During the second year, the individual becomes more comfortable with his surroundings and begins to see how things really get accomplished. In his third year, he has figured it out and becomes adept at maneuvering through the bureaucracy effectively. Then he leaves for another assignment, and some new guy takes his place.

In my case, I generally knew what to expect. The first two years of my second tour were spent as the head of the Ground Officer Assignment Branch for Lieutenant Colonels and below. The assignment officers (or monitors) on the staff were all very high-quality individuals who were handpicked for the most part for those jobs. These are sensitive assignments because the monitors are managing individual careers. The monitors should do whatever they can to meet the desires of the individual if that is possible considering assignment policies. Even then, problems can develop when a specific individual is not happy with his or her assignment and tries to apply pressure with a higher rank than the monitor. Fortunately, we did not have to deal with very many issues of command influence, but it did occur on occasion.

Consistency with policy, as mentioned, is very important, but communication between the monitor and each member of his population is vital. This particular policy was not very effective in that some officers were contacted while others were not. This was changed for a very simple reason. All of our officers would prefer to at least be able to express their wishes, and the job of the monitor was to discuss what was possible based upon several factors. All most of them wanted was a say in the process. Once the policy was established officially, each officer would be contacted by his or her monitor no matter where they were in the world. The result was ninety-five percent of problems created due to miscommunication or no communication at all went away. It sounds fairly simple but difficult to implement in the beginning. This was also a credibility issue between the monitor and his population.

Start with half-truths or some other form of "smokescreen," and you can lose your credibility with your peers quickly. On several occasions, officers would come in to discuss their upcoming assignments. Even the most hardened individual would pay a visit with some trepidation because they knew we had the power. One of the things that I did to ease the burden was to find a 12-inch by 24-inch poster of a Black Panther with yellow eyes, lying on a branch of a tree and staring right at the camera. At the bottom of the poster were the words in white: "TRUST ME." When an individual came in to sit down in front of my desk, he would be staring right at the panther. That tended to break the ice, and the more relaxed individual could start the conversation.

At the beginning of the third year at headquarters, I was selected for the rank of colonel, which drove me to a different assignment. During the summer of 1982, I moved up to become the Head of the Officer Assignment Branch, relieving now Colonel Jim McWilliams, who moved to another assignment. This meant we were now responsible for the assignments of all ground and aviation officers from the rank of colonel and below in the Marine Corps, which was 15,000—16,000 officers at the time. Policies at that level stayed pretty much as planned, although there was more communication from commanders in the field regarding the assignments of colonels to their respective commands. This was expected, and we tried to accommodate their desires as much as possible. Doing your homework so you could discuss each case carefully with the senior officers involved was critical. Arriving at some sort of accommodation, if possible, was mandatory, and in most cases, it worked. Mishandle any assignment at that level, and your reputation can become an issue very quickly.

CHAPTER 16

FROM BEIRUT TO THE ARCTIC

In June 1983, I received orders back to the Fleet Marine Force and the 2nd Marine Division in particular. This was the beginning of what was to be one of the most rewarding four-year periods I experienced in the Marine Corps. The Division was located at Camp Lejeune, North Carolina, which sits both on the Atlantic Ocean and the New River. It is the largest amphibious training base in the world and had been activated since the early years of World War II. The long beach line at Camp Lejeune was perfect for practicing various phases of amphibious warfare. Marine units routinely deploy out of Lejeune to Europe, the Middle East, Africa, the Americas, and the Pacific on occasion.

At the time, the 2nd Division was commanded by Major General Alfred M. Gray, who was an institution in the Corps. He was known for his unconventional, engaging leadership style, training expertise, and innovative vision. Compassionate and always looking out for the troops, he did more to enhance the education of his Marines than any other general officer. He did this through education programs, libraries to include the Commandant's reading list and publication of books on warfighting. When he became the 29th Commandant of the Marine Corps, he founded the Marine Corps University at Quantico in 1989, which encapsulated most of the major educational programs in one organization.

During my tour in the 2nd Division, five major events became priority responsibilities at different levels for me, and all of them had major international implications: The Beirut bombing, followed by a presidential attendance at a memorial service for the casualties of that event. Assuming command of the 2nd Marine Regiment, closely followed by a major Strategic Mobility Exercise supported by the U.S.

Air Force, and winter operations in the Arctic of North Norway during the Cold War. My initial assignment was to be the G-3 of the Division, which meant that I had the responsibility for training, scheduling, and coordinating plans for the deployment of 2nd Division units for exercises in the states or contingencies overseas.

THE BEIRUT BOMBING

Sue and I arrived at Camp Lejeune with Anne and TJ in July 1983. Quarters were not available due to renovations, so we rented a house out on the beach. Emerald Isle was a nice community that sat on the Atlantic about twenty miles away from the base. Early on Sunday morning, October 23, 1983, I received a call from the Division Command Center indicating that I was to attend a meeting with General Gray as soon as I could get to the Division headquarters. Upon arrival, we were briefed on a suicide bombing that had occurred earlier at the Marine Compound at the airport in Beirut, Lebanon.

The Marine units from the 24th Marine Amphibious Unit (MAU) from Camp Lejeune were all part of a peacekeeping force stationed there amidst the sectarian violence ongoing in the Lebanese Civil War. Casualties were reported to be heavy, but we did not have any definitive numbers at that point to judge the impact. As the day wore on and reports began to filter in, it was evident this had been a catastrophic hit on our units there. Indications were the headquarters of the battalion landing team had been decimated.

The final list of mass casualties came to 241 Marines, soldiers and sailors dead, and several more seriously wounded. As the reporting procedures for notifying families of both the dead and wounded went into high gear, we were tasked to organize a replacement headquarters for rapid deployment to the site of the bombing. Its mission was to regain the necessary command-and-control of the surviving units in that battalion. The quickest way to do this was to take an experienced battalion headquarters from one of the regiments stationed at Camp Lejeune and add specific capabilities to that headquarters for deployment to Beirut. This concept was worked very hard all day on the 23rd so that the replacement unit would be ready to deploy by air late that night out of Cherry Point, North Carolina. This was accomplished, and the U.S. Transportation Command (TRANSCOM) had the planes ready to go with the airlift.

The enormity of the loss of so many personnel in the battalion hit everyone pretty hard. Many of the deceased had families located at Camp Lejeune as well as in other parts of the country. The notification of the losses to the families took a long time to be completed, due to the fact the headquarters building at the Beirut airport had collapsed in the explosion, burying many Marines. General Gray did his best to make as many funerals as possible in a process that required a significant amount of time.

Two days after the terrorist strike in Beirut, the 22nd MAU, which was on the way from Camp Lejeune to relieve the 24th MAU as part of the normal rotation, was diverted south to participate in the invasion of the island of Grenada. Landing with forces from both the U.S. Army and Navy, the island was quickly secured, and the pro-communist government was replaced with the queen's representative. Part of this mission was to rescue some 230 American students who were studying on the island but fortunately were not harmed in the fighting. They were safely evacuated off the island. The price for this successful operation was eighteen dead servicemen. When the operation was completed, the 22nd MAU continued across the Atlantic and through the Mediterranean to relieve the 24th MAU in Beirut.

When the 24th MAU and its rebuilt battalion landing team returned to Camp Lejeune, General Gray established a board of colonels from within the 2nd Division to go through the Beirut bombing in detail. The objective was to find out what went wrong and what could be done to prevent something like this from happening again. It was to be a lessons-learned examination and not a drill to find scapegoats. This fact was heavily emphasized to every Marine who testified in front of this board. As I recall, the board was in session for a couple of weeks and interviewed both survivors and other personnel who were not injured by the blast.

It appeared the Marine units that had been stationed there were really caught in the middle of the Lebanese Civil War. This situation allowed the Marines to be left alone until it was perceived that they were tilting toward one side versus another. In the morass, that is the Middle East, this can be a common occurrence which often leads to conflict. In Lebanon, the local security was beginning to wane gradually until the troops started to get shot at for one reason or another. My impression was that they were beginning to hunker down within their positions at the Beirut International Airport as the security situation got progressively worse. On the day of the attack, the sentries on the gate into the compound had noticed the large yellow truck slowly moving around in the distance as if surveying the gate. At some point, the truck started to move toward the gate while gathering speed. As it went by the sentries, who did not have time to react, the driver smiled at them. The truck went through another open inner gate toward the building where several members of the battalion were sleeping. The Sergeant of the Guard, who had his post at one corner of the building, saw the truck roll through the gate toward the barracks and took off running out the back of the building just as the truck struck it and blew up. The actions following the explosion saw the survivors digging and trying to rescue their comrades as well as trying to remove the dead and injured from the collapsed building. The political ramifications from this incident were immense and much too detailed to go into here. Lessons were learned from this tragedy that were implanted into the training for every unit working up to deploy to the Middle East.

PRESIDENT REAGAN ATTENDS THE MEMORIAL SERVICE

On November 5, 1983, a memorial service was held next to the division headquarters and alongside the New River for the dead, both from Beirut and Grenada. This came about following a request from the White House that President Reagan would be in attendance. As the G-3, I became the action officer for the event. I must say at this point that we had a good handle on how to react to a rapidly developing situation but nothing compared to a short notice presidential visit. A White House advance team arrived a week before the event, laid out their requirements, and then went back to Washington the same day. Twelve hours later, the decision was made that the president would attend on the 5th of November. The detailed planning that goes into such an event was unlike anything I had ever experienced. The program, attendees to include service secretaries, congressional members, flag and general officers plus somewhere around 5,000 visitors including families of the dead, all had to be coordinated. Security, communications, media representation, and coverage were other areas that had to be planned for as well. Also, we had reports that a truckload of explosives had been stolen somewhere in southern New England and was reportedly heading for North Carolina. This caused us to place anti-tank teams in various places with jeep mounted TOW missiles covering all the roads leading into the base at Camp Lejeune as a precaution. Twelve of the Beirut wounded would be in attendance wrapped up in ponchos in the front row so the president could speak to each one of them, which he did. The service went off really well even though it poured rain through the entire event. The president spoke to the families privately following the ceremony in the division headquarters and then departed for Washington. We had planned for the traditional "missing man" formation for a flyover at the end of the service. Unfortunately, one of the F-4 Phantom fighters in that formation got disoriented in the fog and rain and flew into the ocean. The crew was lost, which capped the end of a very mournful day.

THE STRATEGIC MOBILITY EXERCISE

One of my final challenges as the G-3 was to organize a strategic mobility exercise featuring units from the 2nd Division supported by the U.S. Air Force. The Air Force has a program called Operational

Readiness Inspections (ORI), whereby they will conduct no-notice operational evaluation inspections of Air Force Wings to ensure the units are up and ready to go if they have to respond to a contingency. During the Cold War, this was an absolute requirement. The inspecting headquarters prefers to have Army units involved so that the ORI is a very realistic lift exercise. We had been approached to see if we could support an ORI with some of our own troop units in the late spring of 1984. The offer was quickly accepted, and planning commenced. The scenario would include an airlift from Cherry Point, North Carolina to NAS, Fallon, Nevada, followed by a 90-mile road march to the Mountain Warfare Training Center for three days of training. The return trip would feature another road march back to Fallon for the airlift to North Carolina. The Air Force gave us 70 C-141 and C-5 sorties for the ORI of one airlift wing on the way out to Fallon. They allocated some 50 C-5 sorties for an ORI on another airlift wing on the returning airlift. The decision was made to execute this operation in mid-July in what could be described as an enormous daisy chain that stretched across the country.

THE 2ND MARINE REGIMENT

The 2nd Marine Regiment was one of three infantry regiments in the 2nd Marine Division based at Camp Lejeune, North Carolina. It consisted of three infantry battalions and a headquarters company. Normally the regiment had 3,000 Marines in its ranks as well as a complement of Navy corpsmen. The 2nd Marines was a proud organization that had gained fame in World War II. It had served on Guadalcanal for months at the beginning of the campaign in the South Pacific in 1942 and then led the bloody amphibious assault on Tarawa in the Gilbert Islands in 1943. That was followed by another amphibious assault on Saipan in the Marianas in 1944, and then as a participant in the campaign to seize Okinawa in 1945. During the years of the Cold War, the regiment had participated in several NATO-sponsored exercises primarily in Northern Europe.

I was fortunate enough to assume command of the 2nd Marine Regiment in early July 1984. A few days after the change of command ceremony, the Air Force notified the Division that the two ORIs were on. The 2nd Marines had been directed to be the lift force for the ORIs. The size of that force comprised one infantry battalion, and an artillery battery, along with numerous other attachments, including truck units. Four helicopters from the 2nd Marine Air Wing were also added to the force list. Brigadier General Joseph Hoar, then the Assistant Division Commander, was designated as the commander under the unit titled the 10th Marine Expeditionary Brigade (10th MEB). Joe Hoar and I had been friends since serving together in my second tour at HQMC. He was a very warm, friendly individual who always displayed a great amount of savoir-faire in his assignments. He later rose to the rank of four-star general and a future commander of the U.S. Central Command. The 10th MEB was a designated headquarters that General Gray often activated for training purposes so that both staffs and commanders could get comfortable functioning at the brigade level.

The air and surface movement out to Fallon and MWTC, and then back to Cherry Point, was successfully executed with no casualties. Training in the mountains gave everyone a taste of what it is like to operate at high altitudes, even in fair weather. The scenario called for strenuous cross-compartment movement in altitudes up to 9,000 feet, which taxed everyone. Before the exercise, participants were also briefed thoroughly regarding the fact that MWTC training areas were actually in a national forest. That meant that destruction of trees and other plant life, construction of LZs, and digging emplacements was not allowed. When the exercise was over, the road march back to Fallon followed by the movement by air to Cherry Point was also completed successfully. The opportunity to see what the regimental elements could do in a potential contingency, as well as what was required by the Air Force, was extremely valuable. The cost of all the air transportation was born by the U.S. Air Force as part of their responsibility for ensuring readiness.

OPERATIONS IN THE ARCTIC

The United States had participated as part of a NATO Force in exercises in Northern Europe during the Cold War with the Soviet Union since the 1970s. Exercises ranged from the Jutland Peninsula in Denmark all the way north to areas above the Arctic Circle. Strategically, in the time of conflict, the plan was for U.S. Naval forces to meet the Soviet Navy's Northern Fleet in the vast seas above what was called the Greenland, Iceland, and United Kingdom Gap (GIUK Gap). The strategy also included the employment of a U.S. Marine Brigade in the mountains of North Norway, along with other NATO forces to counter any Soviet moves overland into that country.

This operational requirement was assigned to the 4th Marine Amphibious Brigade (4th MAB) located in Little Creek, Virginia, for both planning and execution. As a Marine Air-Ground Task Force (MAGTF), the 4th MAB was assigned the 2nd Marines as the ground combat element, Marine Air Group 14 (MAG- 14) as the Air Combat Element and the Brigade Service Support Group 4 (BSSG-4) as its Combat Services Support Element (CSSE). Usually, every winter, elements from these units would be assigned to the 4th MAB for purposes of the winter exercise somewhere above the Arctic Circle in North Norway.

I believe that Marines can accomplish almost anything, given the proper training, equipment, and leadership. Operations in the Arctic can provide many examples that would challenge my previous statement. The leadership is generally there at the small unit level, but the issue for several years was the lack of realistic training and reasonably sound equipment that enabled Marines to operate effectively and survive under very harsh winter conditions in the Arctic. For Norway, that meant that the exercise force would normally be operating 300 to 350 kilometers above the Arctic Circle in wildly changing weather conditions. A combination of varying temperatures, snow, ice, or rain, coupled with high winds driving the "chill factor" well below zero, can destroy a unit's cohesiveness quickly and especially if it is not acclimated. There were many examples of this over the years in Norway because the troops were not grounded properly in the fundamentals of Arctic warfare.

Exercises before my time in the barrel were gradually getting better concerning individual and unit performance, but there were many deficiencies with regard to training and equipment. The first key element was to get the exercising ground units to MWTC for a thirty-day winter course in January before the scheduled NATO exercise, and not after they arrived back from Norway. This was a scheduling issue that was rectified before Exercise Cold Winter 85 in March 1985. At the same time, the aviation units had to conduct winter training of their own, usually in upstate New York or somewhere in the upper Midwest.

The next part of the program was to bring all elements of the MAGTF together under the 4th MAB for joint training in the snow before deploying to North Norway for the exercise. The first winter I commanded the regiment, we went to Fort Drum in upstate New York for the advanced training. In the years that followed, we would exercise at Fort McCoy and Volk Field in Wisconsin. At times the cold and temperatures in Wisconsin could be worse than what was experienced in the Arctic. Deployments to Norway usually followed an airlift scenario with the 4th MAB or by amphibious shipping with units of the U.S. 2nd Fleet. For the first winter that I participated in these exercises, we deployed by air into different Norwegian airfields above the Arctic Circle. When the regiment closed on the exercise area, we drew specific kinds of equipment from prepositioned stocks that were staged in caves in central Norway. Over-the-snow vehicles, Arctic tents, stoves, and numerous other items necessary for operations in that environment were issued to the troop units.

The MAG-14 helicopter squadron (HMM-266) helicopters were broken down at Cherry Point, North Carolina, loaded aboard five USAF C-5 transports and flown to Bardufoss, Norway. There they were staged in huge caves that had been dug into the mountains by

Norwegian laborers under the control of the Nazis during World War II. Reassembling the 12 helicopters in the cave was a challenge that I had not experienced or observed anywhere up to that time. Initially, only one of the C-5s arrived at Bardufoss on time with its cargo, while the other four were down for maintenance issues at various points across the Atlantic. When they eventually flowed into the airfield, the responsibility of putting them back together fell to Major Jim Ledford, himself a CH-46 pilot whose call sign was "Crazy." A fun-loving, outgoing individual famous for doing unconventional things, he had served as a force reconnaissance Marine conducting long-distance patrols deep in enemy territory in Vietnam. Following the war, he won a commission and started out in the aviation community in helicopters. Jim would become a very effective maintenance officer with a razor-sharp mind in aviation matters and one not afraid to go outside the chain of command to get things done. Supervising the installation of rotor heads, transmissions, blades, and tail sections on each CH-46, he accomplished the task in four days. He would later serve with distinction in the 4th MEB in 1990-1991 in the Middle East.

Allied nations that were normally involved annually in these operations were Canada, the United Kingdom (UK), Norway, the Netherlands, and Italy. Most of these countries provided mountain troops or commando units, such as the 3rd Commando Brigade Royal Marines. They lived and worked in that environment, which the U.S. units generally did not do, because of several deployment requirements in other parts of the world. That was one of the reasons it was so difficult to get the American participants up to par with their NATO counterparts. Another reason was the majority of our Marines had grown up in urban areas and had never spent any time in snow and ice. The exercise leadership in the host nation would divide up participating units well in advance in the planning stage, so everyone knew who the opposition was going to be.

An example would be the 4th MAB and the Norwegian Brigade North against the Royal Marines and Dutch Marines, with the

Canadians playing on occasion. In some exercises, the Italian mountain troops would take part as well. Participating in these exercises was not meant to see who wins and losses, but was a great opportunity to test our capabilities against those of our allies in a very difficult environment. The 2nd Marines would be part of the attack force on offense against UK and Dutch units who would be in defensive positions in this exercise.

Exercise COLD WINTER 85 was to be conducted in Troms County in North Norway and was the first opportunity to test out training improvements in the harsh conditions of the Arctic. This part of the environment was characterized by high mountains normally covered in snow and ice with steep canyons that drop into fjords some hundreds of feet deep. The road nets usually followed along the fjords because the canyons are normally solid rock and too steep to accommodate anything else. Many of the mountains are covered with pine forests, but only up to a certain elevation before opening to bare rock all the way to the top. Any movement across this kind of terrain is extremely difficult unless you have experienced ski troops or helicopters.

The major issue was our ability to move cross-country on skis or snowshoes in mountainous terrain both day and night and survive the weather conditions. That part actually worked reasonably well, thanks to the training the troops had received at the Mountain Warfare Training Center in January and then refined in the workup at Fort Drum before the actual exercise. We were still on the old skis, but the snowshoes were new. The utilization of our CH-46 helicopters from HMM-266 (The Griffins), under Lieutenant Colonel John Dennis, combined with the troops on skis and snowshoes, made a significant difference in our ability to maneuver across the snow in those mountains. John was an extremely effective commander. He had a reserved personality, worked well with the ground officers, and demanded results with his pilots. I had great confidence in John and his squadron as he really proved himself in the mountains in North

Norway. We had the mobility no other NATO participant possessed, and this made the difference.

The night before the exercise, the 1st battalion 2nd Marines moved up into their attack positions under a spectacular display of the Aurora Borealis (the Northern Lights) that flashed across the sky. In freezing conditions at the beginning of the exercise the following morning, the battalion was lifted by CH-46s deep behind the UK Parachute Regiment's defensive positions along the Balsfjord southeast of the city of Tromsø. This forced the paratroopers into an unplanned retreat, which threw the exercise schedule off. The controllers had to readjust the scenarios and start the exercise again. The Norwegian head controller did not believe we had accomplished the move until he came down to see for himself. Before the exercise, the 1st Battalion Brigade North (the Minks) had been assigned to the 2nd Marines and given the CH-46 boarding procedures. The exercise commenced, but the Minks were not able to cross Balsfjord due to high winds and rough water. We responded by sending in our helicopters to transport the Norwegian unit high onto a snowfield on the other side of the fjord. That placed them behind enemy positions, which threatened the rear area for the entire exercise opposition force. Again, by outmaneuvering the opposition in defensive positions along the fjords, we were able to throw the schedule off a second time by the end of the exercise. I believe this display of mobility demonstrated to everyone that the preparations in the training workups had paid significant dividends in our ability to function effectively in the Arctic.

One more example of how far the Marines had come occurred late one night in the exercise. A rifle company under the command of Captain Jerry Durrant in the 1st battalion conducted a night march on skis over a mountain range and proceeded to attack downhill and overrun a portion of the 3 Commando Brigade Command Post. This had not been done before, and was another indicator that the training program and individual confidence were beginning to pay dividends.

I was told the Brits, who were the "pros" at doing this, thought the movement was "jolly good."

Clothing was still a problem, but training had helped solve earlier issues with clothing care. General P. X, Kelly, the Commandant of the Marine Corps at the time, visited the units in the field, so we had the chance to show him what we had for clothing and equipment. Things began to change rapidly when he arrived back in Washington. Thanks to the perseverance of the troops, the reputation of the Marines in the Arctic increased significantly, which sent a clear message to the political world the U.S. Marines had come a long way. Even the Soviets had taken notice and requested official observer status for the exercise to be conducted in 1986.

In the fall of 1985, we began the preparations for the next Norwegian winter exercise, which was to be held in March 1986. ANCHOR EXPRESS 86 was to offer a different scenario for the 4th MAB. It was to be located in the Troms area north of the city of Harstad. The northern defensive force had units from Norway, Canada, Italy, Luxemburg, and the United States. The southern force was composed of units from Norway, UK, and the Norwegian Home Guard with armor units. This time the scenario would find the 2nd Marines in a defensive posture and guarding certain fjords against the United Kingdom/Netherlands (UK/NL) Landing force. This force included the 42 and 45 Commando Royal Marines along with the 1st Amphibious Combat Group Royal Netherlands Marines. They were all under the command of the Royal Marines.

The training workup was similar to the approach we used for Cold Winter 85. The participating infantry battalion under the 2nd Marines would be the 2nd Battalion 4th Marines under the command of LtCol Dick Janey. The artillery unit and other attachments remained the same as in the previous year. HMM 266 would be in support of the 2nd Marines again, which was great news because they had done so well in the previous exercise. The difference this year would be that John Dennis had moved the squadron out into the field and established a site for the helicopters in the deep snow. The pilots and flight crews were basically living like the infantry for the exercise. One other addition would be a company of amphibian tractors (AAVs) from the 2nd Tracked Vehicle Battalion. This was in recognition of the various fjords in which we were going to have to operate.

The training sequence would generally remain the same with some alterations. 2/4 would go to the MWTC in January 1986 along with the Headquarters 2nd Marines for the thirty-day winter course designed for units going to Norway. The aviation units would conduct their own requirements at Volk Field in Wisconsin. In February, all ground, aviation, and support units would close on Fort McCoy, Wisconsin, for the MAGTF Exercise under the control of the 4th MAB, then under the command of Brigadier General Carl Mundy. After the ten days of exercise training, units of the 4th MAB would begin preparations for the deployment by air to North Norway. Support elements deployed earlier to draw vehicles and equipment from the prepositioned stocks in central Norway and then move them north to the exercise area around the small village of Brøstadbotn in Troms.

Several of the uniform and equipment issues that had been identified and supported by General Kelly were beginning to get resolved. New Gore-Tex uniforms were being sent to the ground units by the time the battalion deployed to MWTC for the winter training. New skis were flowing into the same units along with new "Mickey Mouse boots." Not the greatest by any means, but very workable when worn in the Arctic areas in North Norway. New Arctic shelters, along with new stoves, were beginning to be received as well. A new design for a mobile regimental command post was to be instituted in the coming exercise utilizing the BV-206, a really effective, wide-tracked over-the-snow vehicle produced in Sweden.

Once the exercise force had closed on Norway, the primary effort was to get all personnel and equipment acclimated to the environment as well as oriented to the terrain and fjords we would be operating in. Patrolling in the fjords at night would be another challenge we had not faced before. The amphibious tractors (AAVs) could operate at night, which would be helpful when trying to intercept raid force units from the other side coming up the fjords. The CH-46s from HMM-266 would be utilized to deposit Marine units on the flanks of the fjords to engage the opposition at night as well. HMM 266 had constructed its own Forward Arming and Refueling Point (FAARP) in deep snow so that the pilots and helicopters were very close behind the attack positions established by the regiment.

In the run-up to the exercise, the weather in North Norway had gone from bad to worse. This was not unusual in the Arctic, but it caused continuous changes in the plans, as well as making the troops miserable between snows, rain, ice, and blowing winds with erratic temperatures. The weather conditions this time were radically different from what had been the experience during Cold Winter 85. This made movement in the mountains very dangerous with the threat of avalanches in the unstable snow. The exercise began with units on both sides moving into their respective attack or defensive positions. Under cover of darkness and driving winds, the Marines in 2/4 moved forward in the snow while the AAVs were poised on the shoreline of a fjord. The regimental mobile command post in the BV-206s was perched high in a covered pine forest looking down the long axis of one of the major fjords where we expected the British to come. What followed was a pause in the exercise for reasons we did not know at the time. Following the wait for most of the night, the reports had come down that there had been an avalanche in the southern area of the exercise that had hit a Norwegian ground unit as it was trying to move through a mountainous area. The result was that 12 Norwegian soldiers had been lost. This sort of loss, bad anywhere, was particularly devastating in Norway. Following a meeting with the commanders early the next morning, the exercise was canceled, and participating units returned to their camps to prepare to deploy back to their respective countries.

Despite the loss in Norway, the Marines had performed exceptionally well under really adverse conditions in the environment. The training workups for all units had proven to be sound, and the new equipment was flowing into the 2nd Marines. The confidence in the ability of the troops to deploy and fight in that kind of environment had increased significantly. The attitude of our allied counterparts regarding Marine capabilities to function effectively had increased as well. This trend would continue in the years to come and until Saddam's invasion of Kuwait in 1990.

My two years in command of the 2nd Marine Regiment were two of the best I had spent in the Corps. The increased responsibility, leadership, and operational challenges made it enjoyable because we were participating in several exercises that stretched from California to Norway. At the same time, we were deploying battalions to the Western Pacific for six months under the unit deployment program. I relinquished command of the regiment in June 1986 and moved up to be the Chief of Staff of the 2nd Marine Division for my final year at Camp Lejeune.

In 1987, I was very fortunate to be selected to the rank of brigadier general. I say that because normally there is not more than a ten percent chance of making that rank. The process begins annually with a precept issued by the Secretary of the Navy to the Commandant that gives the policy guidance for the selection board. The board is made up of senior officers assigned by the Commandant, who will review the records of all the colonels who are in the zone for selection. There may only be 150 officers in the zone who will be considered for 8-10 spots based on service requirements at the time. Following careful deliberation in secret, the board will send the list of recommended selectees to the Commandant. This list will be reviewed by the Secretary of the Navy and the Defense Department and forwarded to Congress via the White House for final approval.

The United States Senate has the authority to review and approve all service selection board results. When the Senate approves a list, the results will be announced. In the Marine Corps, the Commandant will personally contact each selectee of his or her selection when it is approved by the Senate. It is the same process for selection to major general, only the numbers required, and the size of the zone will be considerably smaller. It is safe to say that for every colonel that is selected, there will be twice as many who do not make the cut. Many are just as capable, with some being even better than some of the selectees. It really depends on a lot of luck and the required numbers. No officer should ever consider himself a sure cinch for selection. For those lucky enough to be selected, a whole new level of responsibility not experienced in prior assignments can be expected. The challenges would increase significantly.

CHAPTER 17
FROM DISNEY WORLD TO CONGRESS

In late August 1987, Sue and I decided to take the kids, Anne and TJ, to Disney World in Florida for a vacation. Both of them were now at the age where Disney World and all the characters were awesome. I had not received any indication as to what my next duty station would be and had already been relieved as the Chief of Staff of the Division. Rather than floating around Camp Lejeune, we decided to head south. We had been enjoying various activities such as the Magic Kingdom, Space Mountain, the Haunted Mansion, the train rides, and so on. When we arrived back at our hotel, I had a message waiting for me that asked me to contact the Command Center at Headquarters Marine Corps. I did and was told that the Commandant of the Marine Corps, General Al Gray, wanted to talk to me. They put me through to his office. He picked up the receiver and wanted to know where I was. "In Florida at Disney World" was the answer.

After some pleasant give and take, he indicated I was coming to Washington to be the Legislative Assistant to the Commandant and to get there as soon as possible. So began another two-year tour in the nation's capital working with another entity that I had not been associated with before, the U.S. Congress.

The most intoxicating and corrosive element that drives politics, politicians, and everything else in Washington is power. Power is even more important than money, although that is a major issue in the conduct of political campaigns. The quest for power by individuals trying to get a piece of the action to push their personal agendas in an Administration is never-ending, and that includes well-meaning novices as well as the ideologues. Senior military leaders spend an inordinate amount of time working in that environment, all for the good of their respective services and ensuring that the politicians understand the roles and missions, respectively. This can require much give and take and can have an impact on your credibility if issues are not handled carefully. This is always a challenge, due to competing priorities among service secretaries, members of Congress, and outside groups. Success can be achieved by being truthful about requirements while providing education on service problems as well as roles and missions. Just because an individual political appointee is a service secretary or a member of Congress does not mean he or she is fully conversant on the strengths and weaknesses of your service. Very often, they are not, and in today's world, few have ever served in the military. That requires consistent education and influence at times where appropriate, and especially after an election.

One example of this was in Boston on the USS *Constitution* (Old Ironsides). The freshman class in the House of Representatives was attending a week-long seminar at one of the universities on how to operate in Congress. One evening the Navy Office of Legislative Affairs hosted a reception on the deck of the historic ship for all the new members, none of whom had been onboard before. It was a chance to meet and educate the new members while having some fun at the same time. There were several opportunities to talk with some of the members in the following months as relationships developed during that reception. In that environment, it can be all about relationships if you want to make headway.

This does not mean that things always go well in relationships. There are times when outside organizations are pushing specific social agendas to force the services to change. One of your friends from the *Constitution* reception all of a sudden becomes an adversary for one program or another. This is normal give and take, and you have to be flexible when dealing when something goes against your wishes. Harry Truman once said that "If you want a friend in Washington, get a dog." I think that this is generally true, but one has to learn how to operate in this environment if you are going to be successful. You are going to become one of them if you want to get anything done at times.

The United States Congress holds the key to the wellbeing of the services. It is responsible for providing the necessary funding to support each service's stated annual requirements, either real or imagined. It has the power to review and approve promotion board lists from the services as well as to conduct hearings on the recommended selection of all flag and general officers in the U.S. military. It has several other prerogatives that it guards carefully.

The clear message here is that each service must maintain good relations with both individual members in the House and Senate as well as the professional committee staffers who do most of the work on the Hill. Operating in this particular environment is like nothing else in the services, and one has to understand how to get things done for the good of his or her organization. You are dealing with individual members that may want to support you but are maintaining their own agendas. Committee Chairmen who are very senior hold immense power over the functions of their individual committees as well as the budget process through numerous hearings. The senior leadership in the Marine Corps will participate in several hearings at the request of the Committee Chairman during the months-long budget development process. This normally starts in February following the State of the Union speech by the president. It will continue into the summer or until the Authorization and Appropriations bills reach the floor of the Senate for final approval. The entire process is made up of one compromise after another, all per the political priorities of the parties, the members, along with various other Departments and the White House.

To stay up with what is going on in Congress, each service has a dedicated staff that does nothing else but work in the environment. The Marine Corps has a liaison office in both House and Senate. The Marines there are responsible for responding to constituent requests, congressional inquiries, and coordinating appointments between the congressional representatives and senior Marine general officers. They also escort Congressional Delegations (CODELs) on occasional trips to various parts of the globe. Participating in numerous congressional activities to maintain cordial relations with the membership is a hard requirement. Much of what can be accomplished there depends on relationships developed over time.

The job of the Legislative Assistant to the Commandant is to support the Commandant with anything of interest that may be going on in Congress. It also includes coordinating the Commandant's activities with the liaison offices in both the House and Senate. Also, I was responsible for coordinating queries from the hill regarding activities that may be ongoing in the field. An example of this was when we had a Marine participating in a live-fire exercise in the desert at our Combat Center at 29 Palms, California, who went missing. It was reported that he was lost, and they had not been able to account for him when his unit returned to the base. After an extensive search of the exercise area, he was declared missing and probably AWOL. This eventually boiled over when his family contacted senators from both Iowa and Minnesota, and the story was picked up in the media. This was a PR disaster in the making. I was summoned to the hill to respond to the two senators who rightfully were not happy. Marine Corps' credibility at this point was on the line, and we really didn't have any good answers. All we could give them then was that we are going to get to the bottom of this, as the investigation was ongoing at the base. I assured the two senators (Grassley and Durenberger) I would keep them as well as the family informed of where we were as the investigation and search progressed.

Eventually, we decided we should offer the family a dedicated Marine flight to 29 Palms to tour the area where he had disappeared and talk with the searchers looking for him. The family did accept the offer but were also appearing regularly on national television. To make a very long story short, the remains of the Marine were finally found deep in the desert about five weeks later. It had been clear he was left in the field after being told to stay in place in the exercise, and the unit he belonged to did not adequately hold a muster when they returned to base. They then declared him AWOL. He had wandered off and got lost in an area where one cannot last long without water. General Gray and I were in Minneapolis for a speaking engagement about the time he was found, and the Commandant made a statement to the media there what the outcome had been.

The lessons learned here were several: The best the Marine Corps could hope for with this case was to break even. We kept the Iowa and Minnesota delegations completely informed on every aspect of the investigation along with the continuing search. Legal action was taken against members of this man's unit. When it was finally over, the father went on national television and thanked the service for all that had been done, including the flight out to 29 Palms. I think the Minnesota and Iowa delegations were satisfied; all that could be done under the circumstances was accomplished. It was a sad story that never should have happened, but it also demonstrates what has to be done to try to solve the problem as well as retain credibility in a losing situation.

There are times when we would field a request from some member of Congress regarding a situation that made no sense, at least on the surface. One learns very quickly in Washington that when dealing with politicians, there are always ulterior motives you have to work through to get to the bottom of what the real issue is. In this instance, we had members of the Idaho delegation complaining about a new housing project that was being built for enlisted Marines in a farming area on Camp Pendleton property in Southern California. Why Camp Pendleton? The property had been leased out to local farmers for some time, and there had been no complaints. After a prolonged investigation, it turned out that some of the farmers were growing seed potatoes on the property, which in turn were harvested and shipped to Idaho for distribution to Idaho farmers for planting and growing potatoes in that state. This had been normal activity for several years, and when plans for the new housing development were announced, farming organizations in Idaho went to their members in the Idaho delegation in Congress with the complaint. This became an economic issue one rarely has to contend with as the Legislative Assistant. Clearly, a solution had to be found because the housing development was going to be built. I recall a compromise was reached that made the farmers in California, and farming organizations in Idaho, satisfied with the compromise. We had been caught blindsided when this issue arose, and no solution was possible until it was determined where the seed potatoes were going and why. In the beginning, it can be very difficult to determine just what the issue is behind the scenes, and yet the issue has to be resolved one way or another.

One more blatant example of an ulterior motive on the part of a congressman came to light when our Director of the Marine Corps Systems Command and I were called to the hill at the request of a member from Oregon. Major General Ray Franklin and I were greeted warmly by this individual in his office. After going on about how important it was to have the utmost in readiness and weapons for the troops, he proceeded to tell us that the Marine Corps needed a new "fire-and-forget" anti-tank missile for our ground troops. Our response was we already had a good anti-tank missile in the hands of the troops and had no money for a new program. His response was he was going to help the Marine Corps get this new missile, although we did not need it.

After the meeting, we questioned why this issue had surfaced in the first place. Ray, who was a really easygoing aviator with extensive experience in systems development and procurement, agreed we did not have that answer but were going to have to dig before bringing it to the senior leadership in our headquarters. After looking at what the local election issues might be in Oregon, it was finally determined the congressman had jobs in his district as a plank (his campaign platform and mission). However, he was also pushing the construction of a new plant, probably with the assistance of the corporation that would build the new fire-and-forget anti-tank missiles, in his district. When that determination was discovered, we briefed the senior leadership at Headquarters Marine Corps. When the issue was finally identified, appropriate overtures were made to the congressman, indicating the Marine Corps would not be a part of the scheme.

Another example of what can happen when a constituent issue surfaces in the office of a Committee Chairman occurred toward the end of my first year on the job. As with all hearings on the hill, I had accompanied General Gray to a scheduled hearing in the House Appropriations subcommittee on Defense. This particular committee was chaired by Representative John Murtha (D- PA), a Marine, and backed up by Rep. Joe McDade (D-PA). Murtha was listening to testimony from the Commandant, the Secretary of the Navy, and the Chief of Naval Operations when he spotted me in the back of the room. He sent his aide to get me and come to the front of the room. This was highly unusual, but I complied.

When I got to him, and while McDade and others are questioning the three principals at the witness table, Murtha stated: "I have this letter from an officer at Parris Island, but I can't trust you to keep it a secret." I assured him this was not the case and that the Commandant could keep this secret. What he wanted was to secretly go to Parris Island to see for himself if what the letter said was true. To accommodate his request, a C-20 executive jet belonging to the Navy flew him, the Commandant, and myself first into MCAS Beaufort, South Carolina, unannounced. From there, we went by a prepositioned van driven by Marines from the Commandant's office to MCRD, Parris Island. We then drove through the main gate at Parris Island without raising the suspicions of the Marine Guards on the gate. To be fair, General Gray had taken off his stars and was sitting in the back seat with a coat over his uniform. From there, it was out into the field, first to observe recruits in classes and then to the rifle range to watch recruits firing on various targets.

It was there one of the Drill Instructors (DIs) on the firing line recognized the Commandant and passed the word that General Gray was on the firing line. About halfway down the range, we saw a door of the range shack fly open, and a Marine lieutenant colonel came racing out to meet the Commandant. General Gray saw this and said we need to leave, as Murtha played right along. We were gone before that officer could reach us, but the word was out. By now, the commanding general at Parris Island was now on full alert but unsure about what to do next. His car was spotted out in front of the headquarters building with the engine running as we went by at a distance. The MPs were now alerted as well as they were trying to find the vehicle, we were in. The Commandant told the driver to head through the quarters area where an MP vehicle spotted us as we drove by. They closed on us from the rear but did not attempt to stop our vehicle.

Finally, General Gray told the driver to head to the headquarters and park. We did that, but the MPs never did dare to get close. The Commanding General, whom I knew well, was waiting when we drove up and got out of the vehicle. The first thing he said to me was "You son of a bitch," with a half-smile on his face. Things relaxed when Gray introduced Murtha and told him it was all secret until now. Murtha, for his part, said he "wanted to see how things were going at PI." After some friendly banter between Major General Lynch and Murtha in his office, everyone was satisfied that there were no causes for concern on the part of the Committee Chairman. We then went back to MCAS Beaufort and taxied out for take-off with the control tower, still not knowing who was on the plane. Admittedly this was an extreme case, but it illustrates what can be done when trying to maintain relations with one of the most powerful members of Congress at the time. I never did see the letter or its contents that triggered the whole event.

During the second year on the job, we received another one of those requests from Congress that could not be ignored. This time it came from Senator Robert C Byrd (D-WVA), one of the most senior senators on the hill and an Appropriations Committee Chairman. He was famous for steering numerous projects to his state to increase jobs and improve infrastructure. This time he thought that the Marine Corps needed a mountain warfare training center on the east coast to support training for units deploying to NATO's northern flank. This would be in addition to the Marine Corps Mountain Warfare Training Center already established at Bridgeport, California. A similar request had gone to the Navy, but they had blown the idea off. Remembering the importance of relationships with powerful committee chairmen, we made the decision to go to the area in question, do an honest survey to establish several requirements for sustaining such an initiative, and then report back to the Commandant. I had requested helicopter support for this trip, and the 2nd Marine Air Wing sent a CH-46 from North Carolina for our use.

There is a good reason why the state of West Virginia describes itself as wild and wonderful. Much of it is rugged, forest-covered terrain intersected by numerous rivers that offer spectacular vistas from mountain tops. Except for a few small towns, the mountainous regions are sparsely populated. Coal has been mined there for decades. Often a mining company would move into a location, completely grind down the mountain tops through surface mining to extract the coal. When finished, the company would move on, leaving a destroyed landscape. That changed when the government put restrictions in place for mining and reclaiming the land to a healthy state. I mention this because one of the areas we were to inspect was a reclaimed surface mining site now covered with timber.

We left Washington in the CH-46 and flew to Green Bank, West Virginia, to meet staged vehicles for further movement into the mountains. Green Bank is the home of the Green Bank Observatory and the Robert C Byrd telescope, the largest steerable radio telescope in the world. There was a small runway there where we met up with our guides. The helicopter would fly back to Washington and return the next day to pick us up at a predesignated location along the Cheat River some thirty miles south of the town of Elkins.

The location we were to inspect was timber-covered terrain that offered little space for even a temporary camp. There was no infrastructure in place, which meant everything would have to be trucked to the site. One two-lane road did touch the perimeter of the reclaimed site. The closest railhead was miles away if we wanted to bring in heavy equipment to support a camp and training areas. Water would have to come from wells drilled in the reclamation site. We spent the day moving over steep timber and boulder covered landscape, which demonstrated what the challenges would be for operating there. We ended up at a lodge along the Cheat River for the night. The next morning, we left the guides, met the helicopter, and flew back to Washington.

I reported our findings to the Commandant, indicating only a temporary camp was possible. Anything else was going to have huge costs for sustaining any kind of consistent training activity. There was also another factor looming in the background. We did not need a second mountain warfare training center. After all of our observations were collected, the findings were presented to Senator Byrd, who generally accepted the Marine Corp's position. Here was another example where a very powerful senator was looking for "pork projects" for generating jobs in his home state, which was legitimate. When presented with some of the facts, he backed off. Our effort was necessary to honestly do the research and report our findings to him. Preserving our relationship with Senator Byrd was critical, and honesty won out.

About midway through my first year as the Legislative Assistant, General Gray informed me that I was going to be dual-hatted as the Legislative Assistant to the Commandant, and the Director of Public Affairs for the Marine Corps. This was totally unexpected, as it had never been done in the past at Headquarters Marine Corps. In one occupation, you are dealing with Congress and in the other the media and several news organizations. This is in addition to public information programs, whereby we tried to keep the American public in tune with what is going on in the Corps at the same time. The OLA and PA staffs were loosely combined at HQMC. I had sharp colonels running each staff, so there was not much of a problem in coordinating activities. The Marine Corps had field public affairs offices both in the media centers in New York and Los Angeles staffed with public affairs specialists. In Los Angeles, they often worked with studios in Hollywood when the filmmakers were working on something that related to the service.

There was one principle you could count on almost every time. If we had an issue boiling up in the media somewhere in the country or even overseas, it would inevitably be picked up in the Congress or vice versa. The Rather case at 29 Palms was a prime example. If there had been a series of aircraft accidents reported over time in the media, the Congress would send queries to the headquarters requesting information. These were situations where both staffs could coordinate responses on behalf of the Corps and make sure the message was clear and with one voice. I believe this was the real value of combining the two staffs after we got the bugs out of the very different procedural issues.

Media relations are always tricky if one is not careful with what he says. I firmly believe the American media is one of the necessary evils in our society, and they do abide by a set of standards and procedures. This may be more so with the print media than with television nowadays. Print media correspondents have to do some research to get their stories by their editors. This does not seem to be the case with television because they are always in a race to outdo the competition and get incestuous "breaking news" stories out on their networks. In today's world of round-the-clock news cycles, reporting can often be skewed to one political spectrum or the other and based on speculation as fact. The "talk shows" are some of the worst examples of this. Adding the phenomenon of social media to the mix means that public affairs officers must know how to operate in this complex environment to ensure the correct story gets out to the public.

The bottom line must always be, to tell the truth even if it hurts. Don't do that, and the knives come out. Credibility and mutual trust are vital to any relationship with media representatives. Like members of Congress, if you assume the media know everything about the service, you have made a bad assumption. Very often, the unit public affairs officer is the expert, and he or she has to be able to educate the media representative on the background that led to the story they are working. In some instances, it may be important to brief the local media representative regarding a developing story so one can stay ahead of the event. If you can develop relations like that, it will make the job much easier, and it can enhance your credibility with reporters or commentators. After all, the vast majority of them are trying to do a job, even if some of the network commentators are not as well informed as they think they are.

The Marine Corps has always paid close attention to the media, even to the extent of embedding reporters with units so they can report what they see accurately. The Marines in the field are the very best representatives because they will always tell it like it is. An excellent example of this was when Doug Fain of Mutual News was on 881 South at Khe Sanh, interviewing the troops in the trenches. He had been stuck there for over four days because there were no available helicopters to come out and pick him up. He stopped to talk to a young black Marine in Mike Company about his thoughts regarding the war. The man's response in a slow southern drawl was, "Well, I guess it is better than no war at all," after which Fain almost fell down.

I had developed solid relationships with Washington DC-based reporters as well as media representatives from other newspaper chains. That was necessary to do the job correctly. I never had a situation where a media representative violated that relationship or the rules they live by. Sometimes someone in the media will try to roll over you to get an interview or story. One day I received a phone call from the office of Dianne Sawyer, one of the female star commentators in New York. The caller indicated her boss wanted to get an interview with a Marine who was currently in solitary confinement at Fort Leavenworth, Kansas. He had been convicted of becoming compromised in Moscow and indirectly giving sensitive information to the Soviets. My response was that it wasn't possible to interview him in solitary confinement. Also, we did not have responsibility for this particular prisoner as he was under the control of the U.S. Army while incarcerated. She then suggested she would get network lawyers into this, after that, I told her it would not do any good. The conversation ended there, but I notified my Army counterpart of what was coming. He assured me he would gladly take care of this request, and Sawyer did not get the interview.

I had stated before it is important to educate the media where appropriate because they are generally the outlet to the American public for legitimate reasons. During my tour with the 2nd Marine Division, we had a regular schedule whereby we would stage what was called a MAGTF Capabilities Exercise at Land Zone Bluebird. This was a very compact one-hour demonstration that displayed all the air and ground capabilities in the MAGTF. It was one of those demonstrations General Gray loved to show off, and media representatives were generally invited. It was a terrific display to educate the reporters on our capabilities as well as give them access to both officers and the troops to talk about what they had seen.

I really enjoyed my two years as both the Legislative Assistant and as the Director of Public Affairs. I had developed strong relationships with several members in the Congress that paid off in later years during Desert Shield and Desert Storm. Some of those relationships carried over to my final tour in Washington a little later. In my capacity as the Legislative Assistant on two occasions, I accompanied General Gray to the annual Defense Security Symposium held in Munich, Germany. This was a forum that had been established by German officials to discuss defense-related issues affecting many of the countries in Europe. It was always a magnet for congressional representatives as well as senior Defense Department officials, and that was why we were there. It was another forum whereby we could mingle with the likes of Senator John McCain (R-AR), Senator John Warner (R-VA), and Senator Sam Nunn (D-GA), along with other VIPs at the international level to continue to cultivate relationships. This forum is just as popular today as it was in the late 1980s.

The Marine Corps takes its relationships with Congress and the media seriously and strives to ensure that newly selected general officers understand the importance of these relationships. Each new class of Marine brigadier general selectees is required to attend at least a week in Washington learning the ropes so that they are prepared to deal with the challenges they will face. Part of the course deals with congressional relations. The selectees will spend a day on the hill getting information on how things work, visiting the committee rooms as well as meeting members. The issue of relationships is heavily emphasized again for good reasons because some of the new selectees come into town with preconceived personal opinions regarding Congress.

There was one specific example where this relationship really paid off. We were in a fight to save the V-22—which was being developed in Fort Worth, Texas—from being cut out of the budget. The Secretary of Defense Dick Cheney was against the program and had indicated he did not want the Marines in uniform working this on the hill. Congressman Jack Brooks (R-TX), a Marine who had Fort Worth in his district, had passed the word that he wanted a meeting on the hill with the Commandant, and I was to go along. This was one of those stories one reads about but has trouble believing. The Commandant and I arrived at one of the private rooms that the House owns in the capital. When we entered, Brooks had most of the Texas delegation in there with him, and we quickly got down to the subject at hand. Brooks wanted to make sure that the service was solidly behind him regarding the V-22 and then proceeded to hand out assignments for various members of the Texas delegation. It was

CHALLENGES

the classic example of the give and take that goes on concerning major defense programs Congress wants for the obvious reasons, and the Defense Department is dragging its feet. It is how the system works in many cases. As it turned out, the Marine Corps eventually got the V-22 some years later, but it really showed just how important these relations are.

One rather humorous incident occurred at the meeting that bears repeating. I was sitting next to Congressman J. J. Pickle (D-TX), who represented the same district that used to belong to Lyndon B. Johnson when he was an up-and-coming member of the Texas delegation. Each of us had a booklet of Marine Corps aircraft in front of us for reference. Pickle leaned over to me and assured me he was a full supporter of the V-22. He then pointed to a picture of a C-130 in the booklet at the same time. I politely turned the page and pointed to a picture of the V-22. He politely reiterated that he was a full supporter of the V-22 in the picture. Can't let a little thing like photo recognition get by if you want success.

One final example of how important relationships with members are on the hill occurred one afternoon while I was walking along a hallway in the Senate Russell Office Building. Senator Ted Kennedy (D-MA) was coming along from the other direction. I had worked with his office on several issues, so he knew me. Many people thought that he (being a liberal on any number of issues) was not really a pro-defense supporter. Not true, as he was a senior member of the Senate Armed Services Committee, and they were in session crafting the next Defense Authorization Bill. He greeted me warmly and stated he was on his way to get the Marine Corps two more AV8-B Harriers authorized in the coming bill. This was a surprise that nobody on the Marine side had expected and was partly a result of a positive relationship we had developed with him even to the extent of inviting him to visit Camp Lejeune to see the equipment and talk to the troops. That conversation included Marines from Massachusetts among other states and proved once again the importance of relationships with Congress.

208

CHAPTER 18

THE 4TH MARINE EXPEDITIONARY BRIGADE

My two-year tour in the OLA/PA job was about over when I learned that I had been selected for major general. I was also expecting orders in June 1989, and the next stop would be the 4th Marine Expeditionary Brigade, which was based in Little Creek, Virginia. The 4th MEB (formally the 4th MAB) had a lineage that stretched back to World War I in France. It was one of three amphibious brigades activated at that time in the 1980s. Primarily responsible for operations on the NATO Northern flank, which included Norway, Denmark, the Netherlands, and Germany, it had most recently been involved in the annual winter exercises in Norway.

In addition to the 4th MEB, I was also the Commanding General of the Landing Force Training Command (LFTC), also located in Little Creek. This organization was responsible for most of the formal amphibious warfare training that took place on the Atlantic Coast. It offered a variety of courses that covered most of the technical aspects of conducting amphibious operations. LFTC had a large staff that planned and coordinated the activities of the various schools functioning there, as well as participating in exercises from time to time.

We moved into quarters on the base which had held German POWs during World War II and had been renovated to accommodate families of Navy officers. It was a very pretty area close to the beach, but the quarters, which have since been renovated, left much to be desired at the time. Both Anne and TJ were in Virginia Beach schools, Anne in the ninth grade, while TJ was in the fourth. The quarters' location was nice and convenient for most of what we needed as well as work. Other commands there included Amphibious Group 2, two Navy SEAL teams, and assault craft units, as well as anchorage for some of the amphibious ships assigned to the 2nd Fleet. Due to the ongoing campaigns with the Navy regarding the role and support of the Marines, General Gray had been insistent that the 4th MEB retain spaces on the 2nd Fleet Flagship, the USS *Mt. Whitney* (LCC-20), in Norfolk. The rationale was if we had to deploy for a contingency, both the Navy and Marine staffs on the flagship would be known to each other and could work together as a team.

One of several advantages of being on the flagship was that I had the chance to meet and get to know the commanders of the aircraft carrier battle groups as well as the submarine groups in the Atlantic. These relationships would come back in the form of support during Desert Shield and Desert Storm, and specifically, Carrier Group-6 and Carrier Group-8. The *Mt. Whitney* was designed and built as an amphibious command ship but had been rarely used in that capacity over the years. For me, it meant that I maintained a headquarters on the flagship as the CG, 4th MEB, and another at Little Creek with the same title. My third headquarters would be the one for the CG, LFTC. I did spend much time going back and forth between one and the other.

A general officer can be called upon to represent the service or command on numerous occasions at a variety of events. This can be an interesting part of the job. One of my more pleasant assignments occurred a short time after I had taken command of the MEB as well as the LFTC. The Soviet Army band was doing a tour along the east coast as part of a reciprocal agreement between the U.S. and the USSR. We had sent musical organizations to Russia, and they had come back with this particular band, which staged several concerts along the eastern seaboard. The Russians were hosted by several commands all the way south to MacDill AFB, and they were on the way back when it became the turn of the U.S. Navy in Norfolk.

The Navy was really good when it came to events like this. The band members were housed in facilities in Little Creek and were given a thorough tour of various sites in the Hampton Roads area. Each member was turned loose in one of the major malls in downtown Norfolk with a shopping bag to fill with items of their choice. This was all funded by local organizations. The bandleader was a Soviet Army two-star general, and I believe the senior member of the Soviet Army Bands organization in Russia. I was to host him while he was in our area, and we put him up in the senior VIP facilities on the amphibious base. While the band moved by bus wherever they went, the general rode in my staff car. He was fascinated with the mobile phone I had in the back seat of my car. I told him he could use it to call whomever he wanted no matter where they were located. He shied away from that, but clearly, he had never seen anything like it.

My limited experience with the Soviets was weak, but it was amazing the wit and sense of humor the general displayed on numerous occasions. At one point, he challenged the band members to count the number of cars they would pass by on the bus to see how many were the same make. This was an obvious comparison to what they were used to in Russia. We would be sitting somewhere at some event, and he would lean over and point out one or two of his handlers. He would then quietly state, "See that officer? He is an idiot," or "that tall officer over there is KGB. They think we don't know this, the fools," and then chuckle. We had some very friendly conversations together, which made me wonder if most Russians were as friendly as he was. My suspicions were most Russians were just like that, but they would shy away from politics. When the band was ready to depart on its tour, he gave me some children's books in Russian for Anne and TJ. I reciprocated with similar books in English for his grandchildren back in the Soviet Union.

The Commander, Amphibious Group 2, was my counterpart with the Navy, and he also was headquartered at the Amphibious Base in Little Creek. Initially, the commander was RADM Glen Whistler

USN, and then RADM John "Bat" LaPlante USN. All the amphibious ships in the 2nd Fleet were under the control of Amphibious Group 2 (PHIBGP-2). We had begun to do some advance planning for an upcoming NATO exercise called Northern Wedding-Bold Guard. This was scheduled for the fall of 1990 and would take place in the Orkney Islands, Norway, and down on the Jutland Peninsula to Denmark and Germany. These exercises occurred every other year in various locations on NATO's northern flank and were preceded by extensive planning conferences followed by reconnaissance activities in the exercise areas.

The general plan for Northern Wedding called for an amphibious rehearsal landing in Scapa Flow, the site of the famous British Fleet anchorage in the Orkney Islands during both World Wars I and II. It was also the site of the scuttling of 54 ships of the German High Seas Fleet in July 1919 to avoid surrendering as war prizes to the British. From there, the 4th MEB, along with allies, would move in amphibious shipping to a landing area in central Norway for an exercise ashore. The plan then called for the amphibious force to disengage, backload, and steam south through the North Sea to stage Bold Guard amphibious landings on the Jutland Peninsula in Denmark. We were beginning to get into the detailed planning for this exercise through the early summer months when the international situation suddenly changed. Saddam Hussein and the Iraqi army surprised everyone and launched an invasion into Kuwait to take oil fields that they believed belonged to Iraq. The government in Kuwait quickly fell and fled the country, thereby posing a threat to Saudi Arabia early on. We were watching the activities in the Middle East but were still focused on the Northern Wedding exercise.

One Sunday afternoon in early August 1990, Sue and I were at a garden reception hosted by the 2nd Fleet Commander, VADM Mike Kalleris, at his very spacious quarters on the Admiral's Row at the naval station in Norfolk. I was called away to the phone in the admiral's quarters. Lieutenant General Carl Mundy, the Commander of the Fleet Marine Forces in the Atlantic, alerted me that the 4th

MEB was going to deploy to the Persian Gulf as a result of the Iraqi invasion. Carl Mundy was the senior Marine in the Atlantic who had served in 3/26 during the early stages of the siege at Khe Sanh. He was known as a very sharp Marine in appearance who was a mild, friendly individual and easy to get along with but was from the old school when it came to customs and traditions of the Corps. He had also been the Commanding General of the 4th MAB during the two years that I deployed with the 2nd Marines to Norway for both Cold Winter 85 and Anchor Express 86. There was no execution order for the current deployment for some time, as the call was an alert to commence planning for a very long movement by sea. The setting that day reminded me of what it must have been like at Pearl Harbor with the senior Navy leadership going through normal activities on a Sunday when the attack came. This time the attack was in Kuwait. I passed the information along to the fleet commander and continued to participate in the reception.

The following week grew very hectic quickly. We had not received anything definitive regarding the mission other than to "load and go." PHIBGRP 2 had to supply the available ships, but there were not enough ships to transport a full amphibious brigade. RADM La Plante, who now commanded the amphibious group, did his best to assign what was available that could withstand the long voyage. I had not known RADM LaPlante before we came together at Little Creek. A wry, convivial officer, he was a very able commander with much experience in the amphibious world in the Navy. We would serve together for the entire deployment to the Persian Gulf, and he taught me a lot about maintenance and the sustainability of his amphibious ships. Most of the shipping we had was old and would require much care and attention during the long deployment. The force structure for this movement under the 4th MEB command element consisted of the 2nd Marine Regiment, under the command of Colonel Tom Hobbs as the ground combat element. Marine Air Group 40, the Air Combat Element, was commanded by Colonel Glenn (Smoke)

Burgess, and Brigade Service Support Group 4 as the combat service support element under Colonel Jim Doyle.

RADM La Plante was able to organize 13 amphibious ships that would carry the MEB, which was eight ships short of the basic requirement. It should be noted here the majority of supplies on ships that sustain a brigade in what is called an Assault Follow-on Echelon (AFOE) were not even assigned until after we had left Norfolk. I requested a helicopter and flew down to Camp Lejeune to meet with now Major General Bill Keys, the Commanding General of the 2nd Marine Division, and Brigadier General Chuck Krulak to get coordinated on that loadout. This would eventually take place on five Roll-on-Roll-off (RO-RO) ships when they arrived at Sunny Point, North Carolina. That problem was resolved when the Marines at Camp Lejeune went to work and loaded the five ships. The shortcoming here was that none of the five had an in-stream offload capability, and they were all foreign-flagged, which meant they could not sail in the combat zone.

Despite the confusion that week, the force left the east coast in three Transit Groups: Task Group 1 with four ships on August 17th, 1990, Task Group 2 on August 20th with four ships, and Task Group 3 on August 21 with five ships. Bat La Plante and I, with our staffs were collocated on the flagship USS *Nassau* (LHA-4) in TG 2. The afternoon of the 20th saw several family members on the pier in Norfolk when the ship was ready to cast off. The *Nassau* was a very large (42,000 tons) multi-capable amphibious assault ship that could take helicopters, AV-8 Harrier jets, and all kinds of vehicles were stored in the well deck of the ship. The *Nassau* had the capability of ballasting down and opening the ship's stern gate so that landing craft could go in and out of the well deck with vehicles as large as tanks. Standing on the flight deck and looking down at Sue, Anne, and TJ was kind of sad because nobody knew how long we would be gone. The kids did not seem overwhelmed by all of this and appeared to be a little bored as the ship slipped away from the pier.

Once we cleared Hampton Roads and pushed out to sea, the twenty AV-8 Harriers that would be on this ship began to fly in from Cherry Point, North Carolina. They were bedded down within the ship to make room for the helicopters that were coming in behind the jets. When all of that was completed, the *Nassau* turned to the east and picked up speed while heading into the Atlantic.

At this point, I was responsible for 9,000 troops embarked within the 13 ships, 20 Harriers, and 46 helicopters spread across the force. MAG-40 was also assigned F-18 fighters, A-6A attack jets, and 3 EA-6B electronic aircraft that would be forward deployed and bedded down in theater for our use should the need arise. Due to the Iraqi tank threat on the Saudi border, one squadron of Cobra helicopters from MAG-40 was flown by C-5 transports to the east coast of Saudi Arabia to back up Marines from the 7th MEB. The MEB had flown in from 29 Palms, California, and was already in position along the roads leading north to Kuwait. The Cobras would be returned to MAG-40 when we arrived in theater later. Colonel "Smoke" Burgess was a very likable, friendly, and professional aviator and an experienced pilot who had spent time in both helicopters and jet aircraft over his career. He would prove to be an exceptional commander of MAG-40 and especially when both operational and sustainability issues proved to be real challenges as the deployment continued for the next several months.

What are the issues associated with normal embarkation and loadout of Marines in an amphibious force? U.S. Navy amphibious ships are designed for specific missions and purpose. The specifications for the crew are carefully included in the design, as are the requirements for embarked troops and their equipment. The *Nassau* was not designed to accommodate both the PHIBGP-2 staff and 4th MEB command element along with associated equipment. This meant berthing spaces overlapped with the crew spaces, which caused conflict. Due to the paucity of available shipping, equipment and supplies had to be jammed in wherever it could be accommodated in each ship, which caused more conflict. In theory, there is a definitive plan based on the mission that provides adequate facilities for both personnel and equipment. The only problem with this approach was we had no defined mission before leaving Norfolk and were short available ships, which meant combat loading was not done following a probable scheme of maneuver ashore. What we did was to use the assault planning for Bold Guard, which was different, but it saved time. I think one could call the combat loading effort across the 13 ships a "STUFFEX" because all the amphibious ships were overloaded.

Fortunately, I had one of the best brigade G-4 sections in the Marine Corps headed by Lieutenant Colonel Gary Collenborne, Lieutenant Colonel Bob Dickerson, and Major Chuck Herndon. Gary was a tall, engaging individual from Montana who had started out in the infantry and then made a lateral move to the field of logistics. He had become an expert in Marine Corps logistics, a field that is often ignored by the operators to their peril, and especially if aviation is involved. Along with their G-4 staff, they did wonders during the embarkation, and it was only just beginning. The G-3 of the 4th MEB, Lieutenant Colonel Robert P Mauskapf, would be in charge of most of the operational planning required throughout the deployment. He and his staff would be deeply involved with planning for rehearsals, training ashore when the opportunities presented themselves, and any contingency planning for tasks leveled on the 4th MEB from higher headquarters. My Chief of Staff, Colonel Bill Scheffler, an aviator, would oversee the staff planning for the MEB headquarters for the entire deployment. At the same time coordinating major initiatives with his PhibGru-2 counterpart Navy Captain Andrew Fosina.

The transit across the Atlantic was relatively uneventful. We steamed past Gibraltar and into the Mediterranean in calm seas, still heading east. The Harriers were getting in good flight time and honing their skills. In this situation, nobody was worrying about the number of flight hours per month that they were using up. The U.S. Navy is the best in the world in underway replenishment (UNREP) at sea. The system places oilers or other kinds of replenishment ships at various points along a route. Coordinating is done between units that will place an oiler at a certain point to rendezvous with a task group that is steaming through. It will transfer bunker and aviation fuel, as well as other commodities, to other ships. This way, the task group can continue moving forward at a sustained speed. The linkage between an oiler and a replenishment ship moving side by side with the *Nassau* was a sight to see. Depending on the type of ship, there could also be a vertical replenishment (VERTREP) going on by helicopter at the same time that the two ships were close together, transferring fuel. On this trip, it seemed like we were doing a UNREP every three or four days as we crossed the Mediterranean. This fantastic capability was one reason why the sailors and Marines on all the ships had fresh fruit and vegetables every day for the eight and a half months that we were at sea.

When the MEB was about halfway across the Atlantic, I began to have some trepidation about how I was going to control or influence what was going on in the other ships of the amphibious task force. This would only grow as time went by, and we added more assets to the force. The communications between the MEB Headquarters in the *Nassau*, and the subordinate Marine units spread across the amphibious task force, were spotty at best. That the first task group was a day ahead of us, while the third task group was a day behind, did not help matters either. Communications between the Commander Amphibious Task Force (CATF) (LaPlante) and the 2nd Fleet in Norfolk, as well as U.S. Naval Central Command (NAVCENT) in the Persian Gulf, were not any better initially. This caused messages to be delayed or lost, creating much more confusion about plans for employment in the Gulf.

To accommodate this problem, each day would start with a meeting with the MEB staff that normally lasted an hour. This usually commenced with an intelligence update that quickly demonstrated there was not much going on with the Iraqi Army, as they already had Kuwait. It did reinforce the idea that Saddam might invade Saudi

Arabia, which had everyone's attention. At the time, both the Central Command (CENTCOM) planners and the leadership in the Pentagon thought if that happened, the Marines might be able to do an amphibious landing somewhere behind the Iraqi forces to cut them off from bases to the north. This drove the initial staff briefings each morning. My guidance that came up following discussions would be passed out and down through the chain of command to the respective units across the force.

This assumed the communications were working normally. There would usually be at least one weekly joint meeting with Bat LaPlante, myself, and both staffs to iron out any disputes that may have arisen. There were always arguments between the staffs regarding any number of issues that had to be resolved at the flag level. Most of the time, they were worked out. I regarded this as the staffs maturing together and getting to know each other's problems. One thing that I think was at the base of several issues between the two staffs was the fact we still had no defined mission. I did not receive the first operations order until early in September, due to communications problems. This was a generic order, but not an Initiating Directive, which establishes specific objectives for planning and execution. This situation did not really improve until we were in the northern Arabian Sea.

CHAPTER 19
OPERATION DESERT SHIELD 1990

Toward the end of August 1990, the amphibious task force was off Alexandria, Egypt, and waiting to transit the Suez Canal. We decided it would be a good time to have a deck party on the flight deck of the ship. The weather was good, and both sailors and Marines were lounging across the deck, listening to music from the ship's band while drinking their allotted two cans of beer or soft drinks. It was a nice relaxing day, and the mess decks put on a special feed for the ship's crew and embarked Marines. Early the next morning, we were positioned to enter the Suez Canal and proceed south as far as the Great Bitter Lake. The lake was located about halfway through the canal. The way the transit was managed by the Egyptians stipulated that southbound ships, commercial or military, would proceed south to the Great Bitter Lake, drop anchors there and wait. Northbound ships would pass through the Great Bitter Lake and continue on their way and into the Mediterranean. When northbound ships had passed through, then southbound ships would weigh anchor and continue south and into the Red Sea. The whole process took about a full day.

One interesting observation was as we transited south, the west bank of the canal was covered with Egyptian green farms, crops, and date orchards. The Egyptian side was also lined with gun positions, anti-aircraft batteries, and missile launchers, all pointing east. On the Israeli side, the Sinai was nothing but desert until we passed by the entrance to the Gulf of Aqaba. The transit south through the Red Sea proved to be uneventful until we closed on the border between Saudi Arabia and Yemen. The ship went on alert as we passed by Djibouti, and through the narrow waterway of the Bab Al Mandab, which was heavily fortified on the Yemeni side. Experiencing no incidents there, the amphibious task force proceeded east into the Gulf of Aden and then out into the North Arabian Sea (See Map 8).

The three task groups finally came together in mid-September around the island of Masirah, which belongs to the Sultanate of Oman. There we went into what is called a modified location (MODLOC) for some time. On September 13th, we were joined there by the 13th Marine Expeditionary Unit (Special Operations Capable), which had deployed off the west coast of California and had been in the region for a few months as part of the routine six-month deployment. The 13th MEU (SOC) was to become part of the 4th MEB until further notice. That meant we now had a force of 18 ships and 12,000 Marines. Colonel John Rhodes was the Commander, 13th MEU (SOC), and he was a very experienced aviator who had served in Vietnam both on the ground and in the air. We were also designated as the CENTCOM reserve by General Schwarzkopf and placed under the control of the Commander U.S. Naval Forces Central Command (USNAVCENT).

On September 21st, the first of the five commercial RO-RO ships passed Masirah on the way to the Persian Gulf. They were to be offloaded at Al Jubayl on the east coast of Saudi Arabia and then leave the Gulf. To offload the five RO-ROs, I had to send a working party of 400 Marines under Lieutenant Colonel Bob Dickerson to the port for a job that would take more than a month to complete. Meanwhile, the decision was made by COMUSNAVCENT to establish a logistics hub at the airfield on Masirah, which would serve the 4th MEB initially. The U.S. Air Force would be tasked to fly in sustainment for the MEB, subject to Omani restrictions. The airlifted supplies would come into the airfield and be staged. Then PHIBGP 2 ships would close on the coast of that island. Marine helicopters would fly in and lift the supplies back out to the ships for further distribution across the force (See Map 9).

The Omanis had stated we could only do this in daylight, and nobody could remain overnight at the airfield. The first time I went to the Omani airfield, I spotted a fairly large tent camp off in an open area not far from one of the runways. It turned out this was a USAF camp complete with camouflaged, air-conditioned tents and equipped with SATCOM phones. Upon entering one of the tents to check with the local commander, a young airman greeted me and immediately offered me one of the phones if I wanted to call anyone in the states. This was a nice gesture, but it took me completely by surprise. Here we were aboard ship and were lucky if we could contact each other by radio.

The Sultanate of Oman has a rich and colorful history that dates back centuries. In the southern Dhofar region and along the Yemeni border, frankincense grows in the high plateau and mountains. It has been used by ancient kings from Egypt and elsewhere across the Arabian Peninsula since the middle of the first century AD. The Portuguese occupied many of the coastal cities for some time before they left a mark in terms of forts and mountain watchtowers. That occupation was very harsh despite the architecture, and the Imams spent years in revenge for the repression. At one point at the beginning of the twentieth century, Muscat and Oman were separated into two sections and with little influence in the region. Then in the 1960s, oil was discovered in what was still a very impoverished country. A coup was executed in 1970. The current ruler at the time was removed peacefully from his throne by his well-educated son, Sultan Qaboos bin Said. The son was educated at Sandhurst in the UK and served with the British Army of the Rhine in Germany before returning home. When he arrived back in the country, there were only 75 miles of road throughout Oman. Oil revenues were to become the bankroll that the Sultan used to initiate several programs to upgrade the lives of the Omanis.

Today it is a fairly modern country where education and health care are available for all its citizens. In addition to modern and very creative architectural symbols designed to beautify good roads, the Sultan has constructed a gigantic new mosque in Muscat that dwarfs just about everything else. At some point, the British moved in to provide security as well as develop a fairly modern defense establishment. When we arrived, the British were gradually fading out, but several traditions followed the British model. An example of that occurred when we were standing off of the rehearsal beach area when I received a request from the Defense Attaché in Muscat. He wanted me to meet up with one of their desert patrols at a point in a certain wadi in the desert. I flew off the ship in one of our helicopters to find the spot and meet up with whoever was in charge of the patrol. The helicopter set down in the desert and shut down to wait for the patrol. It was late in the afternoon, and the sun was beginning to settle in the west when we spotted a cloud of dust heading our way. At a certain point, a Land Rover appeared out of the sun with four riders, mounted machine guns, goggles, and some camouflage gear on the vehicle. They stopped, and a young British NCO got out and introduced himself along with his Omani Army companions. This looked like something we would have seen with the British Desert Rats in North Africa operating against the Germans in Rommel's Afrika Corps.

His orders were to brief me on the security situation along the Saudi border that divided the two countries. There had been issues with the Saudis' coming out of a vast desert area known as the Empty Quarter in southeastern Saudi Arabia. Oman had a screen of vehicle-mounted patrols and was constantly monitoring the border. The British were operating with them as advisors and had been doing this for years. While he was briefing me, the other three soldiers started a campfire and were cooking food over the fire. There again protocol, even in the middle of a vast desert, called for a joint meal put on by the Omani hosts. The meeting went very well, and as we got ready to board the helicopter for the flight back to the ship, the British NCO offered me a swig of a cold drink, which I accepted. It was really cold, and it turned out to be scotch whiskey. It was a fine gesture, and only the Brits would have a tradition like that in the middle of nowhere.

I had mentioned earlier the importance of maintaining good relations with the media. One day after the routine morning meeting, we were told that Katie Couric and a camera team wanted to come out to the *Nassau* to do a story on the Marines. At the time, the *Independence* Carrier Battle Group was up in the southern Persian

Gulf. To get to her, the *Nassau* had to steam for a day and a half to get within helicopter range of the *Independence*. They picked Couric up along with the camera crew and brought them back to the *Nassau*. She told me she wanted to do a major story on the Marines afloat and was looking for suggestions. The first thing we did was let her go around the ship with my public affairs officer, Captain Dan Carpenter, and talk with the troops. Dan was another first-class officer who often functioned as my aide whenever that was necessary. An easygoing, friendly individual, he could handle media issues and personal relations with great skill, which came in handy on several occasions during the deployment.

Katie interviewed both Bat and me, and then we took her out to a spot overlooking the flight deck to get pictures of a flight of Harriers. They were practicing taking off and then circling back to a hover just off the port side of the ship. Then they would gradually ease in over the deck and land. After that and more interviews, she left the ship by helicopter for a short flight to the shore to be picked up by someone else. I mention this because every time we saw any coverage of operations in the Gulf, those pictures of the Harriers were almost always included. Excellent publicity for us as well as something real for the viewing public.

OPERATIONS UNDER COMUSNAVCENT

The flagship for Commander U.S. Navy Central Command (COMUSNAVCENT) was the USS *Blue Ridge* (LCC-19), the sister ship to the *Mt. Whitney*. VADM Hank Mauz, who was also the Commander, U.S. Seventh Fleet, was initially the commander under General Schwarzkopf. He had positioned himself on the ship up in the Persian Gulf around Bahrain, At the time, he had only one officer on his staff who had any experience with this kind of amphibious warfare. The perceived threat of an Iraqi invasion of Saudi Arabia and the persistent communications problems across the force presented me with a challenge. The amphibious task force was not adequately combat loaded for a specific amphibious landing, because no plan had been communicated. The hard requirement for rehearsals so we could get the ships loaded correctly for any plan was critical. This became my top priority.

After negotiations between the Navy, CENTCOM, and the government of Oman, we were given a designated area roughly 90 miles long and 20 miles deep along a deserted coastline south of Masirah. This location was near a place called Ra's al Madrakah and was off any of the shipping lanes passing along the coast of Oman and into the Gulf of Oman (See Map 9). The terrain inland was all desert with very little visible vegetation or sources of water. Several wadis crisscrossed the exercise area, which made navigation a challenge. This was before GPS devices were available in ground units. The temperatures were routinely well over 115 degrees, although we could usually count on a slight breeze coming off the ocean in late afternoon. The heat in the middle of the day was brutal. There was an added attraction in that the exercise area could be used to offload everything on the beaches.

We could also exercise all elements of the force without any danger of injuring civilians. Bedouin tribes were moving around in the region, but they generally stayed out of the specific area we were operating in. This became the site of what eventually saw four major amphibious rehearsal landings (Sea Soldier I- IV) both during day and night over five months. Each scenario was different and reflected various conditions upon which an amphibious landing could be carried out. As the intelligence situation changed in the Gulf, we would adjust the next scenario to reflect the current situation and conditions. Most of the required maintenance on all of our vehicles was also carried out on the beach following the tactical landings. After the exercises, all the equipment would be loaded back aboard the ships per current load plans, and we would sail out to sea.

Each rehearsal had to be planned and coordinated with the Omani general staff in Muscat, which was always a formal affair. On each occasion, we were able to use the U.S. Ambassador to Oman, Bill

Bolen, and his staff, to provide details that were acceptable to the Omanis. He proved to be of exceptional help on each one of these planning initiatives, and I grew to admire him immensely. I thought he was the quintessential ambassador of the old school who really was a terrific representative in that country. We later invited the ambassador out to the Nassau to observe the operation as well as address the sailors and Marines on the ship. I sent a C-12 aircraft to Muscat to fly him down to Masirah. There I met him at the airfield, and we flew by helicopter to the ship. He was dressed in a very sharp suit and tie and looked cool even in the blistering heat. Following briefs and lunch in the wardroom, he addressed the combined crew of sailors and Marines on all manner of subjects and thanked them for what they were trying to accomplish. I think Ambassador Bolen was on the ship for 3-4 hours, but it was well worth the effort. He had indicated to me that none of the senior Army or Navy officers had bothered to call on him, which made no sense when operating in someone else's country. At any rate, it paid dividends for us as we saw him every time we were in Muscat.

On one occasion early in the activities around the southern Gulf, the Navy had decided to conduct a GPS survey on an area west of Abu Dhabi that could be utilized as a rehearsal area for amphibious training exercises (See Map 9). This initiative had been approved by the United Arab Emirates, and I was tasked to go in and meet with the Defense Minister of the United Arab Emirates (UAE), Sheikh Mohammed. He was a pleasant, likable individual, well-educated, and very conversant on the role we were playing in the Persian Gulf. I took a C-12 into the airfield in Abu Dhabi to meet with Mohammed. We met at his grand receiving area at the airfield, and after pleasantries, I joined him on a tour of his family's fleet of aircraft. There were several executive jets on the field, including a Boeing 747. Following the inspection, we flew in another jet down to the area where the survey had taken place. There had been some interest in the Landing Craft Air-Cushioned vehicles (LCACs) that I had in the landing force. To accommodate that, we had five LCACs staged on the beach, each with a load of Light Armored Vehicles (LAVs) that I had in my force as well. Mohammed toured the line of LCACs and stopped to talk with the Marines who manned the LAVs. He was fascinated by the fact that one of the LAV crews had built a workbench on their own inside the vehicle to be able to make repairs on the vehicle if necessary. I explained to him this kind of initiative was not unusual with the Marines, as they will make things work one way or another. It had been time well spent, and he came away impressed with what both the Navy LCAC crews and the Marines were doing. We flew back to Abu Dhabi and parted company.

THE REHEARSALS

It was a relief to get the entire amphibious task force together off of Masirah so that we could get the load plans sorted out for off-loading during the coming training rehearsals. With the approval of the training areas around Ra's al Madrakah, which was about 90 miles south of Masirah, we could now start scheduling all facets of amphibious operations (See Map 9). There still was no specific directive outlining missions that the force might have to execute against the Iraqis. I had directed that we try to plan for any possible option which could be carried out by the 4th MEB. I had also forwarded a document with ten potential employment options to VADM Mauz, indicating what the MEB could do if a contingency arose. The normal procedure is for the higher authority to issue what is known as the Initiating Directive. In this document, the commander will find the missions that the force is expected to execute if given the green light to do so. This, in turn, drives the training plans and the logistics requirements to support the training.

On this deployment, the 4th MEB did not receive an Initiating Directive until January 10, 1991. The first exercise, SEA SOLDIER I, was designed specifically to conduct a simple ship-to-shore movement by helicopter, amphibian tractors (AAVs), and air-cushioned vehicles (LCACs). Once on the beach, the troops would go off to conduct training under their own commanders. This was necessary to get the troops somewhat acclimated to the intense heat and complete lack of any shade in the region. The second and most important component of SEA SOLDIER I was to offload all the equipment from the 13 ships and reorganize and maintain it on the beach. Following the effort over eight days, the equipment would be back-loaded following a generic landing plan the force could rely on if we had to execute a contingency. I thought the initial time on the beach gave us the space we needed to get organized for whatever came down the line. It also gave me time to meet with most of the commanders face to face for the first time since leaving North Carolina, and to ensure the guidance I was receiving from higher headquarters was not misunderstood. This continued to be necessary because communications at sea continued to be spotty at best, and there was no way I could get around to each ship when we were at sea.

SEA SOLDIER II was scheduled for November 3 - 9, 1990, in the same rehearsal area west of Ra's al Madrakah. The MEB started to rehearse potential landing scenarios we might have to execute up in the Persian Gulf. This included raids at night as well as the traditional helicopter and surface assaults from distances as far out as 20-25 miles from the beaches. One goal was to get most of the 12,000 Marines off the ships and into the desert for training. This exercise also included off-loading of vehicles and equipment for maintenance on the beach.

Before the landing, I had received an invitation from Ambassador Bolen to be the guest of honor at the traditional Marine Corps Ball that would be held in Muscat on November 10th. The Marine Corps Birthday is celebrated in every Marine unit and facility anywhere in the world on the date of the founding of the Corps in 1775. Ceremonies can be large or small, but it is a tradition held automatically in every clime and place in or out of war. Toward the end of the exercises, I boarded a CH-53 helicopter and flew out of the desert to Masirah and then by C-12 aircraft to the Seeb Airfield in Muscat. The Ball was to be held at the Al Bustan Palace Hotel just outside of Muscat. It was an exclusive hotel originally built to support the Gulf Cooperation Council for the leaders of Oman and the other countries that ring the shores of the Gulf. I stayed at the ambassador's spacious quarters and went from there with him to the event.

Every U.S. embassy has a detachment of at least six Marines, which make up the embassy guard. They traditionally plan the event, which includes dinner, speeches, and a cake-cutting ceremony to honor the Corps as well as the oldest and youngest Marine at the ceremony. This Birthday Ball and ceremony had around 200 guests from the diplomatic community in Muscat, as well as several expats who were living in Muscat. It was a really nice event and an excellent break for me from what I had been doing for the previous three months. I went back to the ambassador's quarters that night and then left the next day by air for the amphibious force, which was now off of Masirah.

In late October, General Schwarzkopf directed Admiral Mauz to conduct an amphibious exercise called "Imminent Thunder" from 15 -21 November along the north Saudi coast. After much discussion between the NAVCENT Staff and Schwarzkopf's staff, the landing area was designated north of Al Jubayl around Ras al Ghar. This was to be a landing to send a signal to Iraq that the U.S. would move amphibious forces deep into the Persian Gulf if necessary. It was also designed to impress the news media with maximum coverage of the event. The directive indicated that USCENTCOM would control the media coverage to achieve its own objectives. The scheme of maneuver for the amphibious force called for movement to positions some 25 miles offshore, and conduct both surface and helicopter-borne landings from that distance to the beach and inland. Also, Bat LaPlante requested additional aircraft sorties for close air support (CAS) for the assault landings by British and French aircraft.

Sea conditions were much different 25 miles out in the Gulf as compared to sea state along the beaches. When the lead LCAC backed out of the well deck of its mother ship, the craft master found the waters too rough for the air-conditioned vehicles, which threatened to damage the propellers that drove the LCACs. The result was the surface assault was canceled, and I concurred. The helicopter-borne landing went off as scheduled with good results, in that 500 Marines and 19 vehicles were deposited on the beach. We organized the air assault into six waves, with 29 helicopters used in the first wave alone. That was a good test to move troops in that manner over distance. I had flown to the landing area to brief the media on the beach, and to also meet with Major General Mike Myatt, the Commanding General of the 1st Marine Division, on future plans. At the time, we had little idea of what was to come some two months later. Following the meeting, it was back to the ship to make preparations for the transit back out of the Persian Gulf. We proceeded through the Straits of Hormuz and south to our assigned exercise area in preparation for SEA SOLDIER III.

SEA SOLDIER III was also conducted at the same location on December 8-18, 1990. In both exercises, increased emphasis was placed on raids, night operations, and movement at longer ranges of up to 25 miles from the ships to the beach via helicopters from MAG-40. One of the goals was to lift most of the ground combat element (the 2nd Marines) with the forty available helicopters to objectives inland. What we found out was that a lift of that size involving three infantry battalions was not possible in the allotted time without moving the four helicopter carriers closer to the beach. By doing so, we would increase the risk to the ships from enemy fire in a real situation. Even so, the sky was black with helicopters as we continued to lift all elements from the ships to locations ashore throughout the day.

This did require changing tactics, as well as increasing CAS missions with the Harriers in support of the troop units maneuvering in the desert. The normal offload and maintenance of vehicles on the beach was carried out in a much more effective manner. In SEA SOLDIER III, the force operated at night in a communications blackout or EMCON conditions to evaluate the effectiveness of our plans in that environment. The one really tragic incident that occurred was with the Harriers off the *Nassau*. They did not have a night capability on the aircraft, so they would operate until a little after dusk before returning to the ship. I was on the flag bridge when the commander of the Air Combat Element (ACE), Colonel Smoke Burgess, came up to inform me that one of the Harriers was missing. An immediate search was launched, and after a short time, they found the wreckage of the aircraft a little inland from the beach. We were not sure of what happened, but it looked like the pilot may have become disoriented and flew the jet into the ground. A memorial service was held the next day on the ship. The remains were escorted off the ship by helicopter to Muscat for further transfer home. This put a very somber end to what had been a successful exercise. Having "Smoke" Burgess as my ACE commander was very important due to the large number of helicopters we had afloat in addition to the Harriers. He did a masterful job of ensuring that the readiness levels in the ACE were high even though his aircraft were spread out over five different ships at the time.

One of the initiatives we wanted to include as part of each rehearsal was a medical (MEDCAP) and dental (DENTCAP) program to provide medical assistance to the local Bedouins in the rehearsal areas. This was a capability that had come to fruition over the many years we had been in Vietnam. The plan was for the Omani military to notify the tribes as to when and where this would occur and to get the chiefs to buy into it. In addition to the obvious positive results for something like this, I wanted to employ some of my 100 doctors embedded with the MEB who were troublesome because they did not have that much to do at the time. The plan called for us to set up a tent site away from the landing area and staff it with several doctors, and all the implements they would need to work with. Keep in mind that this area was beastly hot, and there were no trees for miles. When Omani liaison officers passed the word, we began to get the Bedouin families to come in and participate to get free medical assistance.

The first thing we noticed was most of them came in out of the desert, driving Toyota pickups, usually red. This was because the ruler in Oman, Sultan Qaboos, had decreed families could have a free vehicle if they wanted one. The reports back from the doctors indicated that they were working on medical issues they had never seen because they did not exist at home. It was not unusual for the dentists to pull two or three teeth without the use of any painkiller because the Bedouin chiefs forbid it. It was also noted none of the patients had any complaints, something else not seen at home. If a doctor had to work on a Bedouin female, the husband of the patient or a male family member had to be present. We did four of these in conjunction with each rehearsal, and they were quite successful. The number of patients increased in each event, and some even came in on camels. The doctors were happy because they were dealing with problems; most of them had never had to confront. It also gave them a chance to get off the ships and get really sweaty and dirty.

Communications were still a problem, and it was difficult to make sure the troops spread across the 18 ships were reasonably informed. I had made it a point to go several times ashore during each rehearsal to talk to the commanders in the field along with troops I could find. One thing about Marines is if there is any sense of an upcoming fight, the morale will be really high accompanied by very few problems. I tried to get around to different ships while we were afloat, as well. On one occasion, I requested a helicopter to fly over to one of the Landing Ship Tanks (LST) in the force to visit with both sailors and embarked Marines. The LST had its birth during World War II and proved to be very successful in every conflict since. It could sail right up to a beach and begin to offload troops and equipment. With the older models, this was accomplished through a bow door that opened right on the beach. On the newer models, vehicles would move down a ramp that telescoped out from the bow of the ship until it touched the beach. It could also carry sections of causeway lashed to the port and starboard sides of the ship.

On this particular flight, I had a CH-46 helicopter equipped with a sling for in-water rescue if necessary. We took off from the Nassau for the short flight to the LST. The flight deck on that ship was covered with causeway pieces as well as other kinds of equipment. I had decided to use the collar and sling as the way I would be lowered to what was left of the clear deck of the ship. I noticed one squadron commander was flying the 46 while a second squadron commander was sitting in the back with the crew chief. I think he was along to make sure that the MEB commander didn't get dumped into the ocean. At any rate, I got the collar on and told the crew chief I was ready as soon as the helicopter was hovering over the deck of the ship. I went out and was lowered down the cable to the deck of the LST. The ship was rolling slightly in a swell when I hit the deck and rolled off to my right. The sailor who was charged with getting me off the deck caught me with his eyes wide open. I got out of the sling and signaled to the helicopter to drift off. The kid on the deck had obviously never seen a general officer hit the deck and roll on his ship, but he soon recovered. I slapped him on the back and followed him forward to the bridge. About an hour was spent going around talking to the crew as well as the troops, and both were all ears. On these ships, the troop compartments had the troops stacked three high, which really had not changed much since my time on the first tour with the Navy on Okinawa in 1961. When it was time to go, the CH-46 came back and circled the ship, lowered the cable and sling, and hauled me back up and into the helicopter. It was a good thing to do, and I think it gave the sailors and Marines on that LST the impression someone was looking out for them.

Not all the things worked out that well. In every exercise, I would lay out the mission for the force, give my commanders intent, and then assign missions to the subordinate units so the commanders could go off and develop their own plans following their specific missions. The 13th MEU (SOC) was off doing one of the assigned tasks, which for them, and the amount of time they had been deployed was somewhat routine. Two of their UH-1N helicopters were on a night mission at sea when, for whatever reason, they collided in mid-air and crashed into the sea. The following search found no survivors. Night operations are inherently dangerous, especially with helicopters. Considering the level of training risk necessary for preparation for combat, there would be more of this before it was over.

I had mentioned earlier the Navy and Bat LaPlante was always concerned with ship maintenance, with good reason. Some of our amphibious ships were old and had to be tended to every day so that something didn't develop into a major breakdown. On occasion, he would send a ship into some port, either in Muscat or elsewhere in the Emirates, to places like Dubai or Abu Dhabi. This was designed to give the crew a break as well as fix problems.

On one occasion, LaPlante sent the USS *Iwo Jima*—an LPH, helicopter carrier—to port in Bahrain to make repairs as required. She was the first ship of that class and subsequently the oldest with continuous maintenance issues. *Iwo Jima* was smaller than the *Nassau* but could carry at least a squadron of helicopters, plus embarked troops who would ride in those helicopters on exercises or contingencies. One day the ship was exiting port when she had a steam leak in the engine room deep in the ship. A main steam line had ruptured and blew superheated steam that killed six crewmembers immediately, plus four later on in the hospital ship near Bahrain. The ship was repaired and eventually returned to the force later in the fall, but this incident was a shock to everyone. I continued to learn much from Bat LaPlante regarding the necessity for continuous maintenance on several of the older amphibious ships in the force.

MARITIME INTERDICTION OPERATIONS

In early August, the Chairman of the Joint Chiefs of Staff, General Colin Powell, had issued an alert order for a Maritime Interdiction Operation to enforce the economic quarantine on Iraq. What that basically meant was ships believed to be carrying goods either out of Iraq or into the country would have to be stopped and searched. If found carrying contraband goods, they would be directed to a neutral port for a thorough search. This developed into an allied naval campaign that would, in effect, circle the Arabian Peninsula from the Red Sea around to the Persian Gulf. Eventually, this force would intercept close to 1,000 ships at sea. Interdictions started in mid-August with U.S. Navy and allied ships stopping and either boarding Iraqi ships or others to determine what they were carrying.

We entered into the picture when the 13th MEU (SOC) was tasked to conduct interdiction missions on the Iraqi tankers *Al Mutanabbi* on October 13, the Iraqi ship *Al Sahil Al Arabi* on October 22, and later a third Iraqi tanker *Amariyah* on October 28 in the Gulf of Oman. When intelligence sources indicated a ship was probably carrying cargo banned due to economic sanctions, an order would go out from USNAVCENT to stop the ship. Any available allied ship would be tasked to stop and search the vessel. That sounds easy, but the other side had its own way of circumventing such activities on occasion. If an Iraqi ship was ordered to stop for a search and its captain elected to not comply for whatever reason, then we had the authority to board and stop the ship. In this instance, the tanker *Amariyah* refused to stop for a search. 13th MEU (SOC) had developed procedures for taking down a ship based on the guidance and Rules of Engagement (ROE) as directed by USNAVCENT. They deployed UH-1N helicopters with Navy SEALs onboard to fly over the tanker and try to land somewhere on the deck of the *Amariyah*. Once on the deck, the trained boarding party could move to execute two specific missions. One was to move to take over the bridge and the captain, and the other was to go to the engine room to stop the vessel. There were instances where the crews were pouring water over the side of the ship to prevent surface boarding parties from climbing onboard. Iraqi crews would also spray the decks with fire hoses to prevent helicopters from landing on the decks. To combat this, helicopters would move in and hover over the ship so that the SEALS could fast rope from the helicopter to the deck. Once onboard, they would proceed to stop the ship. The intercepting Navy ship would then send over a U.S. Coast Guard Law Enforcement Detachment (USCG LEDET) team to search the ship and its cargo while checking the ship's documents. We also had another UH-1N helicopter with snipers hovering if the SEALS were met with resistance by crews on the vessel.

In the situation with the *Amariyah*, once she was dead in the water, the captain became very cooperative and submitted to the search of his vessel. Finding no contraband cargo, he was allowed to proceed. Several cases involving the interception of Iraqi ships presented different situations that had to be resolved both at NAVCENT level and with governments where ships were searched and impounded. If contraband was discovered or the captain refused to cooperate, the ship would be escorted to a neutral port and impounded awaiting further governmental action, in this case, Oman.

One of the most interesting intercepts involved the 4th MEB and the *Ibn Khaldoon,* which sailed from Algeria and eventually ended up in Iraq in December 1990. The Iraqi cargo ship, which was billed as an Iraqi peace ship carrying 241 passengers and had a crew of 41 sailors with a cargo of baby food and medical supplies. Many of the civilian passengers were women from Northern Europe, as well as a contingent of Fata widows. Sources knew this ship would transit down through the Red Sea, across the northern Arabian Sea and up into the Persian Gulf to Iraq.

In November, the 13th MEU (SOC) had received orders to begin the long voyage home to California. To retain the ship interdiction capability within the 4th MEB, another team was formed and trained to do ship takedowns if required. The vertical insertion team practiced this technique thoroughly. They also planned for armed crowd control measures for a different type of resistance, most likely to be employed by activists on board ships like the *Ibn Khaldoon.*

On December 26, the ship was first intercepted off of Masirah Island by an Australian frigate, and it refused to stop (See Map 8). The captain was informed that a helicopter insertion team was on the way to insert a team by fast rope to the deck of the ship. The insertion team came off of the USS *Trenton* (LPD-14), an amphibious assault ship, and was composed of SEALS and some force reconnaissance Marines. Both active and passive resistance was used by the civilians on the ship. In one instance, a flare was fired at one of the covering helicopters along with small arms fire. Passengers and crew gathered on the deck to try to prevent the insertion team from landing on the deck. Once on the deck, the insertion team ran into a human chain of women stretched across the deck in front of the bridge. Warning shots were fired into the air as well as the use of flash grenades to regain control of the situation. Then two USCG LEDET members from two other ships boarded the *Ibn Khaldoon* to search for contraband, which was found. In the meantime, many of the activists were locked in their cabins for security purposes while the ship was searched. Some minor resistance from crewmembers in the engine room was quickly overcome as well by the SEALS. This was followed by a chain of diplomatic events over where to send the ship so the contraband could be offloaded. It ended up going into the Omani port of Mina Qaboos near Muscat. After several inspections of the ship over two weeks, an agreement was reached between the Omani and Iraqi governments on the results. The *Ibn Khaldoon* finally left port for Iraq on January 12, 1991. In the debriefing that I received from the SEAL commander for the mission, he indicated that he had never seen such hard-looking women who caused him most of the trouble, the Fata widows.

During the maritime interdiction operations, we received word that the President of the United States was going to make a tour of the U.S. forces currently in Saudi Arabia. It was to take place around Thanksgiving. Along with other requirements, he wanted to hold church services somewhere on the Arabian Peninsula. Our allies, the Saudis refused to approve a Christian service for the President of the

United States in their country, so the decision was made to hold the service on the USS *Nassau*, which would be anchored just off the port of Bahrain. This being my second presidential visit, it went much smoother, and the ship made an excellent backdrop. President and Mrs. George H. W. Bush landed on the flight deck of the *Nassau* in an "H-60 White Top," and were welcomed by some 500 sailors and Marines. Mrs. Bush immediately plunged into the crowd as if everyone's grandmother had just arrived.

The troops just ate it up as she posed for pictures for at least 20 minutes. The president went down the flight deck and climbed into an AV-8 Harrier to get briefed on how it worked by one of our pilots. Following that, the religious service was held on the flight deck for the whole crowd. General Schwarzkopf and four senior members of the House and Senate, including Senator Bob Dole (R-KA), were with him. Bush was on the ship for about two hours, and then he departed for the 1st Marine Division in what was to be several stops in the field. It was a good day, and everyone seemed to be happy to think that President and Mrs. Bush would make an effort, especially at Thanksgiving.

Communications with Sue and the kids in Virginia were much better now than there were at any time in the Far East. Letters would come in regularly to the ship during underway replenishments or when we were up in the Gulf. CENTCOM had a well-established mail system that covered the theater, and I believe that all the assigned forces were utilizing it. There were some limited opportunities to use facilities to call home on occasion as well. We would also make tape recordings that were mailed back to the states so the Navy and Marine wives' organization could show everyone what we were doing.

The Navy had a well-established support organization at home, which provided the dependents of the deployed servicemen in the fleet with all kinds of information. They had been doing it for years to keep families informed on what husbands and fathers were doing wherever they were serving at sea. Sue and the other Marine wives associated with the 4th MEB worked together with the Navy wives associated with Amphibious Group 2, all during the long deployment to keep each other informed. I think it worked out pretty well.

CHANGE IN PLANS

General Al Gray, the Commandant of the Marine Corps, had visited all the major Marine units involved in Desert Shield in October to assess needs for additional Marine planners on various staffs as the U.S. build-up continued. Noted early on was the lack of Marine Corps officers on the *Blue Ridge* with amphibious warfare experience. In early January 1991, a small planning staff headed by Major General Jack Sheehan arrived on that ship. I had worked with Jack Sheehan on several occasions and had relieved him as the CG, 4th MEB six months earlier. He was a very capable individual who knew how to get things done quickly and efficiently. In this capacity, he would serve as MARCENT (Forward), the link between the 4th MEB, NAVCENT, and I MEF in Saudi Arabia. It did not take him long to get the planning process moving on the *Blue Ridge*. Four days later, on January 10th, NAVCENT issued an Initiating Directive, which laid out four missions for planning if war broke out in Kuwait. It featured one amphibious assault at Ash Shuaybah, a major raid on Failaka Island, and demonstrations off Failaka and the Al Faw Peninsula (See Map 11). With the receipt of the directive, we could now start detailed planning, which would be reflected in the SEA SOLDIER IV rehearsal in late January 1991.

Negotiations between the United States and Saddam were not really getting anywhere, so President George H. W. Bush ordered Phase II operation to commence. For the 4th MEB, it meant we were to continue detailed planning on the four missions assigned in the Initiating Directive. It also meant the 13th MEU (SOC), then in the Philippines, would be turned around and moved back to the North Arabian Sea to rejoin with the 4th MEB. On the west coast of California, the 5th MEB was being organized to deploy across the Pacific and Indian Ocean to join the amphibious forces already in theater. When this occurred, I immediately opened lines of communication with Brigadier General Pete Rowe, who was the Commanding General 5th MEB. Pete and I had known and served with each other for years, and the relationship was solid between us. He was an easygoing, athletic individual who was very reliable. I now had the opportunity to pass information to him on the conditions in theater as well as personalities of the commanders and relationships with the Navy.

VADM Stan Arthur had recently replaced VADM Mauz as COMUSNAVCENT, and this was a superb move. Stan Arthur was a naval aviator with close to 500 combat missions over North Vietnam during that war. I had first known him when we served in Washington. He was a warfighter and a superb commander who later rose to become the Vice Chief of Naval Operations. Between VADM Arthur and Jack Sheehan, relations with NAVCENT became much easier. Once the 5th MEB was embarked and on the way, we were able to keep each other informed on what was going on both in theater and what Pete was getting from guidance issued from his parent command at Camp Pendleton in California. We were able to start coordinating planning for potential missions that might come up based on the Initiating Directive. He was embarked in the USS *Tarawa* (LHA-1) along with other amphibious ships assigned to Amphibious Group 3 (PHIBGP-3) under the command of RADM Stephen S. Clarey. The transit across the Pacific would take the better part of a month before arriving on station in the North Arabian Sea. How we would be organized in one force had not yet been determined.

OPERATION EASTERN EXIT

In late December 1990, I was in port in Dubai, with about half of my force at various locations in the UAE. The rest of the force was in the MODLOC position off of Masirah. On January 1, 1991, NAVCENT received incoming traffic regarding growing unrest among factions in Somalia that were beginning to present a threat to the U.S. Embassy in Mogadishu as well as other diplomatic compounds in the capital. VADM Arthur told his staff to alert the 4th MEB/PHIBGP- 2 staff even though there had been no tasks emanating out of CENTCOM. This changed shortly when on January 2nd Schwarzkopf sent a message to prepare for a Noncombatant Evacuation Operation (NEO) in Somalia. The U.S. ambassador was demanding some sort of help because of the fighting going on around the embassy. At one point, he requested a drop by airborne troops onto the airfield in the capital to open it for evacuation of the diplomats and other personnel.

Schwarzkopf turned that idea down and then handed the mission to NAVCENT. Extended discussions between NAVCENT and PHIB GP-2 took place regarding how many ships should be tasked with this mission and still have enough available to respond to any surprises in the Gulf. The Navy made the decision to send two amphibious ships, the helicopter carrier USS *Guam* (LPH- 2) and the USS Trenton (LPD-14). Both had Marines and SEALs onboard, but the Guam had 24 CH-46 helicopters while the Trenton carried 2 CH-53E helicopters. Colonel James Doyle, who commanded BSSG-4 for the MEB and was located in the area around Masirah, was designated the commander of the NEO force. He had about half of my Bravo Command group on the Guam from which he could select key officers and enlisted for support.

The two ships set sail for Somalia late on January 2, 1991. Not long after they had been at sea and steaming toward Mogadishu, the U.S. Ambassador sent another message that the fighting had spread to his location and that insurgents were trying to get into the compound. Upon hearing this, Doyle elected to launch the two 53s with SEALs and Marines when they were within range of the Somali capital (See Map 10). The two helicopters took off and flew 450 miles at night across the Arabian Sea, refueling twice from Marine C-130 tankers staged along the way. In one instance, during aerial refueling, a seal broke and sprayed aviation fuel over several passengers in the helicopter. When the two helicopters arrived over the capital, it took some time to find the embassy because they only had old French road maps to go by. Finally, they were guided by some embassy personnel into a LZ inside the walls of the compound. Lieutenant Colonel Willie Oats, the senior NEO commander on the ground, quickly coordinated with the ambassador regarding defensive measures and evacuation plans for the evacuees. The personnel who were sprayed with aviation fuel went into the embassy to take showers and then help form a perimeter along the wall to keep intruders out.

The CH-53s were on the ground for about one hour, loaded up with 61 evacuees, and took off for the ships, which were then some 300 miles at sea. By the time the crews in the 53s arrived back to the Trenton, they were exhausted and would not make another flight. The two ships continued to close on Somalia, and plans were made to use the CH-46s to start flying in to evacuate the remainder of the evacuees. When the last man was lifted out of the embassy grounds, 281 diplomatic and military personnel had been evacuated. That also included nine ambassadors, including the Russian ambassador and his staff. Both ships then steamed back toward Oman and proceeded to Muscat, where the evacuees were placed ashore under the care of the Omani government. The flight crews in the CH-53s, as well as the CH-46s, performed exceptionally well throughout the entire mission. This operation even included a real "Atta boy" from the Secretary of State when it was over. Again, communications were spotty between my locations in the Gulf and Jim Doyle off of Masirah, although they were better between his location and the two CH-53s all through the mission. This would become less of a problem later in the Desert Storm operations when we all came together.

CHAPTER 20
OPERATION DESERT STORM 1991

On January 13, 1991, the 5th MEB, along with the 13th MEU (SOC), arrived in MODLOC off Masirah. Brigadier General Pete Rowe was in the USS *Tarawa,* along with RADM Stephen S Cleary (PHIBGP-3). It was great to see him again as we hashed over several experiences we had in prior years. VADM Arthur had designated the amphibious shipping in both PHIBGP-2 and PHIBGP-3 under RADM La Plante as Commander Task Force 156. He further placed the landing force of 4th MEB, 5th MEB, and 13th MEU (SOC) under me as Commander Task Force 158. What that meant was that I now had 17,095 Marines under my command embarked in 31 amphibious ships. This would be the largest Marine force at sea since the Inchon Landings in Korea in 1950. Compare our numbers to those of the 1st Marine Division that only had 13,000 Marines available for the initial assault on the island of Wolmi Do and the Inchon Harbor. Their numbers grew significantly as the landing force continued to attack inland toward Seoul as part of the U.S. Army's Tenth Corps. Equipment-wise, we now had 2,610 wheeled and track vehicles, and 52 artillery pieces for eight infantry and artillery battalions. The ACE had 139 helicopters, and 25 AV-8 Harriers spread across most of those amphibious ships.

The span of control, considering the ongoing communications issues, was mind-boggling. Pete Rowe and I had made continuous coordinating efforts as soon as it was clear he was on the way, and I would pass the appropriate information to him for planning purposes. When Stan Arthur designated me as the CTF-158 and the three MAGTFs would be operating together, we started immediate planning for a major amphibious rehearsal that would include the entire landing force. This would involve different scenarios based on the Imitating Directive to thoroughly test the plan for strengths and weaknesses.

Two key meetings I had attended began to frame the picture of what was going to happen if a war was declared. The first was with Lieutenant General Walter Boomer, the Commanding General First Marine Expeditionary Force (I MEF) up in northeast Saudi Arabia in late October. This was to discuss plans for potential offensive operations against the Iraqis. During the first meeting, the Commandant, General Al Gray, held court on all the senior commanders regarding what they might have to expect from the Iraqis. He also went over the various plans for any attack that might be ordered by CENTCOM. For me, I had to fly off the ship via helicopter to Masirah, and catch a C-12 aircraft for the two-hour flight to where I MEF was generally located. While the CTF 156/158 technically supported plans for operations on the ground, we did not work for the Marines in Saudi Arabia. We were under the command of NAVCENT, and VADM Arthur, which carefully followed amphibious doctrine established decades earlier. There had to be coordination between NAVCENT and I MEF on any plans involving the amphibious force. The key point of contact for any coordination would be Major General Jack Sheehan on the Blue Ridge. The best thing I received out of this particular meeting was that I now had a clear idea of what I MEF was planning and could coordinate issues with several of my fellow commanders in I MEF.

The second meeting occurred on January 12, 1991, on the flagship USS *Blue Ridge*. VADM Arthur had called in all of his commanders who were either in the Red Sea or in the Persian Gulf. The purpose was to get everyone acquainted with each other's plans as well as go over the current NAVCENT strategies. At this point, we were attempting to interpret information on what was coming out of CENTCOM that would impact our future plans. For me, it was off the *Nassau* via helicopter and into Masirah to catch a C-130 flight to Bahrain. From there, I flew in another helicopter out to the Blue Ridge. This was the first time that I had a chance to meet with all of

Stan's subordinate commanders, which included the carrier battle group commanders as well as the logistics, mine warfare, and surface fire support units that were supporting us.

The plan called for the five carrier battle groups to eventually participate along with the Air Force and allies in the coming air campaign against the Iraqis. They were interested in what the amphibious force was going to be tasked to do, as it could impact on what the Navy could accomplish during the air campaign. There was a very general discussion regarding the potential amphibious assault at Ash Shuaybah, but it was all that was known at the time. I will never forget a comment from RADM Riley Mixon, the commander of Battle Force Yankee, which was comprised of two carrier battle groups in the Red Sea. After hearing about the assault on Ash Shuaybah, he indicated, "we could lose half of our Marines if we had to do that landing." It was a sincere comment made in front of the assembled group of flag officers that has stuck with me ever since. The value in this effort for me was to meet with all of them and establish relations, which, in many cases, lasted long after the war was over in another tour in Washington. Following the meeting, some of us went ashore to a fairly well-known Mexican restaurant in Manama, Bahrain, and had a really good time. Naval aviators can always put on a great party. Unfortunately, this was the first and last time we were ever able to participate in that kind of social gathering once the war started.

SEA SOLDIER IV

The Marine Corps had a long history of successful amphibious operations, primarily in World War II and Korea. There were several small unit landings in Vietnam, usually under the Special Landing Force, as described earlier. By 1990 the concept, as well as the mindset of Marine officers, was we were the so-called experts in this form of warfare, even though there had not been an operation of this potential size since Korea. Any amphibious landing and especially one that might occur in combat, can be a very complicated and hazardous undertaking. You are basically starting with zero combat power ashore and building through the assault an increased amount of combat power that hopefully will overwhelm the opposition. Commanders have to be able to control a wide variety of maneuvers as well as make sure every supporting element is in place, and the mission is thoroughly understood. Rehearsals with everything in place are the only way to ensure the operation can be accomplished, and any problems which crop up are sorted out before the actual landing is executed.

Friction on the battlefield, which can be composed of many things, can intrude on the plan and throw everything off. This is normal. There is an old adage that says, "The plan goes out the window after the first shot is fired," and commanders have to be flexible enough to adjust to the circumstances. This is true of most finely tuned plans. Friction was alive and well all during the planning process in Desert Storm because we did not have a clear idea of what was going to be required. We began the detailed planning between the staff in the 4th and 5th MEBs, along with the two PHIBGPs for the SEA SOLDIER IV rehearsal (See Map 9). This was scheduled for early February 1991. There still was no clear signal that CTF 156 and 158 would be executing a major amphibious landing at Ash Shuaybah or somewhere else along the coastline of Kuwait. I had decided that once the amphibious task force had closed on the rehearsal areas around Ra's al Madrakah, the missions for the major units in the force would be as follows: the 13th MEU (SOC) would conduct any advance force operations which would include demonstrations, raids, beach reconnaissance and targeting any suspected enemy sites for destruction by attack aviation. They would be responsible for preparing the landing area for the major amphibious landing. The 4th MEB would conduct the actual amphibious landing with both the 2nd Marine Regiment and the 5th Marine Regiment out of the 5th MEB abreast. This would feature both surface and helicopter-borne assaults simultaneously for the landing and movement inland against assigned objectives with about 15,000 troops. The helicopter assault consisted of lifting three infantry battalions by helicopter from nine different ships to objectives inland in what was the largest lift of its kind in several years.

We planned for extensive simulated close air support for the assault waves moving through the water and on the beaches and inland. The planners had also managed to get some Navy aircraft support for the rehearsal from one of two carrier battle groups that were moving through the North Arabian Sea on the way to the Persian Gulf. After the landing was terminated, all units were to stand down and conduct their own training in assigned areas to sort out problems that may have occurred during the landing. For the 5th Marines, who had been at sea for most of a month, that meant getting their troops acclimated to the intense heat generated in the areas behind the beaches. There was another planned period where vehicles would be brought ashore and maintained on the beach before back loading to the ships began.

One other major event was the construction of a large sand table in from the landing beaches that replicated Ash Shuaybah so the commanders could go over the landing plan for this attack if it was ordered. In the first part of the rehearsal, the command-and-control of the maneuver from ship-to-shore would be done with the 4th MEB during daylight and darkness. The 5th MEB was to act as an alternate command group afloat and monitor and follow the communications nets as well as the maneuvers ashore. When the landing was terminated, then 5th MEB would take over training for its organic units ashore. I wanted to give Pete Rowe a chance to test his command-and-control, so three or four days later, he was directed to conduct an amphibious tactical withdrawal of both the 2nd and 5th Marine Regiments from the beaches and back to the ships under cover of darkness. The 4th MEB would act as the alternate command group in that situation and monitor communications and the flow of men and material via helicopter and surface means. With everything back onboard the ships, detailed lessons-learned sessions were held at several levels in each MEB to correct perceived problems. On balance, this rehearsal went as well as could be expected, although both MEBs and the 13th MEU (SOC) were well versed in the theory and practice of amphibious operations. Even with a high level of expertise, there are so many moving parts in an operation like this practice is absolutely vital, and success is not guaranteed.

We did not have a very high impression of the Iraqis, but they had much more equipment than we did, and any fight would be on their home turf. Intelligence was so bad in many respects I had little knowledge of the quality of the Iraqi military leadership. I never did get a decent analysis on individual Iraqi commanders at the division or corps level whom we might have to face if an amphibious landing was ordered. Everyone was aware of their Republican Guard, but they proved to be minimally effective when the war did start.

One last thing we did was another MED/DENTCAP for the Omanis during this rehearsal in an area adjacent to the landing beaches. Business was brisk again, and the reports back from the doctors who participated were it had been another success. Following this rehearsal and with all personnel and equipment back on board, the ships of the amphibious force moved back out to sea. Sea Soldier IV was the last of five major amphibious rehearsal landings conducted by the 4th MEB while afloat before the commencement of hostilities in Kuwait.

THE PLANS BASED ON THE INITIATING DIRECTIVE

The amphibious assault at Ash Shuaybah: This objective was located about halfway up the Kuwaiti coast between the Saudi Arabian border and Kuwait City. (See Map 11). It was the site of one of the largest petrochemical complexes in that part of the world, with offshore wells dotting the ocean along the coast. The complex itself consisted of several processing facilities for oil and gas, but the really dangerous piece was the area had two large Liquid Natural Gas (LNG) tanks that dominated everything else. If one of them blew up, the result would be catastrophic damage for miles around the complex. Also, there were several piers there where tankers could pull in and tie up while taking on oil or other chemicals. The terrain that followed the coastline north from this complex was flat desert and dotted with high-rise apartments belonging to Kuwaiti citizens. About 1.5 miles inland, a large field of oil pipelines ran north to south and paralleled the coastline, with pipelines diverting to the east to the petrochemical complex. Initially, I MEF had wanted to establish a resupply point (Logistics over the Shore, or LOTS) around the Ash Shuaybah area where its vehicles could stop and refuel and re-equip in their drive north toward Kuwait City. This was what drove this objective in the beginning.

Little information had been forthcoming until the detailed planning began, and what we saw was not convincing. The potential location for the LOTs site was in the Arab JFC-E zone on the coast and not in the MEF zone on the ground. While most of the Kuwaiti citizens had fled south into Saudi Arabia, the Iraqis had fortified the clusters of high-rise buildings for small arms and observation purposes, which overlooked the beaches. There was no depth for maneuvering in the landing area, as the surface force and its vehicles would run into the aforementioned pipelines behind the housing areas. Command-and-control of the air would have been a major problem due to conflicting boundaries on the ground as well as responsibility for the various sectors over the battlefield.

After studying this for some time, I made the decision that if we were directed to land and take the petrochemical complex, we would land well north of the facility, and then attack south to link up with I MEF or Arab forces coming up the coast. I wanted to isolate the petrochemical complex if possible, as well as the small town that surrounded that facility, but we would not land at Ash Shuaybah. We would establish the LOTS site at some point along the beach to support I MEF's plan. It was about this time we began getting reports from the Kuwaiti resistance that the Iraqis were wiring the key components of the complex for demolition should an attack occur.

The area selected for the landing was north of Ash Shuaybah at a location called al-Fintas, which sat right on the beach (See Map 11). From there it was a short distance to the Kuwait International Airport. One of the critical reasons for the site selection was the hydrography and beach gradients right off the shoreline. All of our tanks were pre-boated in Landing Craft Utility (LCU) connectors. They could only get in close enough to the beach, depending on the gradients of the sand under the water. This was the only area along the entire Kuwaiti coastline south of Kuwait City, where the gradients would support the connectors in getting close to the beach to discharge the tanks and other tracked vehicles. None of this was a problem for the LCACs, but the LCUs were showstoppers if they could not discharge the tanks and other tracked vehicles where they would be needed.

The Iraqis had placed some beach obstacles in front of the high-rise complexes, but they did not seem to be very formidable to our planners. Mines were another issue, not only in the water but also along the beaches. The mine issue was one of the greatest intelligence failures during the war, and I will elaborate on this a little later. SEALs belonging to CENTCOM approached the landing area in small boats and carried out a careful reconnaissance of the beaches, but neither Bat LaPlante nor I ever saw the results of their effort. This would have left us blind on what to expect in the shallow water approaches to the beaches. To address this problem, mine plows were hastily welded to the front ends of some of the AAVs in the force, and they would lead the surface assault ashore. After doing a thorough analysis of the potential resistance along the beaches, I recommended to VADM Arthur that if we were ordered to conduct the assault, I planned to use naval gunfire from the battleships *Wisconsin* and *Missouri*, along with other ships to level the area in the LZ "one grid square at a time." He supported my recommendation, although Schwarzkopf disagreed with it later in the decision cycle. He did not "want to destroy the country to save it."

The helicopter-borne assault was another matter. The purpose of using helicopters was to outmaneuver the opposition and transport the troops deep into the landing area, hopefully behind any enemy resistance. I had mentioned earlier that there was no depth to the landing area we were to attack, which basically negated any advantage a helicopter-borne assault would bring to the table. The aviation and coalition air control issues over the battlespace were a jumble, and unless we were going to be allowed to maneuver in someone else's assigned space, which was not likely to happen, there would be no advantage to conducting such a maneuver. The end result was we would be forced to land the helicopter-borne unit inside the lodgment that had been created by the surface assault to build up the proper level of combat power ashore. If we were able to accomplish this, then the Marines in Regimental Landing Team (RLT-2) would land on the left, then turn and attack south toward the complex at Ash Shuaybah to isolate it. The Marines in the RLT-5 would land on the right and establish blocking positions along the main highway and the coast to deal with any Iraqi attacks coming south out of Kuwait City. This then was the generic plan which had been rehearsed in SEA SOLDIER IV. In reality, there was really only one location where an amphibious landing could be conducted, whereby it could have an impact on the CENTCOM campaign. That area was the Al Faw Peninsula.

THE FAYLAKAH ISLAND RAID

By the time that the Initiating Directive was issued by NAVCENT, the Iraqis had given some thought as to where the Marines might land along the Saudi and Kuwait coastline. The result was they started to build up forces along a line that ran from Bubiyan Island all the way south to the Saudi border. When the media began reporting that the amphibious force was actively engaged in exercises in Oman and elsewhere in preparation for amphibious landings, the Iraqis continued to build up their forces, especially in the Kuwait City area. Continuous reporting showed the film clips like those Katie Couric had televised back in October on the *Nassau* certainly fueled their concerns.

Over time the Iraqis had somewhere around six divisions deployed either along the coast of Kuwait or back in the Kuwait City area, which could move quickly toward the coast to try to disrupt an amphibious landing. This defensive build-up did not include the Iraqi Republican Guard divisions that were positioned further north around Basra and the Rumaila Oil Fields as a strategic reserve. At the time, part of the CENTCOM plan was to make the Iraqis think the Marines would conduct an amphibious landing somewhere between Ash Shuaybah and Kuwait City. All the indications were the Iraqis were taking the bait. This was done in part to distract the Iraqis from deploying against the Army's 7th Corps and the XVIIIth Airborne Corp formations that were moving into place out in the western desert with the mission of destroying the Iraqi Republican Guard in one great "left hook." If CENTCOM ruled against the major amphibious landing, then a raid against Faylakah Island would look like the Marines were still coming but were establishing a base on the island to support further operations into Kuwait.

Faylakah Island belonged to Kuwait and was located about 20 miles off the coast from Kuwait City. The history of the island goes back to at least 2000 BC when it was occupied by Mesopotamians. There is evidence the island was also occupied by Babylonian kings for a period, then followed by the Greeks. Several ancient sites have been uncovered in the north of the island by archaeologists over time, and that was going on when the island was occupied by the Iraqis. They depopulated the island's 2,000 residents and sent them all to the mainland. The Iraqi military then planted mines along some of the beaches and used buildings for target practice. Several archaeological sites on the north end of the island were off-limits to any airborne attacks by allied aircraft.

VADM Arthur proposed we stage a large raid on the island to continue the deception the Marines were going to land somewhere along the coast, which would continue to hold Iraqi units in place around Kuwait City. We developed a plan which called for a surface landing at night using 12 LCACs carrying eight tanks and 35 LAVs in two waves on the southwest corner of the island and then move north for a couple of miles and stop. The LCAC maneuver would rely on speed of the air-cushioned vehicles to get to the shore quickly to achieve the element of surprise. A helicopter-borne force of battalion size would land behind the surface units and link up. This would be supported by an artillery raid by 13th MEU (SOC) on the small island of Ahah, south of Faylakah. Some M-198 155mm cannons would be emplaced there to support the troops on Faylakah along with aircraft flying from one of the carriers in the central Gulf. The plan was for the raid force to stay on the island for a few hours to give the Iraqis the impression we were going to take the island as a base for operations against the Kuwaiti coast. The force would then withdraw under cover of darkness.

Using carrier air in support of this raid got Schwarzkopf's attention. He did not want to detract from the ongoing air campaign, which was pummeling the Iraqis all over Kuwait. We were summoned to his headquarters in Riyadh to brief him on the concept. I had not been in the headquarters for the entire campaign, which was also the location of the Saudi Prince in charge of the Arab forces in the field. I had flown in from Masirah to Bahrain to meet with Stan Arthur to go over both the plan and the brief. From there, we flew to Riyadh to meet with General Schwarzkopf. His headquarters was underground, and he was surrounded by armed guards when we met him. He had a "volcanic personality" that was well known within the force. One observer indicated that you could see it developing if something was not going according to plan in the numerous staff meetings in his bunker. At some point, he would explode and berate his staff for whatever reason. To be fair, despite whatever occurred with his staff, he generally let his commanders do what was necessary with a minimum of interference.

We moved to his underground briefing room while his armed guards stayed outside. The briefing went reasonably well. Stan Arthur assured him they would dedicate only one carrier air wing to the operation, and that would leave three more on call to in the Persian Gulf to support the CENTCOM air campaign. Schwarzkopf indicated to me he thought we should do the raid, but be ready to execute it on short order. He also said he was having trouble with Washington regarding amphibious plans. I flew back to the *Nassau,* and we refined the plan for the raid. It was now early February, and most of the forces were in place, although the amphibious task force was still in the vicinity of Masirah. It looked like the raid would be executed around 22 February 1991.

When the orders came down to form up and begin movement toward the Persian Gulf, the size of the amphibious task force had now climbed to 34 ships, as two combat loaded Maritime Preposition Force (MPF) ships had been added to the force. The two MPF ships represented another first for Lieutenant Colonel Gary Collenborne, one of the best logisticians in the Marine Corps. He and his staff had combat loaded the MEB AFOE in the two huge MPF ships that would sail together with the amphibs. At the time, the Marine Corps had three MPF squadrons, each comprised of 4-5 ships with enough equipment and supplies for a MEB for 30 days. When the conflict started, the MPF squadron stationed at Diego Garcia moved immediately to support the 7th MEB as it flowed into Saudi Arabia. Following unloading, the empty ships were placed in a common user pool. Our two ships came from that pool. Most of the cargo that had belonged to the 4th MEB and transported to theater in the five RO-ROs in September had been reorganized following planned landings in the Gulf. It was stored in such a manner that we could gain easy access to what might be needed once the troops were on the ground and maneuvering. The loading and actual movement of the two ships with the amphibious force in a very short period was a masterful piece of planning and execution. Following this deployment, Gary went on to a successful career, was promoted to colonel, and eventually retired. He now lives near Boise, Idaho.

The movement toward the Straits of Hormuz was to be a show of force in broad daylight. It represented one very long line of 34 ships that steamed up into the Gulf of Oman, through the Straits of Hormuz and into the southern Persian Gulf. This got the Iranians' attention, and they sent out a couple of their small frigates that harassed the convoy by darting in and out between our ships. This was not much more than a minor distraction, which continued until the amphibious ships had cleared the Straits and moved past some of the Iranian Islands and into the southern Persian Gulf.

The Coalition Air Campaign against Iraq had been going on for some time before the 4th MEB flowed into the Persian Gulf. As the decision to commence the ground war approached, CENTCOM had shifted the priorities for targets from Baghdad to a variety of targets that were in front of the Army and Marine forces on the ground. Several of the amphibious ships led by the *Nassau* had moved up into the central Gulf, although she was the only ship that moved further north to get within range of Kuwait City and areas beyond the city. NAVCENT granted us permission to get our Harriers into the campaign against various targets in front of I MEF. After thorough briefings along with coordination with the Joint Force Air Component Commander (JFACC), we launched the first flights against Iraqi targets on February 20. This was the first time that Harrier jets had ever been launched on combat missions from an amphibious assault ship.

When this activity started, VMA-331 (the Bumble Bees) had 19 Harriers on the *Nassau,* and the plan was to support the daily sortie rates with a 12-plane base up and ready to go. During eight days, the Harriers were in action, the sortie rates grew from 19 on the first day to 47 out of 59 planned on the last day of the effort when the ground war shut down. The 12 sorties that did not get off that day were canceled due to weather aborts. At that time, the ship was slowly cruising through fog, smoke, and oil-coated waters, thanks to the Iraqis blowing of wellheads off the coast. We did suffer one fatality in our part of the air campaign when we had a Harrier shot down over escaping Iraqi columns north of Kuwait City. After an extensive search, the wreckage was found along with the remains of the pilot.

This many Harriers on an amphibious ship had been an irritant to the Navy since we came into the Gulf. At one point, NAVCENT wanted to place all of our AV-8s ashore. The idea failed because there was not enough space at any airfield to accommodate 19 more aircraft. The other reason was all the squadron's maintenance capability was on the *Nassau*. We were not trying to compete with or provide a threat to the carriers, but some people did not want anything to dim the activities of the aircraft carriers. In actuality, we achieved better cycle times with the Harriers than the Navy could achieve with the F-18s or even the F-14s on one carrier, and that led to much better sortie generation rates for combat missions. Toward the end of the air campaign, we were getting a 45-minute turnaround rate with the AV-8s. What does this mean to a layman? A jet would come back from a mission and set down on the flight deck. The pilot would go off to debrief the mission to the staff. The deck crew went right to work to refuel the plane, fill its distilled water tank used for a cooling effect on its turbofan, and then load the plane with ordnance, followed by a systems check. A new pilot would get in the jet, run his checks, and taxi out for take-off. This was a large political issue within the Navy, but one that needed to be explained to see what that little "jump jet" could do at the time.

What I have previously mentioned was the upside thanks to the superb flight deck crews on the *Nassau*. The downside was you would wear out the pilots at that pace before long unless you had several more aviators to pick up the slack. The second point was the LHA did not have adequate magazine space to accommodate that kind of sustained flight operations with bombs and other kinds of ordnance. Through the middle of the eight-day effort, the ship had to go off-line to replenish ordnance, primarily bombs. Finally, the ship did not have numerous ordnance personnel as part of the ship's company. We had no difficulties getting Marines to volunteer to assist the ordnance personnel with readying and loading bombs. In fact, we had more volunteers than were needed, and they even got to decorate the bombs with various messages for the Iraqis. Again, showing the magnificence spirit of the sailors and Marines.

THE MINE ISSUE

There were several reasons for the abysmal performance for the mine-hunting effort in the Persian Gulf. At the CENTCOM level, Schwarzkopf would not let a mine-hunting activity take place north of the Saudi border for fear of starting the war early. Secondly, the Navy believed that there were only drifting mines in the water that had been placed haphazardly by Iraqi mine layers. They figured that the mines might move with the currents in the Gulf, which flow counter-clockwise along the coast. Third, the belief was that mines had probably been laid in close to the shoreline, which was incorrect.

Another reason was that mine-hunting in the Navy had generally taken a back seat to everything else in the programmatic wars that go on in the Pentagon over funding. There was nothing wrong with the sailors in that community, but there was a distinct lack of training and equipment needed to do the job. I will never forget the sight of a lone sailor sitting on a high-back chair on the bow of his ship with a helmet, flak jacket, and binoculars, looking for mines as we sailed by. Now and then, a floating mine would be detected out in the Gulf that would get everybody's attention.

In late January, the USS *Tripoli* (LPH-10) helicopter carrier was pulled out of PHIBGRP 3 with its embarked Marines placed elsewhere and designated as a mine-hunting command ship. She had embarked Navy MH-53 heavy minesweeping helicopters on board and was cruising slowly in waters some distance off of Kuwait City. Early on the morning of February 18th, she hit a moored contact mine in Iraqi minefield number 4 they did not know was there.

Damage to the ship included a 16- by 20-foot hole in the hull below the waterline with some flooding in the forward compartments. The damage control efforts on the part of the crew eventually stopped it. Fortunately, there were no fatalities.

Four hours later, the USS *Princeton*, a billion-dollar AEGIS cruiser on lookout for enemy aircraft or Silkworm missiles fired from positions along the coast, activated a bottom influence mine. It was later identified as the Iraqi mine line 7, another mined area they did not know was there. Shortly after the first blast, there was another bottom mine that had a sympathetic detonation about 300 yards from the ship. The result of the two blasts was damage to the ship's superstructure and jammed rudders, in addition to knocking out radar and missile systems. Fortunately, some injuries among the crew did not include any fatalities. After an assessment of the damage to the *Tripoli*, she was pulled off the line and sent to a dry dock in Dubai for repairs.

NAVCENT then made the decision to take the USS *New Orleans* (LPH-11) out of PHIB GRP-3, remove the Marines and their equipment to other ships, and embark the MH-53 minesweeping helicopters to continue the mission. All of this occurred as a result of the critical failure of intelligence at various levels to adequately address the mine issue. The conventional thought was that any mines would be found close to the shoreline as an impediment to any amphibious landing. That was incorrect, as the Iraqis had constructed ten minefields in two belts, which extended as far as 30 miles out to sea. The outer belt curved in an arc from a position south of the Al Faw Peninsula to the Saudi-Kuwait border. In reality, they had planted over 1,000 mines of various types, although many were found after the war to be deployed improperly.

All of this had an immediate impact on the Marines. Stan Arthur requested we reduce the size of the planned raid on Faylakah Island. We had planned to follow the cleared lane that had been opened by the MCM force between 16 and 20 February. This generally followed a route from just north on the Ad Dorra oil field some 6 miles past Kubbar Island to the cleared battleship fire support area south of Faylakah Island. Following some adjustments to the plan, we waited to see what was going to happen next. Early in the evening on 22 February, I was on the flag bridge of the Nassau monitoring message traffic. Bob Mauskapf came up to inform me that he was getting the word they were not going to employ the MEB in any amphibious raid into Faylakah Island. The way events had been progressing, I was not really surprised.

Early on the morning of February 24, the ground war began in the I MEF and JFCE sectors. Both forces advanced rapidly once they had broken through the Iraqi mine barriers stretched across southern Kuwait. NAVCENT requested that we stage a series of helicopter-borne demonstrations against the coastline of Kuwait, starting the night of the 25th. The first one would be against Ash Shuaybah with a force of ten CH- 46 helicopters from the 4th MEB equipped with sound gear to get the Iraqis thinking the amphibious force was on the way. This demonstration was launched from 50 miles at sea with the helicopters flying on night-vision goggles at 200 feet above the water to a point about a mile offshore, where they abruptly turned around and headed out to sea. This caused the Iraqis to respond by firing two Silkworm sea-skimming missiles at the force, one of which crashed into the sea while the second one was shot down by a British cruiser on patrol off the coast.

The second demonstration was launched on the night of February 26 from 72 miles at sea and included a force of 18 CH-46 and CH-53s from the 4th MEB. The target this time was Bubiyan Island, which was located north of Kuwait Bay. They were escorted by Navy A-6 and EA-6B aircraft from one of the carriers in the central Gulf. As the force approached the Bubiyan coast, Iraqi radars began to paint the helicopters, and there was some sporadic air defense fire that did not hit any of the aircraft. Again, this force was at a low level over the water and made gun runs on the coast before turning around and heading out to sea. The Navy aircraft went after the Iraqi fires, but all aircraft returned to the ships without any problems.

The final demonstration also took place the night of February 26th, when six UH1N helicopters from the 4th MEB took off from the *Nassau* and flew 60 miles toward Faylakah Island, and again low over the water. As they approached the coast of the island, all of them opened up with machine-gun fire and rockets at targets on the ground before turning around and flying back out to sea. I remember being on the flag bridge of the *Nassau* early that morning when they returned to the ship. The crews seemed to be happy at getting into a small part of the action. From the reaction of Iraqis on the coast, these demonstrations helped pin some of their units in place around Kuwait City until it was too late to escape.

THE END OF HOSTILITIES

The ground war for the Marines in I MEF in Kuwait was pretty much over by February 28th. Operations involving CTF-158 had consisted of detaching the 5th MEB so that they could flow ashore and act as the reserve for I MEF. The 13th MEU (SOC) was tasked to go into Faylakah Island and accept the surrender of the Iraqi Marine Brigade stationed there. Then the Iraqi POWs had to be processed and put on board ships for transfer to camps on the mainland. When that was completed, the MEU began the long journey home to California. The 4th MEB gradually moved south to ports in Dubai and Abu Dhabi in the United Arab Emirates to prepare for the movement back to the states.

The 4th MEB and PHIPGRP-2 began the transit out of the Persian Gulf in early March 1991. The cruise across the North Arabian Sea was uneventful until we approached the Gulf of Aden. We were alerted to the possibility that another NEO might be necessary due to the fighting in Addis Ababa, the capital of Ethiopia. Contingency planning began immediately as we entered the Bab el Mandeb off of Yemen. If we had to execute this one, the distance from the ship to the capital to get embassy personnel could only be covered by the CH-53s in MAG 40. From there, the plan was to fly the evacuees to the airfield in Djibouti for further transfer by CH-46s out to the ships that were cruising off the coast. The plan brought back the same issue of distance we had seen with the NEO into Somalia in January.

The evacuation plan was set and ready to go, but we received word to stand down as the situation had changed for the better in Addis Ababa. This had been a good opportunity to go over detailed plans in preparation for just such an operation if something else came up. We were still conducting air operations with the Harriers as we entered into the southern end of the Red Sea when one of the Harriers was having trouble getting back on the flight deck of the *Nassau*. After numerous attempts at landing on the deck, the plane gave out, and the pilot ejected from the aircraft just before it went into the water. The ship that was functioning as the plane guard behind the Nassau for situations like this put a small boat into the water and rescued the pilot. He was not seriously injured, but the incident became the last of the flight operations until the squadron flew off the ship for Cherry Point at the end of the deployment.

The rest of cruise up through the Red Sea and the Suez Canal was uneventful and somewhat relaxing for everyone on board the amphibious ships. The next challenge was provided by our Department of Agriculture. There was a long-standing regulation where all vehicles operating on the ground in the Middle East or anywhere else must be washed down to get rid of any foreign material or parasites that might be on the vehicles. This comes before they can be admitted back into the United States. In the 4th MEB, we had a little over 2,792 tracked and wheeled vehicles embarked in the amphibious ships that would have to be washed down and inspected before they were put back on the ships.

The first issue was: where could a force of this size conduct the wash downs? The solution was to split the Amphibious Task Force and send half of the ships to an Israeli shipyard near Haifa, and the other half of the force to the naval station in Rota, Spain. This I recall was about a four-day effort in Haifa, where we were able to use dry docks in the Israeli shipyard to finish the job. The same wash down procedures would be utilized as well upon the arrival of our ships in Rota, although dry docks were not available there. This was time well spent for me as I had the opportunity to talk to the troops on the ships there as well as see in little of the Israeli countryside.

The USO in Haifa was fabulous, and they treated our sailors and Marines with overwhelming support and activities. The Israeli woman who ran the USO there was known as Rosie to everyone. The Navy had adopted her as the "mother of the Sixth Fleet," and the description was well deserved. I had a car, so I went out to see the old Roman ruins in Tiberius and later had dinner at a hotel on the shores of the Sea of Galilee. It was a beautiful night with a full moon over the Golan Heights, the scene of numerous battles between the Israelis and the Syrians, which still happen on occasion today.

I also visited another site while there in Haifa: Caesarea on the coast. Here there was an old Crusader fort as well as a small Roman Coliseum near an excavated site of Roman baths, right on the beach. It was hard to visualize just what had gone on there over the centuries, and it did whet my appetite to visit and see more. Then it was back to the *Nassau* and preparations for continuing the cruise across the Mediterranean to Rota. We spent two days in Rota transferring some of our stocks to another MEU (SOC) unit. They were currently sitting in Palma de Mojica, waiting to continue east into the Mediterranean. Leaving Rota, we spent a wild day of plunging seas in the Bay of Biscay on the first day out. The weather was clear, but the winds had really stirred up the sea. *Nassau* was plunging through swells so huge that we were taking water over the bow of the ship. The flight deck was 75 feet above the waterline, but we were getting water over the forward portion of the flight deck on occasion. Once out of the Bay of Biscay, the rest of the cruise across the Atlantic was uneventful.

The Navy had a great program for the dependents of sailors and Marines on the *Nassau* as well as on other ships. After we had approached the North Carolina coast, and all the Harriers and helicopters had left the ship for home bases at New River and Cherry Point, we proceeded up the coast to Morehead City. There we picked up male dependents for a "Tiger Cruise." In this instance, male dependents would be allowed to come on board and sail with the ship overnight and into the harbor at Norfolk the next day. The ship would be met by all the families of embarked sailors and Marines, including Sue and Anne. TJ and other kids had come by bus to the landing site near Morehead City, where I met him. Then we all went by LCU back out to the *Nassau*, which was standing off the coast. It was a fun night as the ship moved slowly along the coast and into the harbor the next morning. It was pouring rain by the time we tied up at the pier in Norfolk; everybody was soaked. That did not dampen the spirits of the homecoming after over eight months at sea. In the final analysis, this was the largest Marine force to be deployed at sea for this length of time in USMC history.

CHAPTER 21

AMPHIBIOUS FORCES IN THE 21ST CENTURY

I indicated earlier there was really only one location where an amphibious landing of this size could have taken place that would have had the potential to strategically impact the Iraqis. That place was the Al Faw Peninsula at the northern end of the Gulf. It was protected by a small brigade of Iraqis sitting in the village of Al Faw at the southern tip of the peninsula. Beyond the village, the terrain was wide open for 40 miles north and threatened Basrah. It featured the Iraqi naval base Umm Qasr on the waterway on the west side of the peninsula as well as the port of Az Zubayr. The peninsula was protected on the east side by the Shatt Al-Arab waterway, which ran along the Iranian border. This option had been discussed with Lieutenant General Walter Boomer, CG, I MEF in October 1990. When this option was mentioned to General Schwarzkopf later, he did not seem interested at the time.

Studies that we conducted on this location showed that the Iraqis had constructed three breakwaters out into the main channel of the waterway to Umm Qasr. They were apparently used for bringing supplies into the peninsula, and they made excellent points for resupply of our units either by LCACs or LCU's. The seaward approaches to Al Faw were good, although the mine issue could have raised itself again. However, we knew Iraqi ships that had been cleared in the MIF operations had passed up through the middle of the Gulf and into this waterway on the way to the port. This indicated there was a clear channel into the waterway. Navigational charts showed the amphibious ships would probably have to stand off some distance from the tip of the Al Faw due to water depths and clusters of offshore oil rigs. The early planning, we did called for movement via LCAC and LCU's up that channel to the breakwaters, landing there while being supported by helicopter-borne forces inland.

This would have provided an excellent opportunity to utilize maneuver warfare principles that the Corps had been refining over the previous ten years. One of the key components of maneuver warfare doctrine is to locate weaknesses in enemy terrain or forces and move to exploit the weaknesses, utilizing fast-moving units either inserted by air or from the sea or both. That was certainly the picture we saw in the planning for just such an operation. It would have been a supporting attack to the main CENTCOM effort, and a feint to fix Republican Guard positions in the vicinity of Basrah. It was ironic that the Commandant of the Marine Corps had ordered a plan that could be used for reinforcing a landing behind the 4th MEB utilizing units moving from Saudi Arabia. This was going on by select staff at Quantico and was kept securely under wraps. I never saw that plan either and only heard about it after we arrived back in the states.

There were a variety of reasons beyond political service ramifications in Washington why such an operation did not take place. It was not needed because the Iraqis folded very quickly. The main attack was conducted in the desert by the Marines in I MEF and two Army Corps that quickly overwhelmed the Iraqi army. The threat of the amphibious landing was enough to freeze several Iraqi divisions along the coast of Kuwait long enough to enable I MEF to cut off and trap those units before they could escape. These were all good and legitimate reasons; however, the bottom line is that commanders both in the Marines and especially the Navy should consider using a force of this size for strategic purposes in the future. Throwing the other side off balance through maneuver from the sea at weak points in their defenses, and not outmoded amphibious assaults like Ash Shuaybah, is the way to go. This mindset has been very hard to overcome, and not having to attempt anything near this size since Inchon in 1950, has not helped the cause to change thinking, and especially as we enter into the missile age.

In 1950, it was General Douglas Mac Arthur who drove the concept of landing at Inchon completely behind the North Korean army in the south, and it was a pattern that he followed in his campaign in the Southwest Pacific, hopscotching along the coast of New Guinea in World War II. Nobody in the Navy, Army, and some of the Marines thought it could be done at Inchon, and few of the Marines ever knew about the potential option at the Al Faw.

One of the most impressive stories that came out of Desert Shield and Desert Storm was the logistics effort. I have already mentioned the Navy's Combat Logistics Force operations in the Atlantic, Mediterranean, and Persian Gulf. Once it got organized for supporting not just one carrier battle group but the entire fleet of ships in the theater, the results were outstanding. On the Marine side of this story are the Maritime Preposition Force ships. All three of the MPF squadrons would periodically move to different locations, always ready to close on location in support of amphibious operations or in a humanitarian mission. The one squadron of which was stationed at Diego Garcia in the Indian Ocean had a full load of equipment for a Marine Expeditionary Brigade. This squadron immediately deployed for the Persian Gulf to support the 7th MEB that was flowing into Saudi Arabia by air from 29 Palms in California.

In addition, it supported the Ready Brigade from the 82nd Airborne Division until its Army Theater logistics units came into the country. The initial deployment of the PHIBGP-2 and the 4th MEB was marked by the shortage of ships and no AFOE ships with equipment and 30 days of supplies for the MEB. That came in later with the five commercial RO-ROs that were down loaded in al-Jubail. This kind of arrangement will probably be needed again if there is ever the need to field a force of this size for a contingency. The airhead that was established at Masirah early in the deployment worked reasonably well, as we used our CH-46 helicopters to fly in and pick up supplies that had been flown in by the Air Force. Doctrine would tell you that green helicopters were not supposed to be used for that kind of activity, as it was the Navy's responsibility. When it came down to sustaining the Amphibious Task Force, I made the decision to use our helicopters. The end result of that was my readiness rating for our CH-46s, took a downward plunge, which got some attention in Washington. We continued that process until the Navy's Combat Logistics Force came on line. Some empty MPF ships were placed in a common user pool to be used as needed. The example of initiative and perseverance by Gary Collenborne and his staff in getting two of the empty RO-RO ships, and organizing the AFOE for the MEB, was the first time in history that it had been done.

Supporting the ACE was another major logistics effort, as we had to keep the helicopters and jets at sustainable readiness rates in case we were tasked with a mission. The ACE accumulated a total of 12,000 flight hours, 3,051 of which were posted by the Harriers while the rest were generated by the combined force of the embarked helicopters during the eight months at sea. As the commander of the 4th MEB during this deployment for combat, I expected to spend about 60 percent of my time with logistics. In reality, it was closer to 80 percent, due in part to the ACE and flying requirements. Someone once said that a wise commander is one who pays attention to logistics over operations. I would not use the term "wise commander" in my case, because it was a requirement to make sure that we were as sustained as possible across the force. There really was no other choice considering the circumstances.

The term Amphibious Power Projection is much more in tune with how amphibious tactics and strategy will work today and in the future. It covers so many options that the commander of a MAGTF will have to execute his mission. I believe the term "amphibious assault" is outmoded and no longer describes the tremendous capability that exists in the modern amphibious force for projecting power from the sea. The term in its original context should be ruled out of the dialog to get young officers coming up to think more broadly about how they will utilize high-speed maneuver from the sea, either by air or surface means, to achieve their objectives.

Robotic systems and drones will play significant roles in the future, both in ISR above and below the sea. Drone swarms may become preferred methods for tactical strike missions against enemy targets, thereby relieving the pressure on very expensive fixed-wing aircraft. Cyber and other forms of electronic warfare for deception purposes will also come into their own and will be critical as a major tool for supporting maneuvering forces coming from the sea. As we get deeper into the modern missile age, the threat of "hypersonic missiles, "cruise missiles," as well as tactical lasers, will be game-changers if we don't develop adequate defense systems. Ships like carriers can no longer hide at sea and will be vulnerable. The same comment applies to big-deck amphibious ships traveling as part of a MEU or something larger. New thinking regarding different force constructs, along with technological innovations that will support high-speed maneuvers from the sea against enemy missile threats, will be absolutely critical in order to avoid being targeted.

Amphibious power projection in the future will have to rely on the upgraded LCAC, the MV-22, and, eventually, the CH-53K helicopter. The LCAC, depending on loads and sea states, can achieve speeds in excess of 70 knots per hour on the surface of the sea. The Amphibious Combat Vehicle (ACV) is a 30-ton wheeled vehicle that swims at seven knots in the water or 65 miles per hour on land. It can carry a squad of Marines plus a crew of three. The ACV will soon be fielded to Marine units and will complement the speed and maneuverability of the LCAC. This could provide commanders with dispersed highly mobile formations for maneuver on land.

Clearly, there is a hard requirement for some sort of ground mobile missile system initially positioned on ships at sea. After engaging targets, it could be moved ashore and provide an extended range of fire support for maneuver units. Such a capability mounted on wheeled or tracked vehicles that can move with the formations ashore will provide depth on the battlefield. This could allow for fewer, highly mobile formations on the ground while disrupting and destroying enemy units standing in the way. In the missile age coming in the future, speed, combined arms, and rapid execution of the mission will be critical for any commander if he is to avoid being targeted. If we ever get involved in a conflict where long-range missile attacks can be expected, the traditional methods of old for amphibious landings will have to change. That has become a critical requirement to solve for Marine leadership in the future.

Whether there will ever be an opportunity to field an amphibious force, the size of what became CTF 158 remains to be seen. That will probably depend on the rise of any potential peer competitor somewhere in the world, and the prevailing enemy systems at the time. Today the Navy only has half the number of amphibious ships in service compared to in 1990-1991. The priorities for shipbuilding within the U.S. Navy, coupled with the costs of modern ships across the fleet, indicate no sign there will be a major amphibious shipbuilding program in the foreseeable future. There is no question there is a requirement for a modern and flexible amphibious force sailing as an integral part of the U.S. Navy in the various oceans of the world. Anything short of a major conflict with a peer competitor will have to be mitigated with a balanced fleet approach. The amount of chaos caused by man or as a result of severe weather that exists around the globe dictates the demand for sea-based amphibious forces that are ready to move and can respond quickly to meet a crisis. No other organization exists that can carry out such missions on short notice.

CHAPTER 22

THE WORLD OF COMMUNICATIONS AND INTELLIGENCE

Our return to Little Creek enabled everyone to get reacquainted with families and prepare for whatever came next. For me, that led to another new assignment in Washington, DC, my fifth tour there. Shortly after our return, we were notified there was to be two parades honoring all the forces that participated in Desert Shield and Desert Storm, and a unit from the 4th MEB would be participating in both events. The first parade was to be conducted in New York City and would follow the traditional route up Fifth Avenue. I took the MEB Command Group to New York, and we were put up at the large Marriott Hotel right under the World Trade Center, which was one of the buildings severely damaged by the collapse of the Trade Center on 9/11.

The next day we formed up with all the other service units in Battery Park at the foot of Fifth Avenue for the ticker-tape parade. It went off really well and was witnessed by thousands of people all along the parade route. The U.S. Navy contingent led by VADM Stan Arthur was right behind us in the Line of March. When we pulled off the route at the end of the parade, I called out to Stan; he looked great as they went by. He returned the compliment by stating that his feet hurt. So much for marching fighter pilots.

The second parade was to be in Washington witnessed by President George H. W. Bush, whom I had not seen since he and Mrs. Bush had Thanksgiving services on the *Nassau* off Bahrain. This event was staged about a week after the New York City parade. The route for this one was basically along Constitution Avenue from Capitol Hill to a point on the west end of the Mall. The reviewing stand was located on the Ellipse, and the president was accompanied by General Al Gray as we marched by. This one went off without any problems, as well.

Shortly after the two parades, I received word that the Senate Armed Services Committee was going to hold hearings on the operations of the individual services during the war in the Persian Gulf. This sort of thing was not unusual, as Congress has the responsibility to make sure that they have an accurate appraisal of what occurred, both good and bad. The Navy, although successful in many areas in Desert Storm, was taking a beating over the whole mine warfare issue, and to a lesser degree, connectivity (especially concerning the Air Tasking Order [ATO] transmission problem). Bat LaPlante and I had already briefed Secretary of Defense Dick Cheney on what our experiences were, and now it was the turn of the Senate. I appeared at the hearing with Stan Arthur and several of his battlegroup commanders. The questions were generally friendly, and now and then, a member would drop a pointed question regarding one of his favorite programs. For me, the question was about the battleships, from Senator John Warner (R-VA). There had been an ongoing debate as to how long the Navy was going to keep them in commission, as they were really expensive to man and operate. He was a very large proponent of the battleships and wanted to know how I felt as a Marine amphibious force commander. My response was if we were going to conduct another amphibious power projection mission, I wanted everything I could get that would shoot if I needed it, including the battleships. This seemed to satisfy him.

Now it was back to Little Creek to begin preparations for a move back to Washington. The first major effort that had to be dealt with was the Change of Command for the 4th MEB. I was to be relieved by Major General Carl Fulford, who was a very experienced officer, so the brigade would be in good hands. The ceremony was to be in late May 1991, and the only question was where to hold it. Seeing as how we had spent so much time on the USS *Nassau*, it seemed appropriate we hold the traditional change of command on the flight deck of the ship. I am not sure if this was another first, but I suspect it was pretty close to the first time it had been done at that level on an amphibious assault ship.

The weather was perfect, which helped the ceremony go off really well, and I think everyone had a good time. My experience as the CG, 4th MEB, and the responsibility that went with it was certainly one of the highlights of my career in the Marine Corps. It required leadership and a span of control at a very different level of responsibility from what I had experienced as a Captain at MWTC. The MEB had been able to accomplish many things while we were at sea. While not everything went smoothly in terms of getting out of North Carolina in the beginning, we got much better as time went along once we had an opportunity to exercise both the concepts and the troops. I can also state that we accomplished every mission that came our way and were certainly in position to do more if required. The successful NEO in Somalia in early 1991, our participation in the Maritime Interdiction Force operations in the Gulf of Oman, and the Harrier strikes against the Iraqis in northern Kuwait all pointed to the superb sailors and Marines who were involved. The ability to present the threat of an amphibious landing in Kuwait certainly kept the Iraqis in place until it was too late to escape back into Iraq during the ground war. This was aided by the helicopter demonstrations against the coast of Kuwait on the 25th and 26th of February. All of this just shows how much flexibility exists in a MAGTF in a modern amphibious force. What makes this sort of operational experience so successful is again the dedication of the sailors and Marines who served in it.

Lieutenant General Carl Mundy, the current Commanding General for Fleet Marine Forces Atlantic and soon to be the next Commandant behind General Al Gray, had indicated to me upon my return from the Persian Gulf that I would be going back to HQMC as the Assistant Chief of Staff for Command, Control, Communications, Computers, and Intelligence (C4I) starting in July 1991. On the domestic side, this was good because we were able to move back into our home in Centreville, and Anne and TJ could return to first-class schools. The assignment was to be another new experience as it was hard enough to figure out what the scope of the responsibilities was beyond the acronym.

It was no secret that communications and digital platforms were not the Marine Corps' strengths on the ground in the Persian Gulf, and one of the reasons for the assignment was to try to get control of any number of issues that grew out of the war. The Corps had several slowly developing digital programs at Quantico, but the pipes for moving the data as well as imagery were not in place either on the ground or aboard amphibious ships. Another perplexing problem was the fact the Marine forces on the ground had radios that often were not entirely compatible with what the Army units were using, and that carried over to the developing digital systems. In many instances, the terms for joint operations and interoperability were being thrown around, but not much was really being driven by higher headquarters in the area of C4. The radio issue was a programmatic one that needed funding to procure new systems that were interoperable with the Army. That was going to take time. GPS-based systems were in their infancy in the Persian Gulf, which created more problems for units maneuvering in the desert. We had experimented with some of the technology while conducting two of the rehearsals in Oman, but there were not nearly enough hand-held devices in the hands of the troops to make up a fully functioning GPS architecture in the maneuver units.

It became obvious that if I were going to get anything done in the malaise that is Washington, I would have to go out of the box and try different initiatives to get some of the new or existing capability for units that would be deploying with the Navy. The priority had to be the support of the MEU (SOC) organizations that would be going to sea in amphibious shipping. My counterpart in the U.S. Navy was VADM Jerry O Tuttle, a very aggressive, innovative, and iconic officer who has generally been credited with bringing the Navy into the digital age. VADM Tuttle, who usually operated out of the box, was a genius at seeking out new solutions to continuing problems. Constantly searching for new lightweight systems and experimenting with commercial technologies, he was way ahead of the entrenched elements in the Navy bureaucracy who preferred to conduct business as usual. He understood what had to be done, based on reported shortcomings for passing large amounts of data out to the ships that were positioned all around the Arabian Peninsula.

One example was the inability of the fleet to receive the daily ATO generated by CENTCOM. The fleet lacked a SATCOM capability needed to carry the data-driven orders to support the ongoing air campaign over Kuwait and Iraq. This document was up to 850 pages daily and had to be flown by Navy S-3 aircraft out to the command ships, so it could be transmitted further to the five aircraft carrier battle groups for execution. This was another example of how the rhetoric associated with joint operations had not been translated into real capability among the services.

Jerry Tuttle devised a plan to procure a Super High Frequency (SHF) system for his ships, which would go a long way toward solving the problem. This did not cover the amphibious ships, so we were stymied when it came to having to get the same system on some of the "big-deck" LHA and the new LHD class ships. Without it, we could not support several of the new digital systems which were coming along at Quantico.

This was when Jerry indicated that if I could find a similar capability in our war reserve stocks, and give it to the Navy for installation on the first amphibious assault ship, he would program funding to procure at least six systems of his WSC-6 (shipboard SATCOM terminal for satellite communications) for installation in the amphibious big-decks. I turned the staff loose, and they soon discovered several TSC-93 communications vans were sitting in the woods at the Marine Corps Logistics Base in Albany, Georgia. Staged there in the event of another major war, they had a similar SHF capability, which would work like the Navy system.

After some grumbling at Albany, we promptly gutted a couple of those vans and gave the devices to the Navy to install on the amphibious ships. The first one went on an LPH helicopter carrier in workups for deployment to Southwest Asia. The next step was to break into the bureaucracy at Quantico to get a system that could be put on that LPH to use the SHF capability. I had selected the Intelligence Analysis System (IAS) as the candidate for the deployment. I can still remember the young captain who was the program manager for IAS at the time, coming in highly incensed I had selected his system which was not completely ready for prime time. After I explained the situation to him, he eased off a bit when I told him the system was going on that ship and would sail with the embarked MEU.

As it turned out, the IAS was utilized by the Marines in that MEU as they eventually deployed into the ravages of Mogadishu, Somalia, for the first time. The IAS was not perfect, but backed by the WSC-6 system, the seed had been planted: better systems than what had been in the 4th MEB were on the way. I had learned several years before sometimes one has to go out on a limb to accomplish a given task, despite the bureaucratic resistance to anything different from the standard norm. The Washington environment is one of the worst for having to deal with anything different from perceived notions. Having said that, VADM Jerry Tuttle worked wonders within it every time. For the Marines, the SHF capability enhanced our effectiveness to process information of all kinds at sea and a step toward bringing such capability into the 21st Century.

The assignment as the Director of Intelligence for the Corps was to be another challenge, but more because of the shortages in personnel in the various disciplines within that community. What we had at the time was really good, but there were not enough trained intelligence officers to fill the open billets in every discipline but Signals Intelligence (SIGINT). In the SIGINT world, the Marine Radio Battalions—operating since before Vietnam—were almost a national asset based on what they could do in the field. Beyond that, my experience in the Gulf was not favorable from the products that we did get in the 4th MEB. Among the examples: no real order of battle reports on the various Iraqi commanders that we might meet on the ground, even though it had been requested several times. Imagery products were another area of critical shortage, although I will admit that it is much better and more responsive today some 17 years later. The use of unmanned air vehicles (UAV) was in its infancy in 1991, although we had used the Mastiff System in field exercises at Camp Lejeune in 1986. The Mastiff had been brought back from Beirut in 1983. The results were eye-opening, but the joint acquisition process was way behind the power curve at the time of the war. The lack of UAVs was clearly evident everywhere, except on the Navy's two battleships that were using the Pioneer System for spotting targets in Kuwait for the 16-inch guns on both the USS *Missouri* and USS *Wisconsin*.

The world of intelligence can be both fascinating and frustrating at the same time. The role of the Director of Intelligence can range from managing quotas for the various intelligence schools, following the progress regarding funding for intelligence systems like IAS and others, to participating in the vetting of National Intelligence Estimates (NIE) for the national command authority. I quickly learned, one has to do his homework to stay up with the senior leadership in our intelligence and law enforcement agencies during the vetting process mentioned above. Relationships were again extremely important, especially in Washington, something I had learned during my first tour at HQMC in 1972. We had solid relations with the DIA, NSA, and certainly the intelligence establishment within each service. Relationships with both the FBI and CIA really improved after operations in the Persian Gulf, and the cooperation was excellent in matters appropriate to issues at hand.

The one frustrating part of the assignment was the inability to place effective and well-trained officers in sensitive billets around the world because we did not have the numbers to support everything. In those days, lieutenant colonels and colonels were critically short, which led to cases where we had to cut tours short to fill a billet somewhere else with a specific skill set. An example of this was a requirement for 26 lieutenant colonels when we only had four on active duty, and yet everyone wanted what he rated on the table of organization. This issue eventually became better, thanks to a coordinated effort of my successors to get more officers in the appropriate schools to make them more competitive in front of promotion boards.

As Director of Intelligence, I was required to attend some interesting social events around Washington. In 1992, the Cold War was beginning to wind down, and some of our previous adversaries were beginning to open up a little. I had received my first invitation to a mid-day reception put on by the Soviet Military Attaché. Upon arriving at the designated location in northwest Washington, it was not the Soviet embassy but an old Victorian home in an established neighborhood. There was a security guy who opened the front door and pointed me to the lobby. There, in a room devoid of any furniture except a desk, sat a female member of the staff. In a cool response, she pointed me to a circular stairway that went to the second floor. On the way up the stairs, I noticed that all the paintings that had been on the walls at one time had been removed, and only the shadow of what had hung there was visible. Upon entering the room where the reception was going on, I was greeted by a Russian officer who formally showed me in and pointed to a table full of bottles of things to drink. After that, I was on my own. This reception room was also devoid of furniture other than the two tables for the drinks and snacks. There were small groups of officers from various organizations, all standing around and talking quietly. The setup for the canapes was all right, but Spartan in appearance. It looked to me like this was the first time that the attaché had ever put on one of these events. After moving around for a while and seeing a few people I knew, I left. Generally, the same approach to me by the people on the front desk and door when I came in was the same on the way out.

They had much to learn about socializing in Washington, but at least it was a start.

My second experience on the social whirl was with the communist Chinese embassy. It was located in a different section of northwest Washington in a large, fairly modern building. This time I was accompanied by Sue, who was also invited. This event, in comparison with the other reception, was like night versus day. We were warmly greeted at the front door and escorted into a large, well-decorated reception room, where the hosts were paying attention to everyone. They had created a very warm atmosphere, and the guests seemed to be enjoying themselves. Of course, there was plenty to drink, and they were taking orders from whoever wanted something. There was a very large table loaded with all kinds of Chinese food and delicacies that were laid out in a very attractive manner. There was also some mild music being played in the background and away from the large reception room.

I recall having short conversations with most of the Chinese officers and diplomats who really seemed interested in what I had done in the Corps. They were very friendly and attentive to both Sue and me. It was clear they had been doing this sort of entertaining for some time and were very good at it. Of course, events like this are required both for social reasons and for getting to know who is who in the intelligence field in Washington. It was not uncommon to see various politicians at these events, along with several other government officials from other countries. These kinds of functions were nice to attend, but you had to be on your toes regarding whom you might be dealing with.

It had been a very busy eighteen months in the AC/S for C4I assignment, and I think we were beginning to make some progress. Noted shortcomings in systems highlighted during operations in Desert Shield and Desert Storm were given programmatic emphasis and more funding. School quotas were increased and made mandatory at certain rank levels to get more individuals grounded in necessary skill sets and more competitive for promotion. Gradually the numbers at all levels in the officer ranks began to creep up, and the experience level across the Marine intelligence community improved considerably. It has made significant progress in increasing the development, training, and professionalism of its members. Its technical capabilities have increased exponentially, as well.

CHAPTER 23

LAST TOUR IN THE PENTAGON

I had been the ACS (C4I) for a little over a year when I began to pick up rumors that another assignment might be on the horizon. I had previously mentioned the U.S. Navy and the Chief of Naval Operations had been taking a beating over the mine warfare shortcomings in the Persian Gulf, among other issues. After several hearings, the Senate Armed Services Committee, Chaired by Senator Sam Nunn (D-GA), had decided to direct some changes in the Navy Staff in the Pentagon. In the Defense Authorization Bill of 1992, the Navy was directed to create an Expeditionary Warfare Division on the OPNAV staff and put in a Marine Corps major general as the Director with a Navy Rear Admiral as his deputy. The bill also directed that proper staffing be obtained with both Navy and Marine Corps officers, along with a budget to support the activities and responsibilities of the staff. This was unprecedented in the history of the Navy staff and caused more than a few ripples within the bureaucracy in the beginning.

When the confusion finally cleared up, the Director would have responsibility for developing requirements and maintaining the existing force of 64 amphibious ships within the fleet. He would be developing requirements to improve the Mine Warfare force of 18 ships along with two squadrons of the heavy MH-53 mine-hunting helicopters. In addition, he would manage the requirements for the Naval Special forces (SEALs) programs within the Navy. The initial budget for all of this was about $3 billion annually in the beginning but rose over time.

As the organization and spaces in the Navy's section in the Pentagon were being worked out, General Mundy indicated he wanted me to take the assignment in large part because of my experience with the 4th MEB. This was fine with me, as it would be another challenge in a different world than I had experienced before. Admiral Frank Kelso was the Chief of Naval Operations. He and I knew each other from meetings in the Gulf and elsewhere and got along really well. He was a submarine officer with several commands in the submarine community. He had been the Commander of the U.S. Sixth Fleet in the Mediterranean in 1968. In response to Libyan terrorist attacks in Europe, he oversaw the bombing of Muammar al-Gaddafi's headquarters in Libya during Operation El Dorado Canyon.

It required some time to get everything set up in the Pentagon for this move, as well as to bring in a replacement for me as the ACS (C4I) at headquarters. What that meant was I would be holding down both jobs for two months. The Navy had always funded and programmed shipbuilding for the amphibious force and the Marine Corps generally followed along with requirements of one kind or another. This was the first time there would be a Marine in charge of maintaining the Navy's amphibious fleet requirements, which was a breakthrough for the Marine Corps within the Department of the Navy.

It is safe to say the two services have very different cultures. The Navy culture relies heavily on programmatic processes for shipbuilding and aircraft procurement for both the Navy and the Marine Corps, which is necessary. Career officers think in programmatic terms regarding various systems when in Washington and even to a degree when they are out operating with the fleet. The Marine culture is heavily oriented toward all aspects of operations, the majority of the time, with little emphasis on programmatic issues in most quarters unless necessary. The Marine aviation community is the exception, due to the necessity of keeping its aircraft flying and coordinating with the Navy on all aircraft procurement. The Marine Corps Systems Command at Quantico has grown over time and does have responsibility for major ground programs such as the Amphibious Combat Vehicle (ACV). Relations between the two services can range from good to bad depending on the issues at hand in Washington and available funding for everything needed. Clearly, personalities will play a role, which is normal. Relations between the Commandant and the CNO are generally good, while most of the disputes occur below the three- and four-star levels involving requirements and available funding. This is also normal for Washington, but when operating together at sea, it is more about solving the mission at hand. I have said many times before that when the Navy and Marine Corps come together operationally at sea, they are unbeatable.

Any number of people indicated to me this new job would be trying, without thinking about the possibilities. My thoughts going into the assignment were this was clearly going to be another major challenge, but I had an opportunity to make some progress that would benefit both services. My experience with the 4th MEB in the recent operations had given me some perspective on strengths and weaknesses on both sides that could be solved, but most of this was operational and not related to budgets and programs initially.

Relationships here were again critical if any progress was going to be achieved. Learning how the OPNAV staff worked was the first priority. Any Marine assigned to the OPNAV staff who goes there with a "chip on his shoulder" may as well not go, because he will not be successful and can disrupt relations where everyone is trying to get along. I was fortunate to have several really sharp Navy and Marine personnel assigned to the new staff, which was identified as the Expeditionary Warfare Division (N-75). Bureaucracies can function in many ways, and one of the first moves was to try to change the leadership model for N-75. The legislation stated that a Marine major general would be the director with a rear admiral as the deputy. A request was made from somewhere within the Navy to modify that arrangement and rotate the Director's billet between a Navy admiral and a Marine general. The response to this in Congress was to place the billet in Title 10 of the U.S. Code, making it a law that the billet would be filled with a major general only. It has been necessary in succeeding years to explain this to some Marines who did not understand the importance of that billet and how it can assist the Corps in achieving some of its requirements. This was another example of what Congress can do if a situation warrants such action.

My deputy was to be RADM Dennis Conley, a very experienced leader in the amphibious world, and we worked well together. The other division heads on the OPNAV staff, some of whom I had served with in the Persian Gulf, were all first-class and very smart flag officers with years of experience. I consistently worked and coordinated with my counterparts in aviation, surface Navy and the submarine community (then N-78, N-76 and N-77 respectively), all working for a three-star admiral, VADM William Owens (the N-8), who was my immediate boss. A very thoughtful, open-minded individual, he was not afraid to try anything as long as it could be covered financially. One thing that jumped out almost immediately in my tenure in OPNAV was they all wanted to assist me where they could, but did not know much about the Marine Corps, and experiences indicated the Corps did not do much to help at times. How certain ship programs and systems could also be used to support Marine operations in areas where we needed to get assistance, and where I could offer my support to reinforce some of their key programs, became very important early.

One example of this was the AEGIS cruiser, a very capable platform used for air and missile defense at sea, whose radars can extend far inland from the sea. Nobody had thought much about how the ship could link with Marine radars operating far inland to extend coverage for air defense purposes over Marine forces maneuvering on the ground. This was a seemingly minor issue but had the potential to extend the capability of the ship in the era of ballistic missiles and other threats from far over the horizon. Not a minor idea when one considers the cost of such a program and the rationale needed to support the procurement of a number of those platforms.

MINE ISSUES

The political situation in Washington over the problems associated with mine warfare became the first challenge to be addressed. There were two classes of mine-hunting ships in the inventory, one of which had not finished the build-out of that class. All Navy ships are constructed and tested under the control of the Naval Sea Systems Command, while OPNAV deals with the ongoing requirements for systems in those ships to include necessary funding. It can be a very laborious process, and I will not dwell on it much further. What I was trying to do was to find appropriate systems in development that might solve some of the problems encountered in the Persian Gulf. It was also clear that we had to raise the awareness of some of the shortfalls in the mine-hunting fleet.

The first challenge was in the area of surveillance and reconnaissance. The mindset had been if you can't find the minefields, everything operationally stops or slows down almost to a halt. We saw the results of this problem in the Persian Gulf. While the Iraqis had placed a rather extensive series of minefields, none were basically located in what was to have been the sea echelon area off of the landing beaches at al-Fintas. This was an intelligence failure of major proportions. In the future, the use of overhead systems or unmanned underwater vehicles should be used to find and plot the perimeters of a minefield so incoming forces might be able to avoid the area and maneuver to find a gap elsewhere to exploit. The maneuver doctrine that the Marines had been working on for several years accommodated this approach, but we had to have adequate intelligence to make it work. This was a really tough nut to crack because conventional thinking just could not break away from the mindset that lanes had to be cleared through a field before anything could be done.

I believed in future amphibious power projection missions, we could clear the lanes after the maneuver forces were ensconced on inland objectives, arriving there either by air or high-speed maneuver around the fields. It all depends on accurate intelligence early. This led to a search and development of an overhead system that could identify mines in the water well before any forces were on scene. The second piece of this was the development of unmanned underwater systems (UUVs) that could be launched from either surface ships or even submarines. Arriving undetected in the landing area, they could search to identify and plot the perimeter of any minefield they might discover. If the integrated intelligence picture was good, based upon input from these systems, then deploying forces could maneuver around the minefield. Then the Navy's mine-hunting and clearing ships could move in to deal with the mines while landing forces maneuvered inland. The development of newer versions of UUVs has made significant progress, but the Navy still has a long way to go.

Today there is still no technical capability to find buried mines in the sea bottom. The only system in the U.S. Navy capable of doing such work is the marine mammal. Owning the Mammal Program was discovered—and came as a surprise—while going through program reviews right after my arrival on the job. The issue at the time was we were trying to identify five million in funding to feed the mammals for the coming year. This program had started years ago when the Navy was experimenting with the SEALAB program under the Pacific. They had been using dolphins to run messages back and forth to the submerged lab and its scientists under the sea. Over time the Navy continued to experiment with dolphins in the mine-hunting business as well as harbor defense against enemy swimmers.

The Mammal Program is run carefully with maximum attention given to the care and feeding of the dolphins. Each mammal has a handler who cares and trains him constantly, and each one gets a frequent examination from a certified veterinarian. They are kept in giant pens in quiet ocean water and are trained steadily at night off of small boats specifically designed to accommodate both the mammal and its handler. Using a system of signals, the dolphin will slip off of the small boat and run patterns in the ocean, searching for buried mines. Its onboard sonar, for want of a better term, can detect such an object and will respond by flying out of the water and swimming back to the boat. It will be rewarded with some fresh fish. They will verify the target again, and if successful, it will be fitted with a charge over its nose. The dolphin will then go back over the located buried mine and drop the charge. There is a timer on the device that will not go off until the mammal is far away from the detonation. They have been proven to be very successful with this tactic, but it is a slow process. They can be deployed in specially designed tanks in C-5 and C-17 aircraft with all the necessary support to sustain them in different parts of the world. They have been used successfully in support of amphibious exercises as well as in the waterway leading to Umm Qasr during the Iraq war.

Another initiative was to look at various platforms already in the inventory to see how we might be able to enhance specific capabilities. One of them was the high-speed Landing Craft Air-Cushioned vehicles or LCACs. I had deployed to the Persian Gulf with 14 of these vehicles carried in the well decks of amphibious ships and had used them extensively in the rehearsals in Oman. The Marines required 72 of these very versatile platforms that could go up to 72 knots empty in the water or 50 knots with a 50-ton tank on board. What we were looking for was some new way of blowing our way through potential mines buried in the sand in the surf zone or along a beach. One of the objectives here was to get the Navy SEALs out of the mission of crawling along in the surf and onto a beach looking for mines. This technique had its beginning with the Underwater Demolition Teams (UDT) in World War II with the predictable high casualty rates. The Naval Station in Panama City, Florida, is the location where a significant portion of the Navy's mine warfare experiments with technology is carried out, and this was where we decided to do experiments with the LCACs. There were already line charge kits that could fire long strings of C4 explosive charges over great distances that could help clear paths through minefields in the sand. This technique had been used successfully by the Marines in their attacks into Kuwait in 1991. By placing 6-8 of these kits on the deck of an LCAC and wiring them together, we could get a significant blast coverage in either the surf zone or on a beach. With that added capability along with the normal vehicle hauling, troop transportation in shelters, and casualty evacuation systems, we decided to change the name to Multi-capable Air-Cushioned vehicle or MCAC. That, of course, brought out the resistance from the bureaucracy, but the system worked. Personnel in the Navy Assault Craft Units began to get nervous about being forced to go through minefields in the approaches to a beach. This was never the plan, but such were the fears. The approaches from the sea were to be open or cleared before the MCACs would come into the surf to do their clearing with the line charges. Had there been a requirement to land at al-Fintas in Kuwait, an MCAC- like capability would have worked well in clearing paths through the surf zone and over the beach. My guess is the requirement to use LCACs for the beach clearing mission has probably faded away, but we have everything already in the inventory to reestablish such a capability.

All kinds of experiments have been conducted within the mine warfare community to improve technologies in the fleet. There is a very active mine warfare organization with industry, the labs, and the fleet all working together to get at the problems and find solutions. The training is better for the sailors, and there is now a constant series of exercises within the fleet and the allies that deal with MIW problems. Unmanned vehicles in the air and under the sea have entered the fleet to improve the reconnaissance and surveillance shortfalls, to get significantly better intelligence pictures of what might be out there. New ships such as the Littoral Combat Ship (LCS) are coming on line with MIW mission packages to be utilized if necessary, against this kind of threat.

NAVAL GUNFIRE SUPPORT

The lack of naval gunfire support for amphibious operations is a capability that has been slowly degraded over the years and is a constant complaint in some circles. There is some validity to the complaint; however, we had two battleships and nine other smaller gunfire support ships in the Persian Gulf that would have been utilized to provide the naval gunfire support if it was needed. Add in the large amount of available tactical air support in Desert Storm, and I would have been adequately covered. I also believe that the deeper we get into the missile age, traditional naval gunfire support, as we have known it for years, is not going to be around. The four battleships that President Reagan had recommissioned are now gone from the fleet and float as museum pieces in various ports in the United States. The sixteen-inch guns of the battleships could fire 2400-pound projectile 20 miles at best. Many missiles today can beat that range easily, and I thought this required new thinking.

One of the initiatives that we tried to get going was the possibility of existing military equipment that could be put on board an amphibious ship to give the force a fairly deep strike capability. That led to the Medium Launched Missile System (MLRS). This system was already in the inventory of the U.S. Army. It was a self-deploying tracked vehicle that could carry several short-range missiles with ranges out to 60 kilometers, as well as one larger missile with a range of out to 300 kilometers. The latter was the (ATACMS). We were given additional funding from the Congress needed to carry out the tests with MLRS aboard ship.

The plan was to put one of the MLRS systems onboard an amphibious ship and move the vehicle up on to the flight deck, positioning it so that the back blast would go over the side of the ship without damaging the flight deck. The target was to be on one of the small islands off the coast of California. After going through various tests for communications of the fire control system, the experiment was ready to go. The missile system was brought onboard the ship, moved up on the flight deck, and positioned for firing well off the coast. When the missile was launched off of the tracked vehicle, it flew for 60 miles before hitting its planned target. The test was declared a success and proved a mobile system like MLRS could be brought onboard a ship, conduct fire missions before a landing, and then be offloaded to continue to support units ashore.

Did this get anywhere with the sea services? The answer was not really. Some issues were trying to de-conflict with air operations on the deck of the amphibious ship who would provide the MLRS /ATACMS systems to the Navy while the Marines were looking at something else. Here was another perfect example of how joint ideas do not work without someone at the top or the Congress driving it. The "not invented here syndrome" was alive and well on the part of the Navy and Marine Corps. Twenty-seven years later, the problem of rocket artillery support versus naval gunfire support from the sea is still not solved.

UNMANNED AERIAL VEHICLES (UAVS)

There had been some discussion regarding UAVs being used in the Desert Shield and Desert Storm operations, even though the Marines had been playing around with the Mastiff System as far back as 1983. Both the Navy and Marines were now working with the Pioneer UAV system as the next tactical UAV for the fleet. When I arrived on deck for the OPNAV job, the Navy had three other systems I had never heard of that were all at a very slow rate of development. Part of this delay was the resistance in the Navy aviation culture in that they did not want them on the carriers, and part of it was due to the fact they really were not sure of what their requirements should be. In another quick move, my boss decided to kill two of the systems under development and move toward a system that could be launched off of an amphibious ship. This could have been either an LHA or the new LHD multi-purpose amphibious assault ship. Politically it took the problem away from carrier aviation, yet had the potential of having a system at sea but on an amphibious ship.

This led to another initiative where we were tasked to see what was available, which might work for this requirement. Pioneer was not considered, so the most obvious UAV system at the time was the

"Hunter." The U.S. Army had the Hunter Program that was somewhat funded and under various levels of testing. Hunter was an Israeli system which had worked very well for them. The Army had developed a procurement objective of 50 systems (four birds and ground control stations per system), which was a sizable number of UAVs. This UAV was coming along slowly within the Army and beginning to get the attention of the Deputy Secretary of Defense for Acquisition for the lack of progress.

A comparison between how the Israelis did things versus how we worked in our own acquisition system proved to be very instructive. Over there and under very different circumstances, the Israelis will build a new UAV, test it briefly, and then deploy it operationally along their borders. If it is damaged through hostile action or it breaks, they bring it back to the factory, make the repairs, and send it off again with a minimum of paperwork. In the United States, we wade through a mountain of paper requirements that might lead to a perfect system but can take so long the bird could be obsolete before it ever reaches an operational capability. The amount of money wasted through this process was shocking, and I did not think the Israelis ever understood how we did things.

A decision was made to test the concept of flying the Hunter off the deck of an amphibious ship. Coordination was completed with the Army program office to provide the Hunter System with its ground station to do a series of tests at the Point Mugu Naval Station in California. There was a taped-out section on the runway for practicing landings and take-offs. The plan then called for a series of demonstrations to be conducted off the USS *Essex* (LHD-2), which was lying off the coast. Following the runway tests, the ground station manned by both Army and Israeli technicians were loaded onboard the *Essex*. Control features, as well as the launch and retrieval systems, were coordinated and placed out on the flight deck behind the island of the ship.

I had gone out to the ship to be in a position to observe both the launches and recovery of the UAV. I remember that as soon as I arrived onboard, the captain of *Essex* came on the intercommunications system to announce we were now going to play with a "toy system" brought to him by OPNAV. Such was the Navy aviation culture in those days. The sea states off of Point Mugu were calm, which helped in the execution of the shipboard tests. The Hunter was lined up on a portable catapult designed for the UAV and, in effect, shot off the side of the ship. This went well, and the UAV made several orbits around the ship before lining up in the approach to the deck for landing. When the Hunter crossed the threshold of the flight deck and set down, its small tail hook caught one of the wires that had been stretched across that deck.

The first of several launch and recovery missions proved the concept was sound. I was standing off to one side of the flight deck and watching the approach for the Hunter, and it reminded me of those films of the Navy fighter bombers returning to their ship after missions against the Japanese in the Pacific. The glide path was almost the same, and if the tailhook engaged one of the arresting cables on the deck, the aircraft stopped. If the cables were missed in those days, the pilot and plane ended up in a net that was stretched across the deck.

Today, the pilot adds power, takes off, and goes around to try again. The same thing happened to the Hunter, only the controllers' added power so that the UAV could take-off and come around for another try. We even had one incident where the UAV suffered wing damage on landing but took off after missing the wire and continued to fly around the ship before landing successfully on the second attempt. It would be years of more testing after the Hunter Program collapsed under its own weight and cost, but newer models were coming on line. Those shipboard demonstrations had planted the seed for what was to come some twenty years later.

THE DEMISE OF THE LSTS

I had mentioned we had 7-8 LSTs in CTF-158 during Desert Storm. These venerable ships were the offspring of the famous LSTs of World War II. They had large bow doors that opened up to discharge cargos of vehicles and other equipment over contested beaches from the Pacific to Normandy in Europe and later at Inchon in Korea. This newer version did not have the large bow doors, but instead had a boom system which telescoped out over the bow to touch down either on a beach or the end of a floating causeway. Even these later models were costly to operate and much slower than some of the more modern amphibious ships then in active service. I also want to refer back to my visit to one of the LSTs by cable out of a CH-46 helicopter in the Gulf of Oman. Getting into the troop compartments to see the Marines stacked three high with no room left for anything else brought back an impression that came back to me in OPNAV thirty years after my first experience with the LST.

In those days in OPNAV, division heads received a "bogey" or a tax that required you to find the designated amount of money within your programs to be passed along to support other initiatives in the Navy. This was an annual event in the staff. In my first year, my bogey approached a significant sum in the millions, which was sort of sticker shock not seen before by me anyway and certainly not in the Marine Corps. This was the standard way of doing business in OPNAV, and it really forced us to take a very hard look at what was critical and what was nice to have in terms of programs. The first year I was as able to fence my ship accounts as well as stay away from all the critical mine warfare programs. This occurred because the Navy was getting hammered over the mine warfare problems in Congress. It was also clear this was not likely to happen a second time, and ships were going to get a very close examination when the "bogey" for the next year was announced. It is important to note that you can take one or two ships out of service, but you have to find some other platform where you can absorb the loss but retain that capability in some way.

This is a fact of life that leads to conflict between the Navy and Marine Corps frequently and hopefully leads to some sort of compromise. The OPNAV Leadership had been looking at the LSTs as a potential source of savings that could be applied elsewhere. They also realized there had to be some sort of tradeoff to try to retain the required lift capability for troops and equipment if it was needed. Realizing savings, if possible, through the bogey process was required in the short-term, but the impact for amphibious lift was a long-term problem.

It was about this period in time that advance plans for a new amphibious assault ship were on the boards as a long-term replacement for the Navy's Amphibious Transport Dock (LPD) Austin and Ponce class of ships. The last of the Ponce class was finally decommissioned in 2014 after 46 years of service. What gradually developed was a much more capable and modern San Antonio Class of Amphibious Transport Dock Ships (the LPD-17), of which there were to be at least 13 built. It was clear the beginning of the demise of the LSTs was going to help pay for the new LPD-17s that would be constructed over fifteen years. Negotiations within OPNAV led to a plan to gradually pull the LSTs out of active service but put them into a reserve status for years, so if a major conflict broke out, they could be brought back into service quickly. This was a form of compromise to try to maintain lift capability while the new ships were coming on line. It was also based on the latest intelligence on what our peer competitors were doing around the world.

What was the risk if we started to put some of these ships into a reserve status? Some Marines were hollering about the gradual loss of the LSTs, but this was the best that could be accomplished until the new ships joined the fleet. I remember one incident when I was giving a briefing to the Command and Staff College at Quantico regarding the role of the Expeditionary Warfare Division and its importance to the Marine Corps. One of the students wanted to know who was responsible for getting rid of the LSTs. I responded to him by saying, "You are looking at him, and here is why." That ended the conversation. Over some time, the LSTs gradually disappeared from active service and remained for a considerable time in a reserve status before being decommissioned completely. During this period, there was little increased risk to our national security that required bringing them back on line. Meanwhile, the new construction continued on the LPD-17s. The increased capacity of these new ships made up for some of the shortfall in lift incurred with the demise of the LSTs.

One of the more humorous aspects of the tour in the Expeditionary Warfare Division was when the OPNAV leadership (the N-8) started to experiment with the concept of utilizing airships as a possible way to increase persistent aerial surveillance over the ocean and coastlines. The Navy had several bad experiences with airships in the 1930s and had lost a couple in crashes with heavy losses of life. The concept had died before the beginning of World War II, and nothing other than satellites had come on line that could meet some of that requirement. The fleet was relying on national overheard surveillance from satellites as well as aircraft capabilities over short periods. It should also be pointed out that the era of long-range UAVs like Global Hawk had not yet been developed into a fully operational capability.

After much discussion regarding airships, my boss gathered up his division heads and flew down to Elizabeth City, North Carolina, to go aboard a commercial airship. I believed this one was either owned or at least operated by Goodyear. We all climbed into the operations capsule, which was under the belly of the blimp, and took off at the blinding speed of about five mph, gradually lifting into the air. We all got to get at the controls of this airship and to watch Navy admirals who were very experienced fighter pilots was worth the price of admission. First of all, they did not want to be there, and second, I think this exercise was an anathema to the whole aviation culture within the Navy. In one of these airships, you climb and descend very slowly, and any turns are very gradual at best even if the ship is at full speed.

After the one-hour flight, we were back on solid ground, but I did not think that anyone in the Navy aviation world was convinced that this was something to do. The experience was fun, but I had estimated that to do a barrel roll in that airship might probably take at least five minutes to complete, even if it could do such a maneuver. As one might expect, the concept of this kind of airship doing surveillance within the Navy did not get very far in OPNAV. It would be 25 years before the Navy finally came up with a system of persistent aerial surveillance utilizing the Global Hawk.

One example of how a concept that looks really attractive comes on line does very well in testing, then disappears for a while before returning again for consideration, occurred in the closing months of my tour in N-75. I had met Charles H. Kaman, who, along with Igor I. Sikorsky, was one of the early pioneers in developing helicopters in this country. In 1993 Charlie invited me to visit his Kaman Aircraft Company in Bloomfield, Connecticut, to observe his latest invention. The Kaman K-Max was an aerial truck that ran on one engine with dual intermeshing rotors, no tail rotor, and one pilot. It had the lift capability of 6,000 pounds on an external hook. The design of the helicopter was very simple, and the unit price at the time was around $5 million per bird; the price included a ground station. Charlie also indicated that he had designed the technology that enabled the K-Max to operate as an unmanned drone for aerial delivery if that was required. It looked very attractive for specific missions and was considered cheap when compared to any other aircraft procurement at the time. This prompted extensive discussions on how this capability could be utilized in the fleet. It was not long before the naval aviation community in OPNAV went against the idea, primarily because it had only one engine not considered safe for operating at sea. The naval surface requirements community (N-76) in OPNAV liked the idea for the purposes of VERTREP at sea, which was currently being done with the CH-46 helicopter. The rationale at the time was it would be cheaper to operate the K-Max, which had an advertised less than one hour of maintenance per flight hour characteristic, vice the CH-46 that averaged over 30 hours of maintenance per flight hour. Following extensive discussion within OPNAV, funding was identified to support a demonstration on one of the replenishment ships operating for a period at sea. The results were very positive, with the K-Max showing its reliability in comparison with the CH-46. One of the members of the test team stated that when the day's replenishment activities were over, all they had to do was polish the windshield of the K-Max, while the other crew was all over the 46 plugging leaks. Like so many other potential systems, this one managed to get lost within the bureaucracy due to vested interests and politics. The K-Max had never been a program of record within the Navy and basically went away. Charlie Kaman then turned to sell this helicopter commercially to logging companies as well as customers overseas for firefighting purposes.

U.S. Marine operations against the Taliban in southern Afghanistan began long after I had retired from the Marine Corps. The Marines were back in combat in Helmand Province from 2009 and had outposts of varying sizes in numerous locations throughout the Province. The requirement to resupply these far-flung outposts, due to distances on the ground, and the IED threat, became a major resupply issue. In an attempt to resolve this problem, the Commandant, General James F. Amos, a Marine aviator, turned to the resurrection of the K-Max. This time he wanted it to be manned or unmanned. The development of the unmanned concept was accomplished at the Kaman facilities in Bloomfield, Connecticut. A team from Kaman and Lockheed worked to create both a conventional line of sight and a GPS -based control system for the helicopter. Following extensive tests, the K-Max was deployed to Helmand Province in Afghanistan to work in support of the Marines. From 2011 to August 2013, the unmanned helicopter functioned exceptionally well as a flying truck ferrying supplies and some equipment to outposts throughout the Province. It was limited to 4,300 pounds of cargo per lift due to altitude considerations in the operational area. The accuracy of the system was such that the operator, in the ground station miles away, could hover the K-Max over the site, and drop the load to a spot within five feet of the designated coordinates. This was to be the first time in history that an unmanned helicopter ever served in combat. The K-Max was brought back to the states following the withdrawal of the Marines from Helmand Province. After some time, the system was deactivated and is now stored at the Marine Corps Air Station in Yuma, Arizona. It could fly again if it is needed.

Finally, the MPF squadrons, which provided so much logistical support at the beginning of Desert Shield, have continued to function as floating warehouses for Marine Expeditionary Brigades (MEBs). They have been utilized in several humanitarian contingencies in the years following that conflict. The original three squadrons were reduced to two, again as cost savings. They continue to provide a significant sea base for logistics support for exercises or contingencies and generally move around in several locations between Southwest Asia, the Pacific, and Europe. They have to unloaded in-stream or in a port facility. Until recently, there was no way of transferring cargo and vehicles from one ship to another ship in calm water for further transfer to LCACs for movement ashore. One of the ongoing initiatives was to develop a requirement for a ship that could transfer vehicles and equipment via a ramp from a preposition ship (the LMSR) in a "skin-to-skin transfer" at sea to what became known originally as a Mobile Landing Platform (MLP). From there, vehicles would be further transferred to LCACs for the run to the beach. The MLP now called an Expeditionary Transfer Dock Ship (T-ESD), functions as a transfer station for preposition ships to offload and transfer vehicles and cargo to a ship-to-shore connector like the LCAC. The T-ESD is a double-hulled Alaska tanker that can ballast down in the water to take on LCACs into specially designed parking lanes to pick up vehicles and cargo on its deck. This design represented a huge breakthrough for transferring vehicles and cargo from a sea base in support of Marine forces operating ashore. These ships are commercial hulls and significantly cheaper to build than traditional Navy ships with a similar mission and design. Each MPF squadron now has one T-ESD in its organization.

The Director of Expeditionary Warfare within OPNAV has become a permanent fixture within the Navy and coordinates well with the Marines at the Combat Development Command at Quantico. The links between the two services brought on by the congressional action in 1992 have grown to a point where the many catfights over who was in charge of ship issues have gone away, much to the benefit of both services. There still are and will always be debates about one issue or another over available funds, but the two services working together under the current organization are advancing and making progress in a variety of areas within the amphibious world.

My tour in OPNAV had been very interesting and exceptionally rewarding. The acquisition system, being what it is, did not allow for any quick fixes to any number of problems that we encountered, but the seeds had been planted, and momentum was beginning to get people moving out with some new ideas. One would have to spend a significant amount of time in the same job to make sure some of these concepts and initiatives stay on track until successful completion. This continues to be a chronic weakness in the current system. There is no such thing as the perfect solution, but we spend inordinate amounts of taxpayer money trying to do just that when perhaps the 85 percent solution will be just as effective.

My time on active duty was slowly coming to an end. I had time to do but determined I wanted to go off in a different direction. The thirty-four years on active duty had been a series of immense challenges, heavy responsibility, and many rewarding experiences I would do again if necessary. Above all, serving with the Marines and sailors all over the world and in two wars, along with several exercise-related deployments, was perhaps the highlight of such a career. Only those who have worked with them, sometimes under miserable circumstances, would understand just how effective they really are. This country is fortunate to have people who are willing to serve and, if necessary, sacrifice themselves for such a higher calling.

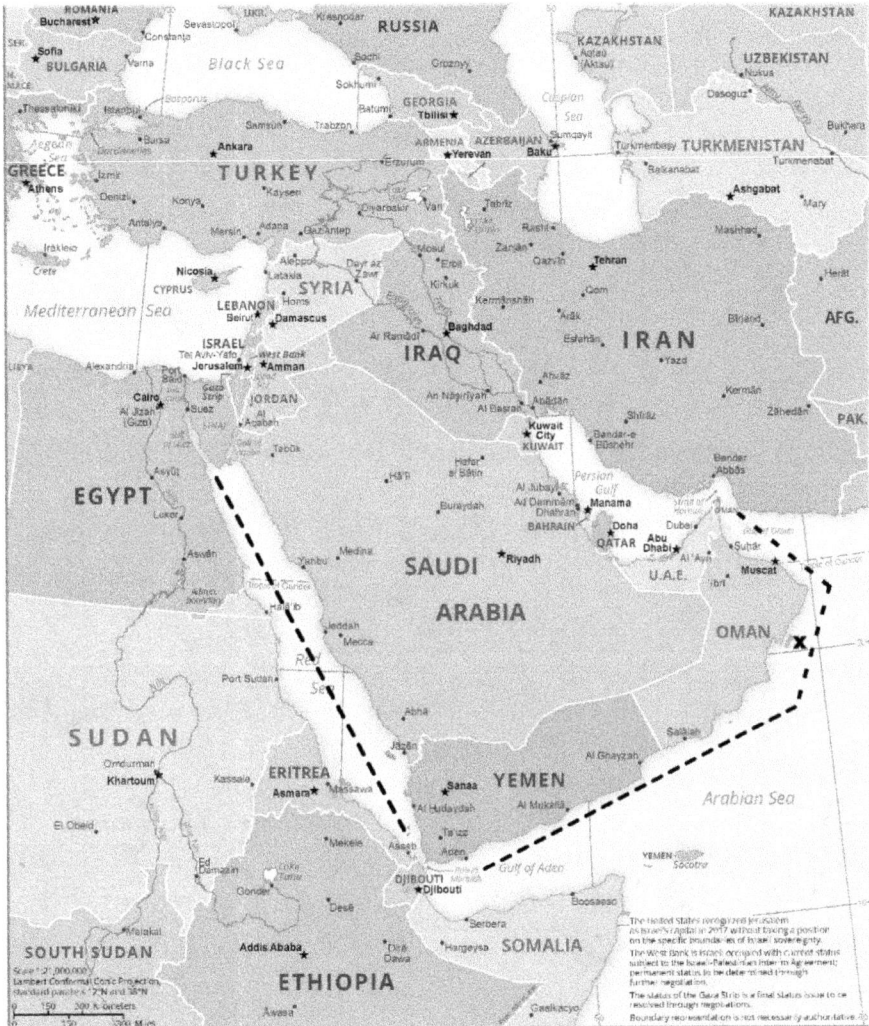

Map 8 The Middle East – Transit and Location (X) of the Ibn Khaldoon boarding.

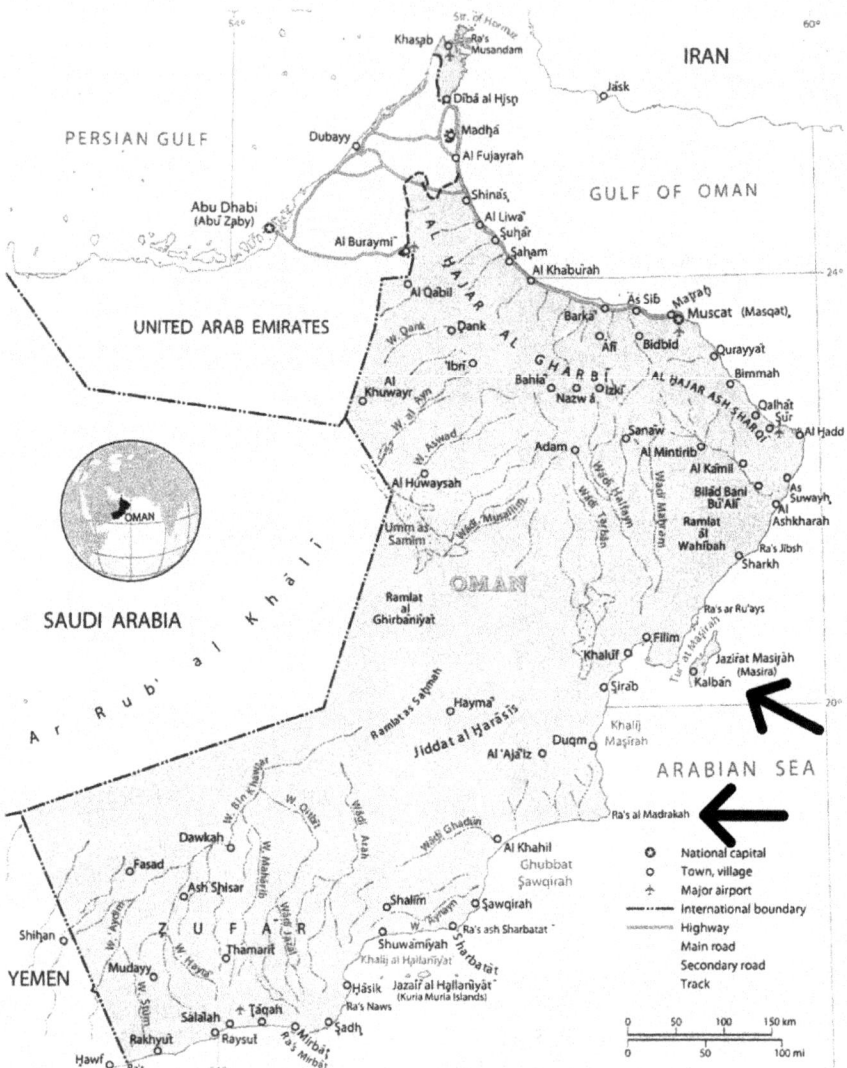

Map 9 Oman - The Amphibious Rehearsals.

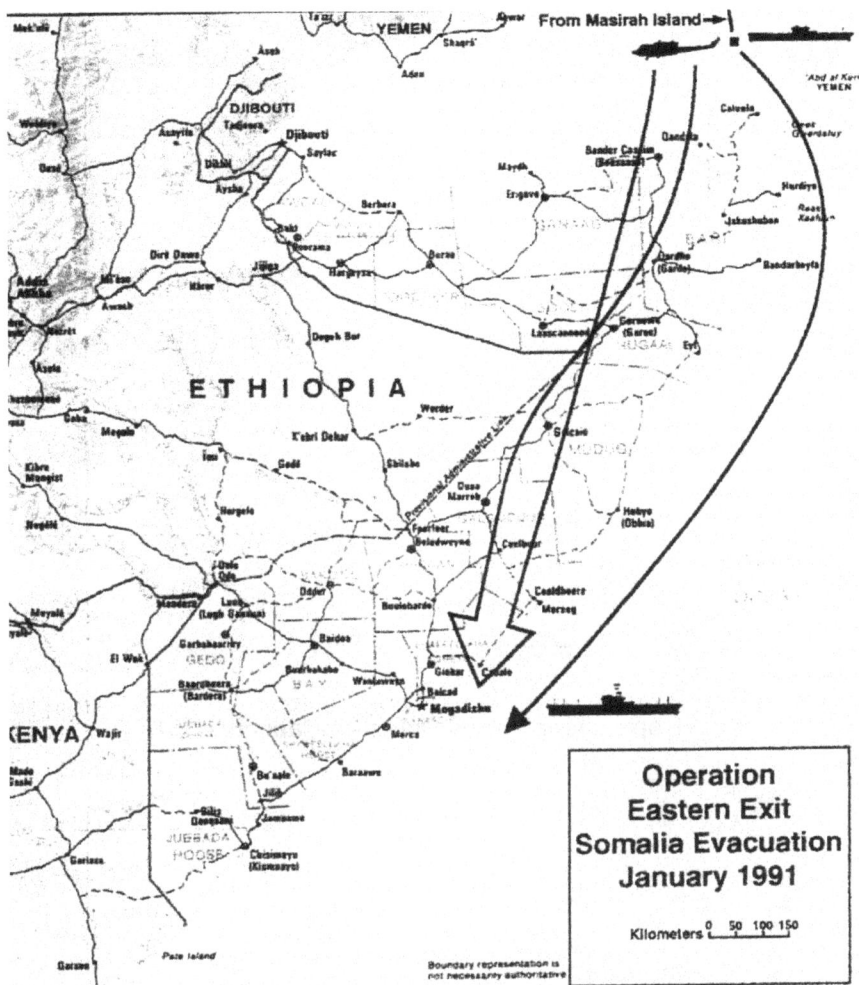

Map 10 The 4th MEB Somalia Noncombatant Evacuation, January 1991.

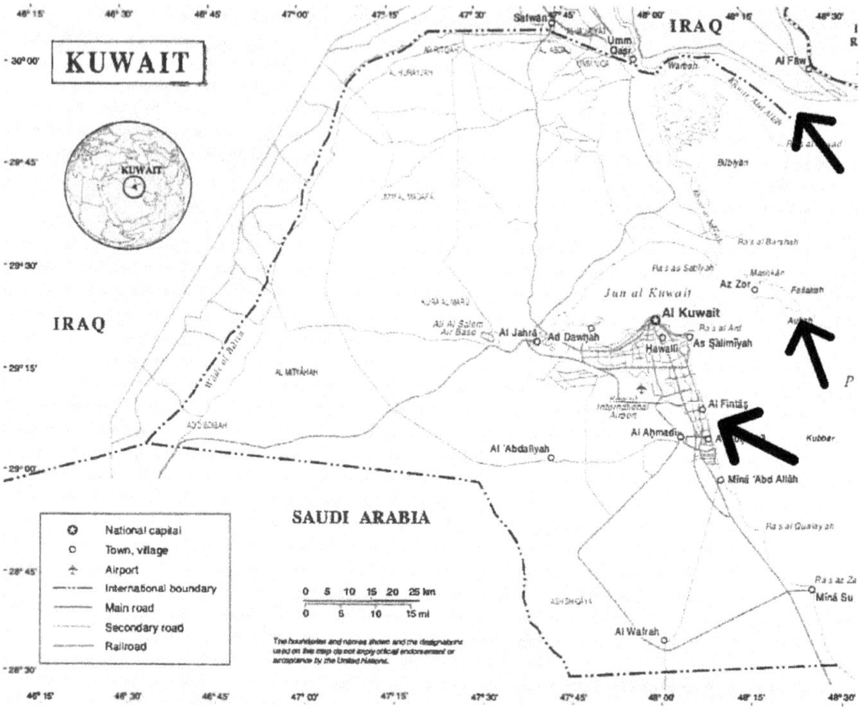

Map 11 Amphibious Options in January 1991.

North Norway 1985, Marines on cross-country skis.

North Norway 1985, Marines' skijoring behind a BV-206.

North Norway, Marines moving to contact in Exercise Cold Winter-85.

North Norway, Cold Winter-85, the author briefing General P X Kelly USMC, CMC.

2nd Marines Command Post, Cold Winter-85.

Amphibious vehicle for patrolling Fjords in North Norway, Anchor Express-86.

USS Nassau- LHA-4. Flagship for the 4th MEB and PHIBGRP-2 in the Persian Gulf.

Underway replenishment in the North Arabian Sea 1990, USS Truckee (AO-147), and USS Pensacola (LSD-38) from USS Nassau LHA-4.

Sea Soldier Rehearsal Area, Ra's al Madrakah, Oman 1990.

The author with Omani liaison officers and RADM Bat LaPlante USN COMPHIBGRU-2.

The author with RADM LaPlante, the Commander Amphibious Task Force ashore during Sea Soldier 1.

Omani liaison officer ashore with the author during Sea Soldier 2.

CH-53E heavy-lift helicopter supporting the Sea Soldier rehearsals.

Desert Storm. AV8-B Harriers line up for an airstrike in Kuwait and Iraq 1991.

Harriers launching from the USS Nassau LHA-4.

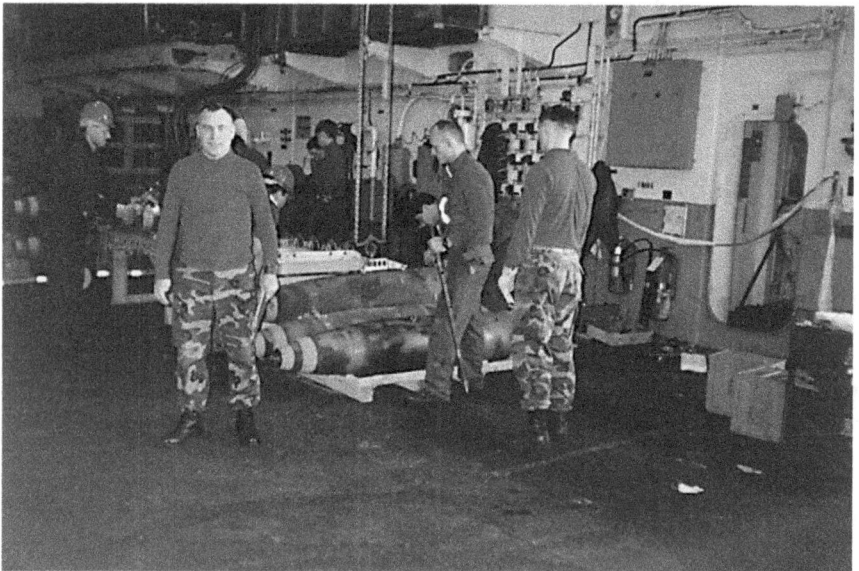

Nassau ordnance men preparing bombs for Harrier strikes in Iraq and Kuwait.

Harriers returning from strike, Desert Storm 1991.

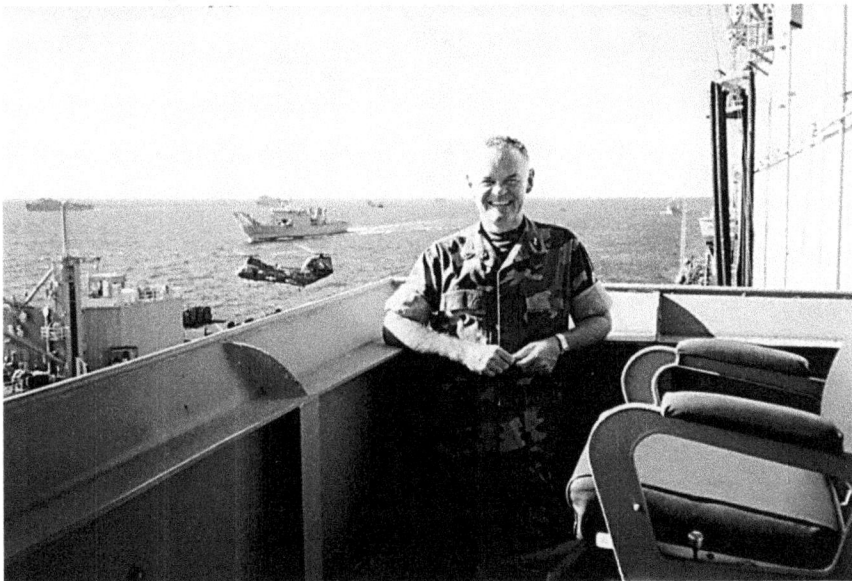

The author on the bridge during underway replenishment in the Gulf of Oman 1991.

LCACs ashore during Sea Soldier rehearsals in Oman.

Marine tanks maneuvering ashore during Sea Soldier II, Oman 1990.

CH-46 helicopters landing troops ashore during Sea Soldier IV in Oman 1991.

USNS Comfort steaming—on the way home—with PhibGP-2 and 4th MEB in the North Arabian Sea, March 1991.

PART IV: TRANSITION TO INDUSTRY

Chapter 24
Dateline ITT

I wanted to spend more time on family-related activities, as daughter Anne was going to Virginia Tech in Blacksburg and TJ was already in high school, and heavy into track as well as the Boy Scout high adventure programs. Sue, who had managed the home front so very well during all the deployments, was still in education but at the adult level now. She had made the transition from middle school to adult education with ease when we were stationed at Camp Lejeune. She enjoyed dealing with Marines, who would often come in from the field for classes in the evenings at the Coastal Carolina Community College in Jacksonville. We had already made the decision following retirement; we would remain in our home in Centreville, at least until the kids were out of school.

In June, I had told the Commandant, General Carl Mundy, I would retire on August 31, 1994. That would give him time to find a replacement for me as well as giving me time to start to chart a course for my second career. Work was generally slowing down for the summer months as both the Defense Authorization and Appropriations Bills involving Navy programs were well into the traditional debate on the Hill. The last major planning effort was to be the retirement ceremony and where and how it would be carried out. The decision was made to hold it at the oldest post in the Marine Corps, the Marine Barracks at 8th and I Streets in Washington, DC It would be a formal retirement ceremony conducted as part of a traditional parade put on by the Marines at the barracks.

Major General Don Gardner, an old friend and decorated Vietnam veteran, agreed to a joint ceremony for the two of us as he was retiring at the same time. This was fitting because Don—a historian of note—had been in our wedding at Quantico in 1968. On the day of the ceremony, the weather at the barracks was perfect, and the ceremony went off without any problems. Don and I were retired by General Mundy, and then we reviewed the traditional parade. Following that, we moved to the Sousa Band Hall at the barracks for a very nice reception attended by the invited guests. After the reception was over, I was now a retired Marine with his first career completed, we headed home.

I had already planned to take the first 30 days following retirement to do nothing and try to get organized for what would come next. Transitions from active duty to retirement and plans for further employment after that can be unsettling. Some of this can be attributed to moving from a very structured environment to another, which is just the opposite. This can produce the fear of the unknown if an individual has not planned out at least a general course on what to do next. Many people I have known had no idea as to what they were going to do, while others had plans all worked out.

In many cases, they had begun the process of job-hunting well before they retired. If you are starting out cold, one can expect it could take four to six months on average before employment options start to clear up, and you get offers. Of course, there will always be exceptions, but the four-six-month rule seemed to be a good planning factor in any transition. In my case, I had generally decided I would look to industry, where I could put some of the experience I had gained to good use. I had started to do some due diligence and networking about two months before I left the service. For some people, this can be a painful experience because one is initially staring into an uncertain future in terms of what he might end up doing. As one friend said, "There is not much need for retired machine gunners, so you have to broaden out."

Here is a situation where your reputation and relationships gained over time can be of great benefit. Of course, flag officers have an advantage because they have worked in the higher echelons of the services, and industry especially likes this background because of the contacts that have been made by the individual flag officer while on active duty. It is no secret that companies will hire an admiral or a general for his expertise as well as contacts within the service or government, but industry will normally not approach you with anything serious until it is clear you are committed to retiring on such a date. I have mentioned industry as that was my focus, but there are any number of different occupations which will vary in other fields where one may be interested in.

One day about six weeks before my retirement, I had been approached about my interest in joining a specific corporation. The idea of joining a major corporation at the time sounded intriguing. There were no real details as to what this job might be about during the initial conversation. Shortly before my retirement, I received another call asking if I would be interested in coming in for an interview with the same corporation, International Telephone, and Telegraph, or ITT. My answer was yes, and the process began to speed up. Shortly after that, I received an offer that came as a surprise, as it had not taken nearly the amount of time that people had told me to expect. I think I can attribute this to relationships and reputation again developed in Washington, as well as a little luck. I accepted their offer, retired, and took my thirty days of leave.

I reported for work in my new job toward the end of September 1994 at the company defense sector facility, which was located in Rosslyn, Virginia. ITT at the time was a $20 billion conglomerate with headquarters in New York and assets in a large variety of businesses in manufacturing, insurance, hotels, and services. ITT had been a power player internationally for many years, both in positive and negative relationships in various regions around the world. The size and reach of ITT were attractive to me because they were in a variety of markets, many of which were well known both at home and overseas. I had not come across any of their activities in the defense sector while on active duty, but the reputation of the corporation was out there. Like most officers leaving the service, my background in business was severely limited, especially on the financial side.

I did have some trepidation regarding my lack of financial expertise associated with business in the beginning. The business world is very different from what I had experienced in the thirty-four years in the Corps. The first part of my education in industry was to learn to function within the culture of ITT. Like all organizations, it had its own and was a far cry from what I had been used to in the service. That came as no surprise, but it still required an adjustment from a fairly rigid military organization where snap decisions have to be made at times. This is especially true where such decisions are required in the crucible of combat. If the leader is unable to make them, people can die. In the business world, processes and decision-making were widely different because everything went to the bottom line.

Loyalty in the service is to the individuals, the institution, and above all, the Constitution. Loyalty in the business world is to the bottom line and money only. Serving in Washington is in an environment where it was all about money for your programs, courtesy of the Congress and the American people annually. This contrasted radically with industry, where you had to earn money for your company if you wanted to stay around. Compensation packages for mid-level executives in business can take several forms but generally will include a base salary, bonuses, 401Ks, and stock options as well as medical and dental plans. Compensation for senior executives often involves secret negotiations that can lead to some of the egregious payouts one reads about in the media. Either way, it can add up to a sizable amount of money.

Consequently, individuals functioning in the business environment were very careful about making decisions for fear of making a bad one, which could bring about negative consequences relating to their jobs. I learned that decisions were often made by committee rather than one individual, and after much discussion and compromise. It was clear there was safety in numbers. In many instances, the company controllers or Chief Financial Officers (CFOs) retained as much power as the CEO in the decision-making process. Early on in my tenure at ITT, I had one individual tell me, "A good controller could dissect the molecules of a penny and still make money." It was all part of the effort to continue to enhance the bottom line within the company. The successful company will not spend money on a whim unless there is a clear opportunity for a substantial return on its investment. If the company does not meet financial expectations for one reason or another, the CEO and other members of the leadership can get called on the carpet for failing to achieve established annual goals.

Does that affect the customers who will be recipients of the product? The answer is no. It could certainly impact the real customer, the shareholder in the company. Company shareholders who begin to lose money in their investments can exercise clout with the company board. The most recent classic example of this is the fallout at Boeing over the problems with the 737 MAX 8 aircraft. Boeing's leadership is getting rough treatment from its shareholders as well as the government over the potential loss in value in their investments. Transfer that to a situation where the Navy builds a $13 billion aircraft carrier, which still doesn't function correctly some two years from when it was supposed to be ready. The ship's ammunition elevators do not work for one reason or another. It still needs millions more too correct the problems not fixed during construction. They get the money after huffing and puffing in Congress and then sail on hopefully in another eighteen months. If a situation like that occurred in industry, the CEO, senior leadership, and maybe members of the board could all be looking for new work. Waste of funds and overruns are not tolerated for very long in industry. In the Defense Department, it is routine. Management of programs in industry is world-class compared to the Defense Department. This is not to denigrate anyone because that is the way the system works. You have to understand it, maintain your outlook to get along and make the necessary adjustments.

My initial responsibilities within the defense sector were primarily in business development and congressional relations. The former dealt mostly with the U.S. Army early on, because there was a one-year cooling-off period for all retiring flag officers restricting them from doing any business with representatives within their former service department. This requirement has since been changed to two years by Senator John McCain, among others, who became tired of the revolving door practices between the services and industry. The people who worked within the defense sector headquarters in Rosslyn were all first-class and generally helpful where possible. As a general officer, one has to learn to tone down his act in the civilian arena because there is no officer/enlisted relationship. Several employees had not an idea what a general was or even cared for that matter. There were examples of this at ITT on the part of retired generals who did not do much more than blow their credibility with the employees. Instead of being reasonable, they tried to ram programs through the process, which usually failed.

Everybody was primarily equal, other than those on different pay scales, at the executive levels of the company. Business practices usually will follow a model where you are on your own to achieve assigned goals annually. I can't emphasize this point enough. The close management decisions come when executives are watching the numbers to see how the goals are being achieved. In the military, nobody has ever heard of the finite inspection of the numbers, because they are not performing toward a fiscal goal. There it is all about requirements and how to achieve them.

All of this was an education for me, but I gained much experience as time went along. Business development is a general term designed to cover a wide range of proposed opportunities for programs that the company is either interested in or is already manufacturing a product while looking at ways to improve on what they are selling.

This requires that you have excellent relationships with the service you are engaged with. It also means the rapport must be developed to interest them in a new technology that might fit one of the service requirements. A good example would be the tactical radio that had a fine voice capability but couldn't send or receive data. The objective would be to develop a data capability compatible with the existing tactical radios. This particular example was worked for years in both the Army and Marines to give their radios the capability which would be interoperable between the services. This was the first part. The second part was requirements still had to be met for increasing amounts of data to be stored in the radio and moved along a tactical internet.

The business development guys were usually in this project, as it was developed to satisfy both the user and the company who was producing the radio. That sounds relatively simple on the surface, but it was not all that easy to bring the capability to fruition over time. If funding was an issue, there were instances where help might be available by working the issue in the appropriate committees in Congress for additional funding. This is where the congressional relations responsibility came in to play with my job. If we were going to try to get some additional funding for an existing product in the services, there had to be a clear, immediate need. It also had to be substantiated and backed up by the service before we could even get started with the Congress. A real-world example of this will come later.

I spent most of my first year learning the issues and developing relationships with the various management levels within ITT Defense. The goal was to be able to assist with specific programs under development in the Defense Value Centers in different locations around the country. In 1995, word began to circulate that the ITT Corporation was going to be broken up into smaller pieces, supposedly to give Wall Street a clearer idea of what we were doing and to increase the overall value of the major new pieces of the corporation. I am not sure if those were the real issues, but I know that specific individuals made a significant amount of money by engineering the breakup. The end result was that the insurance piece (The Hartford) and the Sheraton hotels, including the Chiga chain in Europe, were spun off, while most of the manufacturing was gathered under what became ITT Industries. Each of the three would have new CEOs, and new boards, as well as separate positions on the New York Stock Exchange.

Our defense sector came under ITT Industries and was now responsible for Communications, Night-Vision, Air Defense Radars, and Electronic Warfare Systems, as well as a large services industry that included a spaceport at Vandenberg AFB in California. Each of these value centers (Aerospace Communications Division, ITT Night-Vision, ITT Gilfillan, Avionics, and Mission Systems) reported into ITT Defense headquarters, which had moved out to Tysons Corner, Virginia. The customer base for this new organization included all four of the services, NASA, and the intelligence agencies as well as other segments of the government.

When all the administrative issues with the new organization were sorted out, the new Industries CEO threw a very large party for all the senior management executives in the organization at one of the Sheraton Hotels in Boston. This was followed by a day of briefings and information sessions designed to get people to know each other. It was a terrific way to start out fresh.

Before the breakup, ITT had a really strong program for educating its executives from across the corporation, designed to improve awareness of where the corporation was going, as well as to work through a series of problems associated with the ongoing business operations. It also provided another excellent opportunity for executives to develop and strengthen relationships between all the business sectors in the corporation. This program was run out of the New York headquarters, but the actual specifically designed graduate course was conducted at the Fuqua School of Business at Duke University in Durham, North Carolina. I was selected to attend this course after about eleven months on the job, and it really helped me to get a much better understanding of the corporation, as well as some of the challenges facing ITT. The information learned at this week-long session was extremely valuable. The contacts made really served me well during the twelve years I was with the company. In an organization as big as either the original corporation or the later ITT Industries, this kind of experience was invaluable in trying to get everyone pulling together on the same page.

While my experience was developing at ITT Defense, there were a variety of events happening at home that were very positive to watch. Anne had graduated from high school in 1994 and was attending Virginia Tech. While in school, she joined the Kroger Company and worked in the Kroger stores in Blacksburg. She graduated from Tech in 1998 with a degree in Bio Business. After graduation, she served in management roles in Kroger's Blacksburg-area stores. In 2003 she was promoted to Advertising Specialist for the mid-Atlantic division, handling marketing responsibilities for 126 stores in six states. She was later promoted to Assistant Merchandiser for Drug and General Merchandise, managing a department with huge amounts in annual sales. With her longtime partner, Brady, she bought a home in a nice Roanoke neighborhood with a large yard where their dogs could run.

TJ was in high school in 1994 and very active in the Boy Scouts High Adventure program with a troop in Centreville, Virginia. I supported his activities, but can honestly say I hiked more on these treks than I ever did in 34 years in the Marine Corps. In the summers of 1994 and 1995, he participated in two expeditions to the Philmont Boy Scout Ranch in New Mexico. This sits on 150,000 acres of prime mountains and wilderness donated to the Scouts by Phillips Petroleum some years ago. It is located outside of Cimarron, New Mexico, and is a terrific place for young boys to learn something about themselves. The first trek in 1994 covered 84 miles in all kinds of terrain and weather for eleven days. The second trek in 1995 went for 77 miles over different terrain on the ranch. During the summer of 1996, his mixed crew of girl and boy high adventure scouts went on a third expedition that took them to Wyoming for a trek completely around the Teton Range in Grand Teton National Park. This one covered a distance of some 55 miles in high altitude and spectacular mountainous terrain. Finally, he participated in one more trek with a mixed crew that went into the Rocky Mountain National Park and up and over the Continental Divide in the summer of 1997. TJ received his badge for Eagle Scout, graduated from high school in 1998, and entered Duke University that fall on an Air Force Scholarship. Sue was able to get back into Adult Education in Prince William County in 1992 while I was in the Pentagon. She continued in this capacity for several years in northern Virginia following my retirement.

Several personnel changes occurred within the Industries Defense headquarters during the first three years I was there. One was the hiring of Greg Pallas as the overall coordinator for Defense Political activities in Washington. He was responsible for the Political Action Committee (PAC) and managed the fund we used to support various members in Congress in areas in the country where we had interests. He also kept close contact with various committees on Capitol Hill to stay abreast of changes in defense bills and especially appropriations as it might affect ITT Defense. Greg was a Naval Academy graduate who had served in the Navy for many years. When he joined ITT Defense, he had finished a long tour as the Chief of Staff for Senator James Exxon of Nebraska, who was retiring from the office.

Greg was a terrific guy, and we worked really well together for several years. He had a tremendous reputation on the Hill and knew how to get things done without creating difficulties. He and I spent many hours working National Guard issues and traveled all over the country together visiting Guard units as well as participating in their many functions. We were in San Antonio and preparing to attend one of many Texas Guard functions when he complained of not feeling very well. We backed off from the event and flew home. Shortly after that, he indicated to me he had cancer and was not going to make it. I think he lingered for almost a year and then was gone. We participated in a memorial service for him at the chapel on the grounds of the U.S. Naval Academy in Annapolis. He was buried there, and I had lost a very good and loyal friend.

In addition to my responsibilities in the office, I had the flexibility to branch out in other activities. I frequently attended quarterly operations reviews that were required of the Value Centers by the CEO at ITT Defense. These usually took the form of a two-day conference whereby we would get briefed on the status of all the ongoing programs that a Value Center was working. This was followed by a thorough scrubbing of the numbers associated with each program. Then it would be planning for the future programs they were considering. This was where the CEO would usually lay into the leadership of a particular Value Center regarding the budget for this initiative, the Research and Development (R&D) costs associated with the proposed new start, and what the potential customer was interested in. Here we had to separate the "wheat from the chaff." Many of these proposals were not based on solid research or a thorough understanding of what the military unit in the field or even another service in another country really wanted. In effect, what was the service requirement for the product? There was any number of instances where one of our engineers had this great idea or technology but had no clear view as to what the service required or needed. In effect, it amounted to building something just because the engineer liked it.

In the business development world, the risk assessment and expenditure of R&D funds for something not clearly laid out from all angles would usually get a negative response from the CEO. Again, it was continuously all about managing the numbers and the bottom line. Superfluous ideas were not approved without a thorough understanding of what might be possible, and this was never clearer when someone had a great idea of selling something on the international market. On occasion, it became obvious someone had not really done the required due diligence before presenting it to the CEO. Times could get really hard very quickly for the briefer if he had not done his homework. I remember one incident where one of the Value Centers had a proposal to sell commercial air control radars to India. Great idea, but the due diligence had not been thoroughly vetted, and the CEO launched on the head of that Value Center. There was also an issue at the time that to be successful in that country, you had to "grease some palms," so to speak. That was not tolerated under the current company leadership, which I thought was very appropriate.

On one very bright fall day in Virginia, I was on my way to the office when I began to get reports on the car radio that a plane had apparently crashed into one of the two buildings at the World Trade Center in New York. As the news continued to expand on that incident, a second report came over the radio that a second plane had crashed into the second building at the World Trade Center. By the time I arrived at the office, the first building had already collapsed into a pile of rubble, and the second one would soon follow. This was followed by the third plane, which slammed into the Pentagon, causing significant casualties and damage. Then there was the fourth plane that crashed into a field in Pennsylvania after passengers attempted to retake the aircraft from terrorists. Most of the people at the headquarters just watched the disaster unfold on television in stunned silence.

The events of that day on September 11, 2001, caused a transformation the country had not seen since the Japanese attack on Pearl Harbor on December 7, 1941. Within our headquarters, we tried to calm fears this would go beyond the incidents at the World Trade Center. By the end of the day, a relative calm had returned to our employees as everyone started to go about his or her business and then left for home. The country began to recover as best it could and follow what the Administration would do in response. It had become clear the attack had been predicted by the CIA and others almost to the day, but the warning not been acted on by elements in the government along with members of the National Security staff in the White House. This was stunning, to say the least, and represented unbelievable neglect of responsibility. Could the attacks have been stopped if people in positions of authority had been alert? That will never be known. One would hope those serving the president would have responded differently. The Administration began to unravel the plot and move toward responding in some way. Industry across the board, including ITT, continued to do what they were trying to accomplish with their normal operations that were ongoing before 9/11. It would be a while before the warfighting needs of the services would surface within the Pentagon and addressed the conflict. It continued to be business as usual for ITT Defense for the time being.

CHAPTER 25
OBSERVATIONS IN AFGHANISTAN

Very early in 2002, I was approached by the current Commandant of the Marine Corps, about serving on a Defense Department Team that was going to go to Southwest Asia to observe and report back on the status of the ongoing conflict in Afghanistan. He needed a Marine representative on the team who could represent him, along with other retired flag officers who were representing their respective services. I had received permission to go from my leadership at ITT Defense, so this would be my third conflict, but this time as an observer and not an active participant in any fighting.

Following 9/11, the Defense Department had worked diligently to get a handle on what was going to be needed to achieve any success against bin Laden, al-Qaeda, and the Taliban in Afghanistan. This was a fairly new kind of conflict for conventional forces equipped with high-tech equipment about to deploy to a country that appeared to be not too far out of the Stone Age. This was behind much of the frustration of the then-Secretary of Defense Donald Rumsfeld because there were few viable targets for high-tech bombing throughout the country.

There is a reason why Afghanistan has been called "the Graveyard of Empires." Afghanistan is a wildly rugged country that occupies a segment of the Hindu Kush as well as the vast plains in the south and west of the country. Its narrow mountain passes have, for centuries, been the only way invading armies could either penetrate or pass through on the way to other areas for conquest. It has occupied a strategic position that has been the center of clashes between armies as well as civilizations. It was the scene of conflicts as far back as when Alexander the Great conquered it, starting in 329 BC. The Mongol hordes under Genghis Khan descended on what was

Afghanistan in 1221 BC and laid waste to just about everything that existed in the country. That was followed by the campaigns of Tamerlane in the late 1500s, with the same result. Many invasions or occupations of the country have come to grief because of the fierce resistance provided by the various tribes and warlords who live in the mountains. They are governed on a feudal basis and have refused to be ruled by a centralized government down through the ages.

When the Afghans are not fighting among themselves, they can come together and act as a single force, which usually happens only when there is an outside threat. Some examples of this were in the First Anglo-Afghan War, where the British were driven out of the area around Kabul in the 1840s. In the winter of 1842, they suffered grievous losses in men and materiel in the mountain passes following their retreat from Kabul to Jalalabad. In the Second Anglo-Afghan War in the 1880s, the British suffered almost the same fate in different battles in the same passes as had occurred forty years earlier. The British did fare better in this campaign against the Afghans.

Enter the Soviets to provide support and development for the Afghans with a caretaker government. Political upheaval between factions of the Soviet-backed government and the Afghans, over time, led to a deteriorating situation that caused major revolts to break out in the fall of 1978. In December 1979, Soviet Special Forces units began flying into Kabul and Bagram to establish bases for the follow-on Red Army. Major elements of the Red Army then began deploying into Afghanistan from various directions to take up positions to control the country. Over the next ten years, the Afghans fought the Soviets to a standstill, which devastated the country again. Increasing pressure from the mujahideen and continuing defeats in the field drove the political leadership in Moscow to quit the country, leaving another satellite government in place.

By February 1989, the Red Army had left Afghanistan. What followed was another civil war between former mujahideen commanders and warlords within the country. Beginning in 1994, the Taliban began to rise out of the carnage in southern Afghanistan and gradually take over large sections of the country. Sustaining thousands of casualties in constant fighting against the warlords in the north, the Taliban finally controlled around 90% of the country by 2001. Al-Qaeda and Osama bin Laden first appeared in Afghanistan in 1996. From there, he plotted several terrorist attacks, which eventually culminated in the attacks on 9/11.

The Taliban refused to give up bin Laden as demanded by the United States. That led to the beginning of airstrikes by U.S. and British bombers on the few valuable targets that existed in the country. The Taliban were not impressed with the effort, which gradually increased over time. The United States got involved on the ground by deploying U.S. Army Special Forces with CIA field representatives. The objective was to support the Northern Alliance forces under General Rashid Dostum and others. Special Forces A teams, some on horseback and backed up by extensive U.S. airpower, began to decimate Taliban forces in the field.

When the Northern Alliance went over on the attack in December 2001, the Taliban began to break and flee south across the Somali Plain. In the retreat toward Kabul, they were pounded all the way by U.S. and British aircraft. At the same time, U.S. Marines of the 15th Marine Expeditionary Unit had landed on the coast and moved overland to establish positions south of the airfield at Kandahar. As winter closed down operations in the field, the United States had some success initially against the Taliban but had been frustrated by the inability to find bin Laden. We found out later he had escaped into the hills and eventually to Pakistan.

The team started to get together in early February 2002. Initially, we were to receive briefs in the Pentagon. Then we were to fly to Florida to meet with General Tommy Franks, the Commander of the U.S. CENTCOM, and responsible for the operations in Afghanistan. In the initial meetings in the Pentagon, we were given a basic understanding of the objectives at that time. The one thing I remembered from the briefing from the Air Force commenting on conducting close air support with B-52s from 35,000 feet. This got my attention because the Marines had perfected close air support tactics decades earlier, going back to the late 1930s in Central America. The difference now was technology had progressed to the point where accuracy via GPS could make bombing much more effective at those altitudes. Another issue was with the Navy and the requirements for tanking Navy jets going to targets in Afghanistan and returning to the carriers on station at sea. The distances were such that missions were exceedingly long and had to be covered by Air Force tankers for refueling. This became routine as the build-up of airpower continued around the Gulf regions.

In the meetings with General Franks in Tampa, Florida, we received accurate assessments of the conditions that existed in the country and the relations with the Northern Alliance. I noted he had a picture of himself sitting with the various warlords who commanded the Alliance. It looked like one American general with several "hitmen" in period costumes of the area. I complimented him on the picture and received a rather colorful description of his new friends, including Abdul Rashid Dostum, the Afghan politician and general/warlord who has sided with the winners during several wars in Afghanistan.

In one of those meetings, I sat beside a retired four-star Army general named Peter Schoomaker. I had heard about him, as he had tremendous credibility within the Army and the other services. A very friendly individual, he was a quick thinker who would later play a major role within the Army as the conflict developed in Iraq. We continued to get the latest updates on the conflict from several agencies as the itinerary came together for the trip to deploy to Southwest Asia.

The plan was to be gone around twelve days and then come back, report our findings, and be prepared to go out again if required. The first stops were in Saudi Arabia, the UAE, and Qatar. Most of the issues were the development of the airfields where strikes were being run out of at the time, along with expansion plans necessary for facilities to support the air effort for Afghanistan. We had an opportunity to be briefed by B-1 bomber crews regarding what they were doing, as well as their impressions of the air effort so far in the campaign. From there, it was on to Oman to be briefed on air medevac plans for casualties coming out of Afghanistan and passed through an Air Force expeditionary field hospital located near Muscat. This was very important because of the great distances any casualties would have to be transported before they could be treated for very serious wounds. The staff at that facility really had their act together and were extremely professional.

One of the things I thought the team should do was to go out to a carrier, so the team could get Navy impressions on items like the tanking issues, or any command-and-control problems with any joint or allied air activities. The visit could also give them a firsthand account from battle group leadership on the status of tactical operations over Afghanistan. Also, the team would get a chance to observe air operations onboard a carrier to achieve a better understanding of just what was involved.

For me, this was almost like going back in time as the Commanding General, 4th MEB in the Persian Gulf in 1990-1991. We had a Navy Rear Admiral who had been assigned as an escort for the trip, and he was able to get us time on one of the carriers on station in the region that was conducting strikes in Afghanistan. He had requested a Navy C-2A Greyhound Carrier Onboard Delivery (COD) to fly us out to the USS *Theodore Roosevelt* (CVN 71), where we would land on the deck of the "*TR*."

We were on board the ship for the better part of three hours. The team received briefs from the battlegroup commander and his staff and observed both the launching and recovery of the aircraft on the ship. Then it was back on the COD for the catapult launch off the *TR* and the flight back to Muscat. After two false starts in Muscat, we flew by an Air Force C-130 to another advance base for flying troops and sustainment into Afghanistan. There we had an opportunity to visit with both Air Force and Special Operations personnel who were generally working in the southern part of the country. This was also the first location where I had the opportunity to observe units of the Army's 101st Airborne Division who were staging for further deployment into Afghanistan. The paratroopers were well organized, looked great, and ready to go.

Late that night, we boarded the C-130 that had been assigned to the Task Force for the flight to Kandahar, Afghanistan. The purpose of this stop was to visit the Marines of the 15th MEU (SOC). They were in positions around the airfield and were running several POW compounds that were occupied by Taliban prisoners. After the normal briefs and a tour of the compound the Marines had constructed, we got into discussions over their impressions of what they had experienced so far. There were now special operators working out of that position, including the first Navy SEALs that we had encountered on this trip. The MEU also had a representative from the FBI who was there to question the Taliban that was brought in.

During the briefing, he had indicated they were required to read every Taliban prisoner his "Miranda Rights" before processing him further. I was about half-listening, but that brought me right out of it. What were we doing reading the Taliban "Miranda Rights"? Most of them were illiterate and had no knowledge of what that case was about, which occurred in Arizona some years before. I never did get a satisfactory answer, but it went a long way in showing just how screwy things were in Washington. This went back to the superfluous argument between inexperienced civilian lawyers in the Administration over who was a combatant and who was a terrorist. History now shows that very few if any Taliban ever made it to a court in the United States.

The next stop was going to be Bagram in north-central Afghanistan. We arrived there at around 2:00 AM after having to make three attempts at landing on that airfield on night-vision goggles (NVGs). Bagram had played a key role during the Taliban retreat south from the Northern Alliance attacks. Special Forces operators had run numerous airstrikes against the retreating Taliban forces from Bagram. The entire airfield had been shot up, and there were wrecked old Soviet aircraft all around the airstrip. There was no power available for lights on the airstrip, which may have contributed to the difficulties that the C-130 crew had in trying to land there. Once on the ground, we were warned not to wander off of the runways because of active minefields that were all over the area. We toured a much larger cantonment where there were many more Taliban prisoners locked up in outdoor compounds with high barbed-wire fences. There had been no sign of trouble with the POWs as the guards were heavily armed and all around the compound. That visit continued to be peaceful, and we were soon out of there.

The last stop of the night was at another former Soviet Russian airfield in Uzbekistan. The airfield itself was a muddy and dreary place with Soviet planes sitting in the mud and covered with tarps. We were told that they usually flew them two or three times a year to make sure that they were still operable. There were several U.S. aircraft coming and going from this location, and we could see old Soviet concrete bunker-like hangars where Soviet aircraft had probably operated out of in the past. They were now occupied by U.S. units and personnel. We arrived there at around 5:00 AM and immediately went to a Special Forces compound for breakfast and briefings. We were given a series of briefs as to what had been going on from this location and how Special Forces teams had deployed south to marry up with the Northern Alliance units for the fight against the Taliban.

The Special Forces officers who gave the briefs were absolutely low-key, very forthright, and totally professional. All of them were much older and mature than the hotshot paratroopers we had seen earlier, and I was extremely impressed with the way they carried themselves. When asked if there was anything, we could do for them, the answer was they were fine, and things were going well. This was the understatement of the evening. The next series of meetings there were with the Commanding General and the staff of the Army's 10th Mountain Division. This was intriguing to me because it had been the Army's premier mountain division that fought in major battles in Italy during World War II. Many of the training techniques that we had used at the Mountain Warfare Training Center in California had been copied from the experiences that 10th Mountain had used while training in Colorado during the run-up to the war. The division had been deactivated after World War II but was brought back to life in the late 1980s and based in Fort Drum, New York.

After the usual round of pleasantries, it became obvious there were frustrations among the higher echelons of the division. Part of it was due to the fact whatever the strategy was for the campaign, it had not been clear what the division was supposed to do now that they were here in Uzbekistan. My initial thoughts were this was symptomatic of the overall malaise which existed in the U.S. plans for Afghanistan that would bugger the effort for years to come When asked what their concerns were at this point, the response was they could not get USAF C-130 support to move personnel and equipment around from where they were located. I suspected this was a matter of airlift priorities within the country, but it was brought to the attention of senior Air Force leadership responsible for airlift later in a stop in Germany. After some discussion on the matter in Germany, we could find nobody there who knew there was a problem. This was resolved much later when the headquarters for the 10th Mountain was tasked to conduct operations in the Shah-i-Kot Valley in Operation Anaconda. The objective was to get bin Laden and more al-Qaeda. I thought the leadership in the 10th Mountain Division was very aggressive, as they should have been, and wanted to get into the action anywhere in Afghanistan. It looked like CENTCOM, and political leadership in Washington had not come to grips with what the strategy would be after the initial success by the Northern Alliance backed by U.S. Special Forces and allied airpower.

We left Uzbekistan on an Air Force C-17 for the big airbase at Incirlik in Turkey. The flight over the high mountains to Turkey was spectacular, as they were all covered in snow with absolutely no sign of human habitation on the ground. Upon arrival in Turkey, we were on the ground for a few hours before transferring to another aircraft for the flight to Wiesbaden in Germany. There we had to brief the Air Force leadership on some of our findings in Afghanistan to include command relationships as well as the complaints regarding the lack of C-130 support for the 10th Mountain Division. Following the briefs, the team was involved with the write-up regarding what had been observed as well as getting ready to fly back to Washington.

It has since become clear that the Bush Administration had no sound plan for what to do in Afghanistan following the defeats of both al-Qaeda and the Taliban in Operation Anaconda. Many of the warlords in the country simply went back to doing business the way it had always been done. By mid-2002, it was evident Bush was going to launch his unnecessary war in Iraq. To do that, the Pentagon began to draw down many of the assets which had been working in Afghanistan, and this tended to water down even our meager efforts to gain some level of stability in the country. In effect, we lost what little momentum we had gained during the first six months of the campaign. The end result was we have now been involved there for nineteen years with no end in sight. We are still trying to create stability by supporting a rampantly corrupt government and with inadequate security in a country historically and culturally not capable of sustaining such a concept for very long.

The most glaring example of a lesson not learned is the political leadership in Washington has not learned a thing from history and continues to be culturally ignorant when it comes to dealing with countries in that part of the world. We keep making the same mistakes over and over again, no matter how nice it sounds to make glowing statements about how we can bring democratic principles to countries in that part of the word. The various administrations continue to put forth muddled strategic plans, which are generally hollow when it comes time for execution. Except for very few individuals, Congress has not a clue on how to solve a myriad of these issues, much less take responsibility for its actions. Then there is any number of "think tanks" around Washington, all with their own expert agendas we hear nightly on television. Despite the rhetoric, it is certainly not for lack of trying on the part of the troops who have been there for the last nineteen years and have paid the price.

In March 2003, George W. Bush initiated the invasion of Iraq under the bogus pretenses that Saddam had weapons of mass destruction. In what turned out to be one of the biggest strategic blunders in the history of the United States, we captured Iraq and Saddam but succeeded in upsetting the status quo in countries around Iraq, which continues to have implications today. As bad as Saddam was, he formed a bulwark against the spread of Shia influence into the Sunni heartland in the Arabian Peninsula. Iran is now a major player in Iraq; that was not the case before the invasion. The rise of ISIS and the ongoing destruction in Syria can be traced back to the unintended consequences of our invasion of Iraq. The combat forces succeeded in defeating both the Saddam Fedayeen and the Republican Guard in a very short period and captured Baghdad. Then the Administration's appointed Proconsul got rid of most of all the key bureaucrats that ran the Iraqi government because they were members of the Baathist Party. Yet in Iraq, if you wanted to work in that government or teach school, you had to belong to the Baathist Party.

Next, he disbanded the Iraqi Army, which put an estimated 125,000 armed soldiers on the streets, all with weapons but no jobs. Following the capture of Baghdad, the society collapsed into an orgy of looting and destruction. We found out later, and in a similar fashion as in Afghanistan, that there was no real plan developed by CENTCOM, the Pentagon, or the Bush Administration for rebuilding either the government or the destroyed infrastructure in Iraq. We have paid dearly for that in lives and treasure. The ideologues who were responsible for that disaster were never held accountable for their actions.

The whole episode had been an eye-opener for me, and now it was back to the mundane and somewhat less active business reality ongoing in industry.

Not very long after my return to Defense headquarters, I was tasked to attend the International Defense Exposition (IDEX) in Abu Dhabi. It is the capital of the United Arab Emirates and sits on the southern end of the Persian Gulf. The exposition takes place every two years and is attended by many of the major international corporations doing business in that part of the world. We were there because of various communications and electronic warfare programs we were working in several countries in the region. I was there for a week before traveling to Riyadh, Saudi Arabia, to coordinate ITT activities with the company's agents working radio programs with the Saudi National Guard. Riyadh is an interesting place in that the architecture is modern in many ways but sterile in appearance. Most of the Americans were living in cantonments on the edge of the city and somewhat isolated from the rest of the population. The ITT office was run by a retired U.S. Army major general who was well-established with the Saudi procurement officials. While there, he took me out to the camel races and to a camel market where Arabs were buying and selling some of their stock. I had never seen so many camels in one place. From Riyadh, it was off to Kuwait City to meet with our agents as well as meet with the Defense Attaché at the American embassy. Our issues there were again over tactical radios and the status of ongoing programs within the Kuwaiti defense establishment. In subsequent meetings with our local agents, I met one of the supervisors who had been in the Kuwaiti underground during the Iraqi occupation in 1990-1991. It turned out he was the one who had passed along the information to us that the Iraqis were wiring the two LNG plants for destruction at the Ash Shuaybah petrochemical complex, the initial objective for the amphibious assault in 1991. I thanked him for his brave efforts and the impact that information had been on our planning—another example of how small the world can be on occasion. Two days after that meeting, I was one my way back home.

CHAPTER 26

THE SPACEPORT AND THE GUARD

THE SPACEPORT

The old ITT under Harold Geneen was famous for acquiring something it didn't have in its inventory of businesses. One of the holdings was a spaceport in California. When the breakup of the ITT Corporation occurred, much of the work and contracts regarding technologies for space-based platforms was transferred over to the ITT Defense sector and placed under the Systems Division. Defense was already doing a significant amount of business both in navigation and sensor systems for some of the predominant intelligence agencies in the country. What came out of the negotiations with the Air Force was a 25-year lease of Launch Complex 6 at Vandenberg AFB in California. It was located at the southern end of the base overlooking the Pacific Ocean. Vandenberg was also the location of several other launch complexes that accommodated larger rockets used by the space industry. The ITT facility had originally been constructed to support West Coast Launches of the Space Shuttle. It consisted of a huge payload processing facility which had three bays where classified payloads could be prepared for a launch and then rolled across a concrete ramp to be married up on top of the booster already in place on the launch pad. Of course, it was all tied into the command-and-control networks at Vandenberg, NORAD, and Houston, among other locations.

After the *Challenger* blew up shortly following its launch in Florida, a decision was made to not use Launch Complex 6 for Space Shuttle operations. ITT then entered into a joint partnership with the Air Force for the use of the payload processing facility as well as the launchpad for possible commercial space operations if the potential ever developed. I got interested in this business because nobody else was paying much attention to the possibilities, and the rent for the use of the facility to the Air Force was unbelievably cheap. The complex was world-class in terms of what could be done there if you could generate interest in either payload providers or booster manufacturers in doing business with ITT Defense. This meant dealing with the "big boys" in the space world, which clearly was a challenge. We had a retired Air Force colonel by the name of Earl Severo, who had served for several years at Vandenberg and was responsible for the operations and business development activities at the spaceport.

Earl was a very persistent, never-say-die individual who generally would not take no for an answer. This had put him in a position as a transactional pro who could work with the likes of Lockheed Martin, McDonnell Douglas, and a few others in a fairly effective manner. After making some modifications to the office spaces in the processing facility designed to make them more user-friendly, he began to generate some interest from companies who were in the payload design business. Several of them were already working with the government, including NASA. Generating interest within the major booster manufactures was really hard. First of all, they all had their own preferences for launch pads for their ongoing programs, some of which were already in place at Vandenberg. Second, there was much resistance regarding the arrival of a potential competitor for future space operations. This I clearly understood, but it is the essence of business to try to provide the customer, in this case, the government, the best possible deal for the services rendered.

I remember one meeting with a potential client in El Segundo, California, that degenerated into a shouting match between the client and the president of ITT Systems. The point being with this incident, the client was not interested in coming together with any kind of partnership with such a small competitor. Most of the other meetings on the same subjects were much more civil once the two parties realized both were after the same thing, and there was more safety in numbers when dealing with the government. I had found this whole process much more different from anything I had experienced with other customers in different fields. It certainly was not like anything I had experienced on active duty.

Over time, business began to be generated with the payload developers as well as NASA. Initially, there were small payloads that were developed and then processed in our facility before being moved to another launch complex at Vandenberg for launching into space. Interest was generated in the university and science communities for launching small payloads on smaller boosters in support of their ongoing programs, and we did achieve some success with those activities out of Launch Complex 6. Finally, they were able to interest NASA in bringing in a large classified payload to be processed in the payload facility, which gave the complex new life. On the commercial side, there was great interest in having commercial spaceports compete for business both in and outside of the government customers. That led to competition between three spaceport companies, one in Alaska, the second one in Virginia, and the ITT facility at Vandenberg. This was fun to watch, but the concept was a little ahead of its time as business did not develop as fast had been forecast. For any customer, including the government, this is a very expensive process with high risk and continued delays for any number of reasons in a launch schedule. Smaller companies in this business, including ITT Defense, did not want to lose money continuously with nothing coming in until the problems could be worked out. The commercial providers could offer their services cheaper than what the government was doing, but it was going to be a very long, slow process.

In the fall of 2004, ITT Defense acquired the Remote Sensing Business from the Eastman Kodak Company to add capability in space and imaging programs it already had. Most of it had been located at the Aerospace and Communications Division (ACD) in Fort Wayne, Indiana. Following the completion of the sale, a new Space Systems Division was created, and much of the space sensing business at ACD was transferred into the new division, along with the piece from Kodak. This was a key acquisition for the space business because Defense was already involved with remote sensing as well as GPS programs that were already in the ITT portfolio. I visited the new facility in Rochester, New York, to get a better understanding of what they were doing. One of the items that stood out immediately was the grinding and polishing capability they had for producing high-resolution mirrors for uses in space. One of the major projects was the competition for placing mirrors for the James Webb Telescope NASA would eventually position in space to observe the heavens. Also, there were several other technologies which added more depth to what was already going on within ITT Defense. I really enjoyed working in this field because it was mostly new and a totally different world in terms of programs and technology enhancements. The bottom line, though, was nothing ever happens quickly in the space world, and a company has to be willing to stay the course if it wants to be successful - usually at great expense.

THE GUARD

The most challenging and rewarding programs I had while at ITT Defense were learning about and working primarily with the Army National Guard. It had become obvious that the U.S. Army could not accomplish its assigned missions without a significant amount of support from the Army National Guard and the Army Reserve. This was due to the fact a large amount of combat support and combat service support capability was in the Guard and Reserve by design because it was not really needed in a peacetime environment. In the build-up to the coming invasion of Iraq, the requirements for the invasion force started to change.

The Army National Guard had its roots all the way back to the Minuteman concept during the Revolution when State and local militias were activated to protect and defend their homes and villages against attack. The National Guard has served in numerous capacities and in most of the nation's wars down through the ages.

Until recent decades, the United States has never had a large standing active Army but had relied on both the Reserve and the National Guard to fill out formations needed for combat operations in times of conflict. During World War I, Guard divisions were activated for service in Europe and performed very well in action against the Germans. One good example of this would be the 42nd Rainbow Division of the New York National Guard, in which General Douglas Mac Arthur had served. It was activated in 1917 for operations in Europe and again in 1943 for operations in the same theater. During World War II, eighteen National Guard divisions fought in Europe and the Pacific alongside active U.S. Army units.

The best example of this would be the landings at Normandy on June 6, 1944, when the 29th Division of the Virginia and Maryland National Guard landed on Omaha Beach next to the Army's 1st Infantry Division (the Big Red One). During the Battle of the Bulge, in the Ardennes in December 1944 and January 1945, the 28th Division of the Pennsylvania National Guard sustained heavy casualties in action against some of the elite German formations during that battle. Guard units fought in Korea, Vietnam, and Southwest Asia, as well. In recent times the Guard is well known for being activated in response to earthquakes, hurricanes, and floods as well as civil disturbances that occur on occasion across the country.

The National Guard belongs to the governors in each state in the union, and not to the Defense Department in Washington unless it is federalized for war or other missions by the president. The regular defense establishment is guided by Title 10 of the U.S. Code, whereas the National Guard is guided by Title 32 of the U.S. Code. This has implications for funding and the development of programs that could be of benefit to both the active units and Reserve and Guard establishments. An example of this would be the rebuild of M-1A1 tank engines. The Guard has a tank rebuilding capability at Fort Riley, Kansas, while U.S. Army has one at a depot in Anniston, Alabama. Some years back it was cheaper, along with better warranties, to get the job done at Fort Riley, but if the Marines want to get engines for their tanks rebuilt, they have to go to Anniston rather than Fort Riley because it takes Title 32 funding to get the job done there. The Marines (as well as others) do not get funding under Title 32. They get funds under Title 10. I had run into this problem a few years ago when we were trying to get the funds switched to save the Marines some money. We even tried to get support from the Kansas Guard because it was a jobs issue for them, but they could not get by the title restrictions.

There is a long-standing policy whereby the U.S. Army is responsible for funding and procuring major equipment for the Army National Guard, as the Guard does not have a procurement budget for major end items. The same thing applies to the U.S. Air Force and the procurement of aircraft and related equipment for the Air National Guard. It was common knowledge many units in the Army National Guard were operating with old and somewhat outdated equipment at all levels. There were shortages everywhere due to the lack of funding within the Army necessary to support the Guard. This problem had gone on for so long that the guardsmen just took it for granted they were stuck with the hand-me-downs.

At the start of the invasion of Iraq in March 2003, there were signs this was going to become an issue that had to be addressed. On one of my first trips out to the headquarters for the Oregon National Guard in Salem, Oregon, discussions with the Adjutant General in the state gave me a clear idea of what they were facing. They had shortages in both tactical communications and night-vision goggles in their 41st Infantry Brigade Combat Team (BCT). The radios were the earliest models of the Single Channel Air-Ground Radio System (SINCGARS) with very little data capability, and the night-vision goggles the soldiers carried were very old and of poor quality. In doing research on the equipment conditions in several other Guard BCTs in other states, I heard the same common complaint regarding both pieces of equipment. After much discussion within the business development section of ITT Defense, it was agreed that we develop a

345

plan to address these issues as well as try to generate business for ITT.

In dealing with the Guard, the approach was very different from when we were working an initiative within the active services. The Guard had gone on for so long, only getting hand-me-downs from the Army; they were very supportive and included the appropriate industry representatives in on their planning sessions for what they needed. They were also open to encouraging industry representatives' participation in their local and national conferences and expositions. This is different from what you experience when dealing with the active services, which can be very difficult at times. The plan had to take into account the source of funding for this initiative, the real requirement within the BCTs for both new radios and NVGs, as well as the priorities for each Adjutant General. What were the priorities for this initiative concerning the individual governor's own state priorities, and what kind of support could we get from the National Guard Bureau in Washington? What roles could the National Guard Association of the U.S. (NGAUS) as well as the Adjutant Generals Association of the U.S. (AGAUS) play in supporting lobbying efforts in Congress if it came to such activity?

I mention both NGAUS and the AGAUS because the Guard and the respective political organizations in each state have had a reputation for years for lobbying the Congress for one thing or another as the only way to get around the lack of funding coming from the Army or the Air Force. The Guard needed so many kinds of equipment at the time that it almost looked like "mission impossible." For some time the Congress had set up what was called the National Guard and Reserve Equipment Account, or NGREA, and each year it would put a lump sum of money into this account and direct the Guard Bureau divide it up according to the priorities of both the Army and Air Guard. This was helpful, but it did not get anywhere near to the resolution of the equipment shortages. The political clout the National Guard and its friends have on the Hill is legendary because the Guard has units in many cities as well as in all the states. Congress is well aware of the clout because the guardsmen do vote!

What we were faced with could be best described as a six-pronged approach that required coordinating with the state adjutants general in specific states, the BCT commanders, the NGAUS representatives, the AGAUS, the Guard Bureau, and finally the appropriate committees and state delegations in Congress. While the Army National Guard was almost as large as the U.S. Army, it was determined we would focus only on the BCTs that were lining up to deploy to Iraq. Greg Pallas and I had the lead for this effort. He would cover the Congress when it became necessary, and I would be responsible for the marketing with the Adjutant Generals and BCTs in their respective states.

This was the beginning of an effort that would last for the better part of six years and was at its height during the first four years that the United States was operating in Iraq. It did not take long for Army Guard units to get federalized and called to active duty for what all knew would be deployments to Iraq, which was now in total chaos. Initially, it was very slow going in terms of outfitting Guard units that could operate with the same kind of communications equipment the active Army was using. In a surprise move by the Pentagon, Army four-star General Peter Schoomaker was pulled out of retirement in August 2003 and nominated as the new Army Chief of Staff. After getting oriented in his new job, he issued guidance that no Guard BCT would deploy to Iraq without the same kind of equipment currently in the regular Army BCTs already operating in that country. This certainly was a help for us, because we were now not just fighting the Army bureaucracy over the funding for either radios or night-vision goggles.

The marketing effort for me resembled a mini-marathon in that I had to first go out and visit the state headquarters for the Army National Guard, to brief the Adjutant Generals in 24 different states. In some instances, there would be a requirement to go to another location of the state BCT because they were not always collocated at the state headquarters. In most cases, the guardsmen supported the effort through the normal vetting process for funding in each state to try to get the governor's support along with his or her own priorities for that state. The Adjutant Generals are political appointees in uniform made by the governor in each state and are critical for generating support for initiatives on behalf of a governor. At the same time, we had hoped they would pass on their desires to the state delegation in both the House and Senate in Congress. Clearly, whatever success we would have with funding over and above what came annually through the NGREA would end up as a congressional add-on to the annual Defense Authorization and Appropriations Bills. Individual state desires for this equipment would also be passed up through the state and national organizations like NGAUS, as well as the AGAUS, for inclusion in their annual campaign plans in Congress. NGAUS is really a political organization that has representatives in each state to coordinate with and support whatever the Guard units in their respective states need. They can be a potent lobbying organization when it comes to supporting various initiatives that can affect the Guard, and they are closely tied to each state's political organization for grass-roots support.

Equipment was not the only item for support; many other issues impact National Guard units all over the country. During their annual conventions, resolutions are debated and then passed on as a prioritized list for support for the coming political season. An example of how effective NGAUS can be, occurred a few years ago when the Guard was pushing for a billet on the Joint Chiefs of Staff. The Administration fought it, as did the services. The result was that NGAUS and other organizations began to lobby for just such a billet through each state. That led to a declaration signed by the governors in all 50 states strongly supporting the resolution to place a guardsman on the Joint Chiefs of Staff. That effort carried the day, and there is now a four-star guardsman who sits on the JCS.

When the state Adjutant Generals and their BCT headquarters were briefed on the plan, we then began to generate support through both the NGAUS and AGAUS. The Director of the Army Guard at the Guard Bureau in Washington was also working his priorities through the Adjutant Generals, but his priorities initially were for SINCGARS radios and not night-vision goggles in the first two years of this effort. At that point, both Greg Pallas and I began to work the appropriate state delegations in Congress as well as the professional staffs in the appropriate committees. In Congress, the professional committee staffs in the defense and appropriations subcommittees are the continuity for the ongoing initiatives associated with legislation that is going to be acted upon. They possess the corporate memory on history as well as the status of such a program. They are also the ones who do all the work for their committee chairmen in either the House or the Senate. In the offices of a congressman or senator, we had to brief the Military Legislative Assistant (MLA), as there is one in each office who will do the research as well as brief the boss on possible positions and where the political pressure is coming from.

At this level in a state as large as Texas or New York, there may be three or four key congressmen who need to be briefed on the radio issue with the BCT in their state. Consequently, the number of briefings that had to be done ballooned very quickly as we worked our way through the House in particular. Some people have said all you need to do is get to the individual congressman or senator, and that will suffice. That is nice, but not correct, as the MLAs do the work and coordinate closely with the committee staffs on the issues. They are usually the ones who develop the positions for their respective members, as well as coordinate issues with other MLAs in the state delegations. When all of this was done during the spring of our first year of this activity, I had completed 42 briefings to both MLAs and professional staffers on the SINCGARS initiative in the BCTs in the Army Guard. Many of the MLAs were very enthusiastic about the assistance, while others were not as warm, which seemed normal.

It was now of a matter of waiting to see how things would turn out as the various defense bills passed through the deliberations in Congress that eventually led to a bill signed by the president. In the meantime, we were following up with the various Guard organizations that had a vested interest in learning what the outcome would be. Late in the fall of 2003, the defense bills were signed by the president. The result of a large amount of work to get all the players moving in one direction to support this initiative resulted in a multi-million-dollar congressional add-on for SINCGARS radios for the Army National Guard. We now had another three months before the process started all over again. The second time around would be concentrated on keeping the support at all levels in line because we were a long way from completing the task. As a sign of the culture within ITT Defense, they were satisfied with the effort as well as the results, but now it was time to go out and do it again. It was all about the money!

The drive to continue to get both Guard and congressional support for this initiative moved at about the same pace as in the first year. By the end of the third year, our relations within the Army Guard were solid, and we were all working as a team through the annual process with Congress. Some years were better than others, but the support continued to show results when the Defense Authorization and Appropriations Bills were enacted. By the end of the second year, we were continuing to push the Army Guard on the new night-vision goggles that were now flowing into the regular units in both Afghanistan and Iraq.

The Oregon Guard had a facility in that state that was repairing not only the first generation NVG but also some of the newer goggles. It was a slow process and nowhere near keeping up with the demand from the field. After several meetings with the Director of the Army National Guard in Washington and elsewhere, a decision was made which directed the staff in the National Guard Bureau to procure only the latest model of the NVG, which was the PVS-7, for the guard BCTs. This was another critical decision for the support of the soldiers operating in the combat zone in Iraq. It also represented increased business for ITT on top of what was already coming in from the services.

The flow of the PVS-7 NVG would continue over the next three years as the Guard units rotated in and out of Southwest Asia. It was personally gratifying to me after so much effort throughout the process, our soldiers were deployed into the combat zones in both Iraq and Afghanistan with the best equipment in terms of radios and NVGs. I had flashbacks to my tour in that war, because of the equipment we had along with the inability of the system to provide the very best in support for the soldiers and Marines in the field. Not only the incident regarding the toothbrushes and other like personal items among Marines on Hill 881S but new M-16 rifles that did not work because they were not sufficiently tested before giving them to the troops who were in combat early in that war. This cost lives because the weapons would jam when firing or when the individual was in the attack. That was malpractice on the part of both contractors and those within the Defense establishment who failed to meet their responsibilities.

My previous experience in the Expeditionary Warfare Division on the Navy staff caused me to make any number of contacts, both in industry and in some of the professional study and analysis organizations that are all over Washington. I had been asked if I would like to serve as a member of the Naval Studies Board (NSB), which is part of the National Research Council in the National Academy of Science. That seemed like the thing to do, and the company had no objections. The Naval Studies Board, under the effective leadership of Director, Dr. Charles F. Draper, was one of several organizations that the Navy uses to do research and analysis on several subjects that were of interest to the Navy and (to a much lesser degree) the Marine Corps. The NSB was comprised of some of the best scientific thinkers that I had ever worked with. Several of the premier laboratories around the country would very often provide representatives to the various studies, depending on what the subject was going to be. Several very senior flag officers in the Navy would make appearances to lend support and opinions to whatever the subject was under consideration. Each assessment generally lasted for about six months, as established in the contract with the Navy. Some examples of this work included Navy Theater Ballistic Missile Defense, an assessment on Navy Unmanned Vehicles, another on the National Security Implications of Climate Change for U.S. Naval Forces, and one on C4ISR for Future Naval Strike Groups, among several others. In one assessment on Sea Basing, I served as the chair for the work that had to be done on this subject. My time as a member of the NSB continued from 1999 to 2006, and I enjoyed every minute of that experience. It was a great intellectual challenge, and some of what we accomplished had ramifications for today and well into the future.

Another activity that had connections to the Expeditionary Warfare Division was an industry-related committee under the National Defense Industrial Association (NDIA). There are several of these organizations around Washington that are designed to provide industry representatives a forum for determining what the potential business opportunities might be for the large and smaller defense-related companies and the Department of Defense. NDIA is similar to NGAUS in that it also has a lobbying function as well as the mouthpiece for industry-related issues in the policy world of the Department of Defense. Most, if not all, of the defense-related companies, belong to the NDIA. Several committees that fall under the NDIA are generally organized to support some form of warfare within the services, and that is where you can find the companies that produce whatever is needed in that form of warfare. Examples of this might be a committee on tactical wheeled vehicles or another on cybersecurity. There you are likely to find representatives from both the large manufacturers and smaller companies that might be in the business of making parts or logistics systems to support the platforms.

One of my successors in the Expeditionary Warfare Division decided to create an Expeditionary Warfare Conference (EWC) within the NDIA around 1996. He was assisted by now, Major General Mike Hough, who was serving as the Deputy Assistant Secretary of the Navy for Expeditionary Warfare (DASN (EWC)) in the Pentagon. Mike had progressed through several prominent command and staff assignments within the aviation community and was destined to run the Joint Strike Fighter Program (the F-35), a multi-billion-dollar Department of Defense aviation initiative for the services for 2-4 years. He later became the Deputy Commandant for Marine Aviation. Mike was an expert in all facets of aviation and very effective in the bureaucratic battles with the Navy over aviation programs in the Marine Corps. He eventually retired as a lieutenant general and now lives in Southwest Virginia.

It was decided that the EWC would focus its program on the three major programmatic areas that made up the Expeditionary Warfare Division in the Pentagon. This included amphibious shipping, Mine Warfare, and Naval Special Warfare (SEALs). There were a vast number of lesser programs that now fell under the overall field of Expeditionary Warfare, where industry representatives could go to listen to briefs, network, and attend meetings regarding what was going on in this particular area. I had been a member of this organization almost from the beginning and assumed the position of the Chairman of the committee in late 2000. We held the Expeditionary Warfare Conference annually in Panama City, Florida, for several years. It was usually a four-day conference that drew many industry representatives with interests in the three major program areas previously mentioned. The organization of the conference fell under the very effective leadership of Capt. Andy Fosina, USN (Ret), the former Chief of Staff of Amphibious Group 2 in 1990-1991 in the Persian Gulf.

We would get senior flag officers from the Navy, Marine Corps, and Coast Guard to come in and brief the audiences on what was going on in their respective services, as well as some of the requirements needed in the future. Panels would be formed to address any number of topics that were of particular interest to the attendees. Industry representatives were invited to participate or chair specific panels to get communication going between both sides. It was remarkable just how many of these representatives from any number of first-line companies did not know what was going on in the real world of defense, and yet they were pushing programs that had no relevance to what the service requirements really were. I held the position of Chairman of the EWC for over five years while still working for ITT. Significant progress was made in opening lines of communication between the services and industry that actually made some programmatic issues easier to solve. This was another challenge that appealed to me: to try to break through lines of resistance within some elements of the Navy and Marine Corps that really did not want to spend much time dealing with industry. This latter peculiarity was alive and well in many circles within the active services. New products going to the field should be the result of close industry and service coordination.

All good things must come to an end at some point, and my second career this time with ITT was approaching that point. It was time to retire for the second time and get on to new challenges. My work with ITT had been very rewarding personally as it related to our efforts with the National Guard. At last count, we had generated millions of dollars in funding for the SINCGARS radios for the Army Guard and several million more for night-vision goggles through the NEGREA. It should be noted that the ability to generate funding through add-ons in Congress is no longer a possibility due to changes in regulations within that body. Having said that, it helped solve some of the shortages in an organization that needed help while providing units for combat, so it was worth the effort we put into it.

My transition and experience in industry were both interesting and rewarding. The environment was totally different from what I had experienced in my thirty-four years in the Marine Corps. There was a steep learning curve initially as I tried to understand how the corporation functioned and how daily business was conducted. The whole process was different from what I had previously experienced. The bottom line was that it was all about making money for the corporation, and anything else (including snap decisions) was frowned upon for fear of making a mistake and jeopardizing a program. This did take some getting comfortable with. In the service, nobody is concerned about a bottom line or what shareholders in a company might be thinking because Congress will give then an allocated amount of money annually to continue what they are doing. That is legitimate, but it also leads to a huge waste of funds due to poor management processes and misguided strategic planning. The management and leadership styles were radically different, but that too was legitimate when I eventually determined how normal things were accomplished.

ITT did develop some spectacular systems and technologies over the years that made them one of the major players both in domestic and international business. This was what had attracted me to the company in the first place. My counterparts in the corporation were all professional and hard-working for the most part and tried to do the right thing in support of our various programs. The CEO, in the beginning, was a taskmaster, but very effective, and looked out for his employees. As long as you were not blowing smoke in the briefings, you had a great amount of leeway to conduct business as you saw fit. I enjoyed my time with ITT because it gave me valuable experience in how to navigate in the business world beyond the various programs that we were marketing. The demise of the corporation following my retirement was not pleasant to watch because it had been a powerhouse for decades. Like so many others in the past, it could not adjust to the realities of a changing business world. A case study on how and why that occurred would be of value in any business school in the country, so students and business leaders do not make the same mistakes. A lack of strategic vision, weak leadership toward the end, and greed all played a significant role.

CHAPTER 27
THE GOOD LIFE

Following my second retirement in 2006, I continued to be involved in a variety of activities and initiatives. I did not want to quit working but wanted to continue at a slower pace. In the meantime, events with the family continued to proceed really well. Anne was promoted in 2015 to Division Customer Communications Manager with responsibilities for all marketing, media, public affairs, and loyalty programs for the Mid-Atlantic Division for Kroger. TJ had graduated from Duke in 2002, had been commissioned in the U.S. Air Force, and was now flying C-130s. He transitioned to the Air Force Special Operations Wing at Cannon AFB in late 2007 and served there until getting out of the Air Force in 2014. He married Crystal Penney, also in the Air Force Reserve, on October 9, 2010, in a beautiful ceremony in Orlando, Florida. Following their honeymoon, they moved into a home he had purchased in Clovis, New Mexico, which was a short distance from Cannon AFB. Our first grandchild, Maya Grace, was born there on September 2, 2013. After leaving the Air Force, TJ joined the Pennsylvania Air Guard and is now flying EC-130s in addition to flying with Southwest Airlines. He is now a lieutenant colonel in the Air Guard. Crystal, who is an intelligence officer in the Air Force Reserve, was recently promoted to lieutenant colonel as well. The best news in 2015 was the birth of their son Max on June 29th of that year. Both kids are doing fine, and Sue and I were back in the babysitting business on occasion.

Shortly after retiring from ITT, I formed my own consulting firm, "Soaring Eagle Consulting L.L.C.," which was still active until late 2018. I gained almost immediate activity that came on line from clients requiring consulting services in a variety of programs all within the defense arena. My background and experience within the government were very helpful, and this set me up for many efforts in the consulting world where any number of potential clients could use my services if desired. That led to an agreement with another consulting firm in Washington that was primarily interested in work with the National Guard. Also, I was brought in to do some work on the international level. This effort continued until the end of 2018.

I have been a member of the Marine Corps Association (MCA) since I was a lieutenant as it had been required back then. Today you can't require Marines to join the association, so you have to have programs that are attractive to both Marine officers and enlisted that motivate them to join the association. I had been asked if I would like to join the Board of Governors for the MCA in 2007. That offer had been attractive to me, as it was a way that I could pay back to all the troops with programs that hopefully would be attractive to them. MCA was their organization and had been in existence since 1913 and dedicated to supporting all Marines. In addition to the two magazines (the *Leatherneck* and the *Gazette*) that are published monthly, we had a variety of programs that involved professional military education, battlefield tours, a very special Marine Shop at Quantico that marketed uniforms, books, and first-class tailoring services. Also, several professional dinners were conducted annually, and insurance programs were offered, along with several Leadership contests for writing.

I eventually became the Chairman of the Board of Governors in 2010 at a time when we were going to establish a foundation with the express purpose of generating funds to support all of our programs. After resolving all the administrative details associated with this initiative, the Marine Corps Association and Foundation (MCA&F) was formed. I maintained the position as Chairman of the Board until the summer of 2015. The foundation has grown in capability, and it has worked really well since its inception. It continues to play a key role in supporting various programs for its members while adding new programs and initiatives. Like several others around the country, we were involved with the Wounded Warrior Program to try to help those wounded warriors on their long road to recovery from injuries sustained in both Afghanistan and Iraq. The services generally had excellent programs to help their wounded members recover, but organizations like the MCA&F were able to fund activities that could take this process further.

One example of this was one event that illustrates not only the effort that support organizations like ours tried to accomplish but the unbelievable response and determination that were displayed by the wounded members at this event. It took place at the Gettysburg National Battlefield in the spring of 2015. We had sponsored a group of Marine Wounded Warriors that were both from the Naval Hospital at Bethesda, Maryland, and the recovering Wounded Warrior unit stationed at Quantico. The Marine Corps had created two battalions (one at Quantico and one at Camp Pendleton in California) for the express purpose of allowing wounded Marines to recover within the military environment, but geared to recovery programs only. This trip was to be an overnight tour by bus from Washington to Gettysburg, Pennsylvania, with all expenses paid by the Association and Foundation. The plan was to have a dinner for them at a hotel in downtown Gettysburg the first night followed by a guided tour of the battlefield the next day.

The group consisted of Marine veterans who were in various stages of recovery. Some from Bethesda were double amputees, with at least two of them without lower limbs but accompanied by nurses and one wife. Others were missing upper limbs, and all of them had PTSD at one level or another. The attitude for most of them was really superb considering their medical circumstances. The tour the next morning started at the headquarters for the Gettysburg Battlefield, where they were introduced to the historians with maps who were to guide them throughout the day. One lady at the display area in the headquarters building came up to me wanted to know who they were because she had never seen an amputee before. We were polite but seething under our jackets and USMC windbreakers.

The tour over the battlefield went really well, as the guides were outstanding. At one stop along Seminary Ridge, the participants climbed or were helped over a low rock wall and moved through the trees to be able to see more of where Confederate General James Longstreet launched his attack against Little Round Top on the second day of the three-day battle in 1863. While there, two buses full of junior high school students arrived to get the same view. The kids were curious as to who we were and wanted to know who the Marines were, even though some of the Marines had USMC windbreakers on. I gave the students a very quick overview of the Wounded Warrior Program, and what the results of war can do to the participants. I suggested they go and mingle with the veterans and talk to them, which they did. The Marines were great and let the kids take all kinds of pictures as well as answering questions. We had organized a picnic for the veterans on Seminary Ridge and not too far away from the Lee Monument. The final event of the day was to stop at the Lee Monument to get a description of Pickett's Charge, which covered a mile from Seminary Ridge across open terrain to Union positions on Cemetery Ridge. The attack on July 3, 1863, was conducted with 15,000 Confederates under the command of General George Pickett.

At the end of the briefing, one of the Marine Noncommissioned officers accompanying the Wounded Warriors wanted to know how many of them would like to follow him across that same battlefield. To my surprise, all of them who could walk, including two in wheelchairs, got off the bus and were ready to follow him. That said something to me about the human spirit and the "never give up" attitude of those Marines despite their injuries. When I left them, they were almost halfway across the field. I have often wondered how each one of them made out following their release from the Corps.

Beginning around 2006, Sue and I had decided that we would start to do more traveling now that we were both operating at a reduced level of activity and were in a position to visit different places. I have believed that you should never stop learning no matter where you are in life. In addition to the leisure side of river and ocean cruising, it is a nice way to get educated on different parts of the world. I have learned over time you can read about several exotic places but rarely get the correct impression unless you are fortunate enough to travel and see places for yourself. We have been able to visit locations in Europe, the Middle East, and North Africa. Canada, Central, and South America have also been on our travel list for several years. Each region and its countries have their own unique history and cultures. Many are fascinating, and the more one can see them in person, the more you find out just how much you do not know. At home, I still have a strong interest in our National Parks, which we try to visit whenever we get the chance.

In 2018 and 2019, we continued to travel but also focused much more on family activities. We are living in Virginia and are equidistant between Roanoke and Mechanicsburg, where the kids live. That made things very convenient, especially if someone needed help or support. Having two grandchildren added a dimension that Sue and I had not experienced in several years. Both of them are very bright and active kids that do bring much joy as we watch them grow. We try to get together frequently, whether as babysitters or for some event like a Thanksgiving or Christmas. We celebrated our 52nd wedding anniversary in February 2020 but held off the festivities until we could get everyone together for the event. Fifty-two years is a long time, but it went by rather quickly. I owe much of my success to Sue as well as Anne and TJ for having the patience to endure the long deployments away from home while continuing to run a warm and secure household.

Chapter 28
The Finale

I have been extremely fortunate to have so many varied experiences over my lifetime. Some of this was due to being in the right place at the right time. The progression of several of my responsibilities grew exponentially as I continued to serve in the Marine Corps. They were unique and normally not a traditional career pattern. Some of it was most certainly luck on my part. All of my assignments presented me with leadership challenges that had to be met, and none more so than the command and staff assignments in Vietnam, North Norway, and in the Persian Gulf. That was the ultimate in responsibility, and I owe much of my success to the thousands of Marines and sailors who served so ably with me, both in peace and in two different wars.

I also owe a deep sense of gratitude to the sacrifice of those who did not come back, as some were my friends. Despite the flag-waving and "thank you for your service" statements, the American public owes a huge debt to those service members who are really the only ones who stand between them and the mongrels of the world. Nobody else does! Perhaps an even better statement to the American people should be, "Never forget!"

Looking back, it looks like Vietnam has recovered and is now a viable, stable country. The situation in the Middle East is far from anything that looks like success, and only time will tell how it will turn out. Iraq is stumbling along under the influence of Iran that was not there until we got rid of Saddam. Syria is a festering sore with no end in sight, and Afghanistan can be best described as a bottomless pit for American resources. In March 2019, while U.S. negotiators were trying to arrive at some satisfactory solution with the Taliban, some of the Taliban's agents ambushed a column of vehicles carrying former General Abdul Rashid Dostum, who was the Vice President of

Afghanistan. He escaped, but several of his bodyguards did not survive. This is business as usual in Afghanistan. If the ongoing negotiations between the U.S. and the Taliban ever amount to anything, and we reduce our presence in that country, rest assured the Taliban will attempt to drive Afghanistan back to the dark ages to where it was in 2002. One other thing needs to be said: We are never going to solve the centuries-old cultural conflict between the Sunni and Shia elements within Islam. The sooner our political leadership in Washington understands the cultural ramifications of that, and learns to accommodate it where appropriate, the better off this nation will be.

I have been fortunate to have been challenged in a variety of situations down through the years and have experienced awesome levels of responsibility both in and out of the service. My experiences with ITT gave me insight into how a major corporation is organized and how it has to function if it is to survive in the very tough world of business.

Some of my success can be attributed to the hard work, standards, and perseverance of some of my ancestors who either came by sea or overland to the west. They, like so many others, blazed the way forward while suffering hardships that do not even exist today. The result is that the newer generations have had a much easier way of life. To those who made me what I am, I owe a profound level of gratitude.

This has been my story. I will continue with several activities well into the future. If I had to do it all over again, I would do so gladly to try to make this country even better than it is now.

Semper Fidelis.

Retirement Ceremony, Marine Barracks, Washington, D.C., August 1994. Major General Don Gardner and Major General Harry Jenkins.

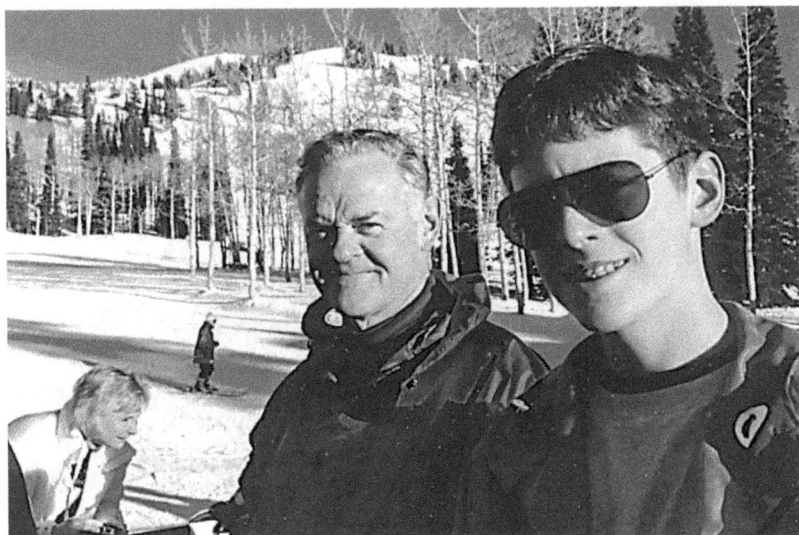

The author and his son TJ skiing at Grand Targhee in Wyoming.

The author and ITT representative with "Cimarron," Texas Guard Conference in Austin, Texas.

The author's daughter, Anne, with his wife, Sue, in Passau, Germany, 2018.

Brady, Anne, Sue, and the author, Salzburg, Austria 2018.

Author and family at TJ's promotion ceremony to lieutenant colonel in the 193rd Special Operations Wing, Pennsylvania Air National Guard, July 2018.

ABOUT THE AUTHOR

Major General Harry W. Jenkins served for 34 years on active duty in the United States Marine Corps. Following a distinguished career in the service, he went on to complete a second career with ITT Industries in Washington, DC, and then a third as the president of his consulting firm in northern Virginia.

Born into a newspaper family in 1938 in Oakland, California, he lived in the Bay Area and Paradise, California, in the early years. After attending schools in Paradise, Oakland, and San José, he graduated from San José State with a BA degree in Physical Education in 1960. Upon graduation, he was commissioned as a second lieutenant and went on to serve in command and staff billets in the Fleet Marine Force, and in high-level staff assignments in Washington, DC. He is a graduate of the Naval War College and holds an MS degree in Curriculum from the University of Wisconsin in Madison.

The author served as a company commander, operations officer, and executive officer in an infantry battalion in the Republic of Vietnam in 1968, and as the commander of the 2nd Marine Regiment in Arctic operations during the Cold War. He later commanded the 4th Marine Expeditionary Brigade and Task Force 158 at sea in Desert Shield and Desert Storm in 1990-1991.

General Jenkins's individual decorations include the Navy Distinguished Service Medal, the Legion of Merit Medal, four Bronze Star Medals with Combat V's, and the Navy Commendation Medal with Combat V.

Upon retiring from the Marine Corps in 1994, General Jenkins joined ITT Industries in northern Virginia and served for twelve years in business development and congressional relations for the Defense Sector in the corporation. During this period, he was a member of the Naval Studies Board in the National Research Council in Washington for six years, and he served on the Board of Chemical Science and Technology also in the NRC. Simultaneously he was the Chairman of the Expeditionary Warfare Committee within the National Defense Industrial Association (NDIA) in Washington for five years.

Following his retirement from ITT Defense in 2006, General Jenkins created a consulting firm and served as its president for the next twelve years retiring again in 2018. A long-standing member of the Marine Corps Association, he joined the Board of Governors in 2006 and assumed the position as the Chairman of the Board of the Marine Corps Association and Foundation in 2010. He served in that capacity until 2015.

General Jenkins and his wife of 52 years Sue have one daughter and one son and two grandchildren. When not spending time with the family, they frequently travel to locations across the country or in Europe and South America. They live in northern Virginia.

ABBREVIATIONS

AAV	Amphibious Assault Vehicle
ARG	Amphibious Ready Group
ACE	Air Combat Element – MAG - 40
ARVN	Army of the Republic of Vietnam
ATF	Amphibious Task Force
ATO	Air Tasking Order daily listing all theater missions
AWS	Amphibious Warfare School
BCT	Brigade Combat Team
BOGEY	used in the OPNAV for annual program taxes
BSSG	Brigade Service Support Group (BSSG-4)
C&SC	Command and Staff College
CATF	Commander Amphibious Task Force
CG	Commanding General
CENTCOM	U.S. Central Command
CIA	Central Intelligence Agency
CIDG	Civilian Irregular Defense Group
CINCCENT	Commander-in-Chief, Central Command
CLF	Commander Landing Force
CMC	Commandant of the Marine Corps
CNO	Chief of Naval Operations
ComUSNavCent	Commander, U.S. Naval Forces, Central Command

CP	Command Post
CSSE	Combat Service Support Element – BSSG-4
CTF	Commander Task Force
CVBG	Aircraft Carrier Battle Group
GCE	Ground Combat Element – 2nd Marines
GPS	Global Positioning System
KCSB	Khe Sanh Combat Base
LCAC	Landing Craft Air Cushion Vehicle
LCC	Amphibious Command Ship
LCU	Landing Craft Utility
LEDet	Law Enforcement Detachment, U.S. Coast Guard
LHA	General-Purpose Amphibious Assault Ship
LPD	Amphibious Transport Dock (dock landing ship)
LPH	Amphibious Assault Shop (helicopter)
LST	Amphibious Landing Ship Tank
MAG	Marine Air Group (MAG 40 or MAG 50)
MAGTF	Marine Air-Ground Task Force
MarCent	Marine Forces, Central Command
MCAC	Multi-capable Air Cushion Vehicle
MEB	Marine Expeditionary Brigade – 4th MEB or 5th MEB
MEDEVAC	Medical Evacuation
MEF	Marine Expeditionary Force – I MEF
MEU	Marine Expeditionary Unit – 13th MEU

CHALLENGES

MEU (SOC)	Marine Expeditionary Unit (Special Ops Capable)
MIF	Maritime Interdiction Force
MPF	Maritime Preposition Force
OCS	Officer Candidate School
OSO	Officer Selection Officer
NSB	Naval Studies Board
NVA	North Vietnamese Army
OPNAV	Office of the Chief of Naval Operations
PhibCru	Amphibious Group – PhibGru- 2 or PhibGru-3
PhibRon	Amphibious Squadron
RLT	Regimental Landing Team – RLT-2 or RLT-5
Regt	Marine Regiment
TBS	The Basic School, Quantico, Virginia
USS	United States Ship

BATTALIONS

1/1	First Battalion, 1st Marines
1/5	First Battalion, 5th Marines
1/2	First Battalion 2nd Marines
2/4	Second Battalion, 4th Marines
2/7	Second Battalion 7th Marines
2/9	Second Battalion 9th Marines
3/26	Third Battalion, 26th Marines

Marine Aircraft and Helicopters

AV-8B Harrier Jump Jet

CH-46 Medium-lift Helicopter (18-20 Marines)

CH-53 Heavy-lift Helicopter (30 Marines)

C-130 Four-engine transport (passengers and cargo)

www.ingramcontent.com/pod-product-compliance
Lightning Source LLC
Chambersburg PA
CBHW070819100426
42813CB00033B/3438/J